100 PEOPLE WHO ARE SCREWING UP AMERICA

(and Al Franken Is #37)

100 PEOPLE

Who Are

SCREWING UP

AMERICA

☞ *(and Al Franken Is #37)*

BERNARD GOLDBERG

HarperCollins*Publishers*

For Harold and Muriel

100 PEOPLE WHO ARE SCREWING UP AMERICA (AND AL FRANKEN IS #37).
Copyright © 2005 by Medium Cool Communications Inc. All rights
reserved. Printed in the United States of America. No part of this book
may be used or reproduced in any manner whatsoever without written
permission except in the case of brief quotations embodied in critical
articles and reviews. For information, address HarperCollins Publishers,
10 East 53rd Street, New York, NY 10022.

HarperCollins books may be purchased for educational, business, or sales
promotional use. For information, please write: Special Markets Department, HarperCollins Publishers, 10 East 53rd Street, New York, NY
10022.

FIRST EDITION

Designed by Elliott Beard

Photo of Michael Moore courtesy of Jemal Countess/WireImage.com.

Printed on acid-free paper

Library of Congress Cataloging-in-Publication Data
    Goldberg, Bernard,
        100 people who are screwing up America (and Al Franken is #37) /
    Bernard Goldberg.—1st ed.
            p.   cm.
        ISBN 0-06-076128-8
        1. Mass media—Political aspects—United States. 2. Political
    culture—United States. 3. Liberalism—United States. 4. United
    States—Politics and government—2001–   I. Title: One hundred
    people who are screwing up America (and Al Franken is number 37).
    II. Title.
    P95.82.U6G65 2005
    302.23'0973—dc22   2005046014

05 06 07 08 09 ❖/RRD   20 19 18 17 16 15 14 13 12 11

INTRODUCTION

I'M SITTING ON A JET PLANE at Newark Airport, minding my own business, waiting to take off for Miami. A few seats away is this lawyer right out of Central Casting—wire-framed eyeglasses, dull gray suit, red tie, mandatory suspenders. Attached to his ear is another mandatory accessory, the cell phone, which he's using to talk to a colleague about some legal brief.

Actually, "talk" isn't exactly the right word. "Yell" is a lot more like it—which is the way a lot of people "talk" on cell phones. Anyway, just about everyone on the plane who isn't clinically deaf can hear the whole conversation, loud and clear, including the part where Mr. Lawyer actually invokes the name of a U.S. Supreme Court justice—Antonin Scalia—to give a little weight to his brief. Pretty impressive, I'm thinking. I mean, how often does a guy on an airplane drop Antonin Scalia's name into a conversation? How about never? Then this obviously well-educated, sophisticated man makes another important observation about his important legal case, another observation you could hear all over the airplane.

"It's all f**ked up," he tells the guy at the other end of the phone.

And here's the thing: No one within earshot raised an eyebrow. The remark drew as much attention as if he had said to the flight attendant, "Got any peanuts?"

Not that I'm suggesting that I was shocked, either. Who are we kidding? In today's world, some anonymous guy dropping the F-bomb in a crowded airplane doesn't move the needle on the give-a-crap meter. In fact, if you even think about making an issue of it, some people start dropping the P-bomb. And who wants to be called a *prude*? So you just sit there and either make believe you didn't hear what you and everybody else just heard or you tell yourself it's no big deal.

But the truth is, it's getting harder and harder to tell myself that stuff like this is no big deal. Instead I find myself remembering that there was a time in America when not even a drunk in a bar would say the word "f**k" out loud. Today, Chevy Chase calls the president of the United States a "dumb f**k"—not in some dingy beer hall but in front of a packed house at a Kennedy Center gala in Washington, D.C.

Yes, we've come a long way from the old days when "Frankly, my dear, I don't give a damn" caused such a ruckus. But that, of course, was a different time, and a different America, long before genuine crass vulgarity polluted not only our relatively private lives but our public, civic lives as well.

And you know what? It's an America that, in all kinds of ways, a lot of us miss.

Of course, every time you say something like that, every time you feel even a little nostalgic for "the good old days," you can count on one of your (almost certainly liberal) friends to come back with "Oh, yeah, you really think things were better when blacks couldn't vote or sit down at a lunch counter? You really think things were better when women and gays were kept in their place? Is *that* the America you think was so wonderful and want to go back to?"

No, if it even needs to be said, that is *not* the America I want to go back to. I want an America where black people have all the rights white people have; where women have all the rights men have; where gays can walk down the street, holding hands if they want, and not have to worry that some jackass is going to call them names—or worse; where little girls can aspire to be scientists just as little boys; where minorities don't get called spic or gook or kike or anything else like that—and, yes, I also want an America where people don't think it's perfectly okay to yell "f**k" on a crowded airplane.

And you know what else? While I may not pine for "the good old days" when Lucy and Ricky had to sleep in separate beds and couldn't even whisper the word "pregnant" when she so obviously was, I'm not thrilled with the endless junior-high sex jokes on *Will & Grace*, either. Or the farting contests on Howard Stern's show. Or rap lyrics on the radio that go on about slitting the bitch's throat and tossing her dead ass out the window. Or those nauseating paternity-test theme shows that Maury Povich puts on the air every other day, featuring losers trying to figure out who knocked them up.

If that's progress, count me out.

And just in case you're wondering: No, I'm not the Church Lady. If Courtney Love or Drew Barrymore wants to flash David Letterman around midnight on national television, frankly, my dear, I don't give a damn. If Janet Jackson wants to show me her breast—and anything else she's got—that's good with me, too, but not during the Super Bowl halftime show, when all sorts of people are watching, including *one-fifth of all the kids in America under age eleven*. It's not the vulgarity that bothers me as much as the rudeness. We invited her into our house to sing—not to undress in front of the whole family. You don't have to be a bluenose to be bothered by that, or by the cheap towel-dropping episode on *Monday Night Football*, either. And if HBO or Showtime wants to run the *Sopranos* or *Deadwood* or *Queer as Folk*, or a lot of other stuff that would give the Church Lady a coronary, no problem with me—because *grown-ups* have to pay for it, which, in my book, makes it *private*, which means it's nobody's business but their own.

To tell you the truth, I didn't even care when Dick Cheney told Senator Patrick Leahy what he could do with himself, which, I admit, struck me as a very good and long-overdue suggestion—because he said it *privately*. If Leahy hadn't leaked it to his pals in the media, it would have stayed between the two of them. Now, if the vice president had told Leahy to go screw himself, say, on *Meet the Press*, well, that's something else entirely.

Here's the problem, as far as I'm concerned: Over the years, as we became less closed-minded and more tolerant of all the right things, like civil rights, somehow, we became *indiscriminately* tolerant. *"You're so judgmental"* became a major-league put-down in Anything Goes America—as if being judgmental of crap in the culture is a bad thing.

A slow poison is running through the veins of this great country, and our tolerance of crap is just a small part of it. Because the stuff that comes out of the television and radio is only the most obvious evidence of how far south things have gone.

Yes, it's easy to believe that it's really nobody's fault, that this is just the way society has evolved, that it's just the end result of impersonal forces beyond anyone's control. But that's not true. There are specific individuals who, in various ways, are not only screwing things up in this country, but who often are *succeeding wildly* by screwing things up. This is a book about those people, a whole bunch of different people who are screwing things up in a whole bunch of different ways.

It's about the Hollywood blowhards who think they're smart just because they're famous and who—when they're not saying other really dumb things—casually compare politicians they don't like in this country to a bunch of Nazis, but think dictators like Fidel Castro are really cool.

It's about the cultural-elite hypocrites, like the Beverly Hills environmentalist-to-the-stars who screams at total strangers for driving SUVs while she's tooling around the country in a private jet that sucks up more fuel in one hour than most small countries use in a year.

It's about the people who make us laugh even when they're not trying, like the congresswoman who thinks hurricane names—I swear I'm not kidding—are too lily-white and that we need more hurricanes with "black names"—like what? DeShawn and Shaniqua?

But it's also about the ones who infuriate us, like the America Bashers, who, just days after September 11, couldn't wait to tell us that "Patriotism threatens free speech with death" and that the American flag stands for "jingoism and vengeance and war."

It's about the intellectual thugs at some of our *best* universities who make rules about what you can and cannot say at school—in order to ensure that none of the little sensitive hothouse flowers on campus ever gets his or her feelings hurt by an unkind word.

It's about those well-dressed crooks at some of America's biggest corporations, who went to some of our finest business schools, who cook the books and steal the future of their own employees because, according to their warped value system, making a measly 10 or 20 million a year just isn't good enough anymore.

It's about the American jackals, the trial lawyers, who file the kind of frivolous lawsuits that are so ridiculous they actually make us laugh . . . just before they make us scream.

It's about a country where as long as *anything* goes, as a friend of mine puts it, sooner or later *everything* will go.

A few words about the list and how I came up with the *100 People Who Are Screwing Up America* . . .

First, I didn't take a poll. Forgive me for stating the obvious, but this is *my* list. There won't be two people in the whole country who agree with every name in the book. "*Why in the world did you put him on it?*" someone is going to yell at me. "*How come you left her off the list?*" Because the people on it are the ones *I* think are screwing things up.

And it won't take you long to notice that there are a lot of liberals on the list, which, of course, is just how it ought to be. If I were compiling the list years ago, say, when I was in college, there'd be a lot of conservatives on it. But this isn't years ago, and besides, I'm smarter now than I was back then. And, believe it or not, it's not so much because of their left-of-center politics that they're on the list, as because of their willingness—make that their *eagerness*—to live up to the most embarrassing stereotypes many of us hold about today's cultural-elite liberals: that they're snooty, snobby know-it-alls, who have gotten angrier and angrier in recent years and who think they're not only smarter, but also *better* than everyone else, especially everyone else who lives in a "Red State"—a population they see as hopelessly dumb and pathetically religious. And it is precisely this elitist condescension—this smug attitude that Middle America is a land of right-wing yahoos who are so damn unenlightened that they probably don't even know where the Hamptons are—that hurts liberals and their causes way more than it helps them. It's one of the reasons John Kerry is still a senator and not the president of the United States.

I understand that Al Franken and Michael Moore may not agree with this analysis, but one can only hope that over time even they will grow and begin to see the light. Maybe Janeane Garofalo could help.

But *100 People Who Are Screwing Up America* doesn't just round up the usual suspects, the big-name windbags who, through their words and deeds, we have come to know and detest. It also exposes some of the people who operate away from the limelight and behind the curtain, but still manage to pull a lot of strings and do all sorts of harm to our culture. And there are even a few "pioneers" on the list, people who no longer are screwing things up the way they used to in their prime—but because they're the ones who laid the groundwork for the many screwups who followed in their considerable footsteps, they also deserve notice in this book.

And in the end, you know what else this book is about? It's about that lawyer on that airplane at Newark Airport. Because, whether we like it or not, in all sorts of ways, I'm afraid he got it right: It really is all f**ked up.

100 PEOPLE WHO ARE SCREWING UP AMERICA

(and Al Franken Is #37)

AMERICA BASHERS

WHY DO SO MANY AMERICANS who ought to know better find the United States such a terrible place?

Maybe "terrible" isn't exactly the right word, but it's pretty close. So are "corrupt" and "immoral" and "dishonorable" and a whole bunch of other words just like those. America never quite seems to get it right, as far as these people are concerned. If something bad happens someplace in the world, it's got to be our fault. And not just because our plans went bad, but because our motives were all wrong. Day in and day out, in their eyes, America comes up short. This country, as far as they're concerned, is a never-ending source of embarrassment. They just don't trust America to do the right thing—because, to them, this is a land of bottomless stupidity and eternal sin.

Whom exactly are we talking about? Unfortunately, not just drugged-out revolutionaries on the fringe, the kind of people we could simply write off as crackpots. And not mainly college kids, either, which would at least be a kind of excuse. No, the America Bashers these days are in the mainstream, in the top ranks of the nation's intelligentsia and cultural elite—professors at some of our top schools, journalists at some of our most important news organizations, celebrities in Hollywood, and, of course, Michael Moore, the reigning king of America Bashers, who deserves a category all his own.

Moore once told a British newspaper that the United States is a country that "is known for bringing sadness and misery to places around the globe." And just hours after the attacks of September 11, he posted this lovely message on his Web site: "Many families have been devastated tonight," he wrote. "This just is not right. They did not deserve to die. If someone did this to get back at Bush, then they did so by killing thousands of people who DID NOT VOTE for him! Boston, New York, DC, and the planes' destination of California—these were places that voted AGAINST Bush!"

Can you imagine if Rush Limbaugh had said something like this? Not even the lunatic fringe would have embraced him. But Michael Moore says something this dumb and it doesn't even register with the cultural elite as over the line, let alone flat-out disgusting. To the contrary—or *au contraire*, as they say in France where Michael Moore is even bigger than Jerry Lewis—liberals continue to celebrate him as a national treasure, as a courageous voice of sanity. When his documentary, *Fahrenheit 9/11*, premiered in Washington, he invited to the gala some of the city's most elite Democrats, who applauded enthusiastically throughout the movie, then, when it was over, gave him a standing ovation. Make no mistake: Michael Moore isn't the court jester. He's not a Yippie like Abbie Hoffman in 1968. Millions of *mainstream* liberals who once looked up to JFK are now idolizing *this* guy!

And the fact that so many America Bashers are middle-aged, like Michael Moore, helps explain where they're coming from, to use that old phrase. They are of a generation—or, more precisely, they are of a part of a generation—that long ago defined itself by its skepticism about everything America is and everything America does. Most of these people came of age during Vietnam, and in some important ways, they've never moved beyond one of the core beliefs of those days: that America is a bully, that it is an oppressor, and that standing up and saying so automatically defines you as a decent and moral person—no matter how you behave in the rest of your life.

With that in mind, consider the reaction of such people to the abuses at the Abu Ghraib prison in Iraq. Decent Americans, of course, were offended by the revelations of what went on there. But was it a horror comparable to the 1968 My Lai Massacre in Vietnam, where hundreds of unarmed men, women, children, and old people were taken out and slaughtered in cold blood by American troops?

The very question is obscene.

But not to the America Bashers, including many in the mainstream press. To them, what happened at Abu Ghraib was less a tragedy than an opportunity—one more chance to reveal America as depraved and dishonorable.

Take Frank Rich and Paul Krugman, two of the most popular liberal pundits at the *New York Times*.

If you read Rich on Abu Ghraib, you sense his thrill at the chance to relive glory days gone by, when he and his pals were running around the Harvard campus playing at revolution. "It was in November 1969," he wrote in his May 9, 2004, column, "that a little-known reporter, Seymour Hersh, broke the story of the 1968 massacre at My Lai, the horrific scoop that has now found its match 35 years later in Mr. Hersh's *New Yorker* revelation of a 53-page Army report detailing 'numerous instances of sadistic, blatant and wanton criminal abuse' at Abu Ghraib."

If Frank Rich were as stupid as he seems to think most Americans are, such an absurd exaggeration might be understandable, if not excusable. But, much as he may lack common sense, he is not stupid. What he is (aside from snide and vicious) is deeply committed to a false vision of America and its people. It's exactly the way alienated rich kids (like Frank Rich) used to write for their college papers back in the 60s. The difference is, now they do it in the pages of the *New York Times*.

Or take Paul Krugman, the most ideologically left-wing columnist on the *Times'* op-ed page, which is no small feat. On May 11, two days after the Frank Rich column, Krugman hopped on the My Lai express with this brilliant observation: "Seymour Hersh is exposing My Lai all over again." For Paul Krugman, and for many of his devoted readers who eagerly embrace his warped view of America and its military, this blatant absurdity had become a simple fact. It was, after all, in the *New York Times*. What more does anybody need?

There's just one problem: My Lai was one of the most egregious war crimes in American history, and Abu Ghraib didn't come close—unless you were one of those moralizing nitwits who deliberately wanted to paint America as a monster. But no matter how hard they tried to draw comparisons, there were none. Forcing Iraqi prisoners to undress and lie in a pile on top of each other is something that has to be punished, but it is not the same as shooting a baby in his mother's arms. Putting women's panties over a prisoner's head is not nice, but it is not the same as machine-gunning hundreds of innocent civilians outside their straw huts.

As I say, decent Americans are embarrassed and offended by what happened at Abu Ghraib. But, as always, the America Bashers are selective in their outrage. American abuses are page-one news for weeks and weeks and weeks. The decapitation of innocent Americans by Muslim terrorists is a one-day story. Blink, and you miss it.

Sorry, but I'm with Dennis Miller. After you see helpless people begging for their lives just before they get their heads cut off, Abu Ghraib looks like nothing more than a "Boys Gone Wild" video.

Ah, but the very sight of Muslim prisoners with dog leashes around their necks sends a lot of liberals heading straight for the Valium. But where, I wonder, is their visceral outrage, their utter disgust, when they see four burned and mutilated American civilian contractors hanging from a bridge in Fallujah, put there by blood-thirsty Islamic fanatics? Of course they don't like it. Who does, be-sides the fanatics? But somehow, it just doesn't get them as agitated as Abu Ghraib.

And have you noticed how these same sensitive people who fight back tears over so-called American atrocities and torture never seem to cry over the *genuine* atrocities and torture that are com-monplace in prisons throughout the Arab world?

Have you noticed how they always seem ready with excuses for terrorists, like radical Palestinians, who blow up little children in Is-raeli pizza parlors? How they lecture us with *moralistic* drivel, like, "*What do you expect from people who are forced to live under such op-pression?*"

But every *American* misdeed is *horrifying* in their eyes, a sign not just of personal bad conduct, but of nothing less than American moral decay. It's as if the America Bashers have arrived at a kind of intellectual truce with the terrorists; it's as if they've made accom-modation with them. America, of course, gets no such generosity from these people. So, you will be forgiven if you think the America Bashers actually *welcome* news that makes our country look bad. You will be forgiven, too, if you believe it somehow invigorates them.

How, I wonder, could so many of them who should know better—including the ones who have had so many opportunities in America—not understand what the lowliest peasants in the poorest countries in the world grasp with absolute clarity: that for all our problems, America is still the freest country on earth, that it is the most generous, and yes, that it is also the greatest hope for hu-mankind, which is precisely why so many people from everywhere in the world want to live in the United States.

For the record, I'm not saying the America Bashers hate Amer-ica. Only they know what's inside of them. And I know that many of them will say that they're the real patriots, because they're the ones holding the country up to the highest standards; they're the ones criticizing America to make it better.

On the surface, it sounds good. But it's only when you listen closely that you discover what they really mean: They love some *hypothetical, idealized America*—one that would redistribute wealth and outlaw gas-guzzling SUVs and celebrate every aspect of "multiculturalism" and tolerate every kind of thought and behavior, except, of course, conservative thought and behavior. But they don't—God forbid!—love the America that we *actually* live in. Only a simpleton could love *that* America!

These are the same people, after all, who went nuts whenever Ronald Reagan called the old Soviet Union an "Evil Empire" but somehow could never muster the same rage over the *reality* of the Evil Empire—a place where no one could speak freely, or worship freely, or even assemble freely, and where anyone "crazy" enough to disagree with the government could wind up in the gulag. But when you think about it, it makes perfect sense, because, as far as a lot of these America Bashers were concerned, the real "Evil Empire" under Ronald Reagan was—correct!—The United States of America.

None of this, if it needs to be said, is an argument against criticizing America when America is wrong. I'm all for that. The problem is that too many America Bashers *only* criticize America.

So how did we get this way? James Piereson, in a piece for the *Weekly Standard*, has a few ideas about why so many liberals today see America through such a dark glass. He says that gradually, since the Kennedy assassination, a doctrine that he calls "Punitive Liberalism" has taken hold on the Left.

"According to this doctrine," he writes, "America had been responsible for numerous crimes and misdeeds through its history for which it deserved punishment and chastisement. White Americans had enslaved blacks and committed genocide against Native Americans. They had oppressed women and tyrannized minority groups, such as the Japanese who had been interned in camps during World War II. They had been harsh and unfeeling toward the poor. By our greed, we had despoiled the environment and were consuming a disproportionate share of the world's wealth and resources. We had coddled dictators abroad and violated human rights out of our irrational fear of communism.

"Given this bill of indictment, the Punitive Liberals held that Americans had no right at all to feel pride in their country's history or optimism about its future. . . . The Punitive Liberals felt that the purpose of national policy was to punish the nation for its crimes rather than to build a stronger America and a brighter future for all."

Most of us don't think we should be punished for the sins of past generations. We try to make things right, as best we can, and move ahead. Most Americans are decent and optimistic about the future. The Punitive Liberals, on the other hand, are mired in the dark past. This is why—despite the fact that the United States has helped to free millions and millions of people who once lived in tyranny, despite the fact that we have spent billions to help poor people all over the world—the Punitive Liberals will never be satisfied. They will never trust their own country. They will always see America as corrupt and immoral and dishonorable. No matter how much we Americans do today, it will never be enough to make up for the past, as far as the Punitive Liberals are concerned.

Because for them, it is always yesterday.

HOLLYWOOD BLOWHARDS

THERE WAS A JOKE GOING AROUND Hollywood a few years ago, which really made them howl.

"What's the difference between George Bush and Hitler?"

"Hitler was elected."

I don't know just who came up with that one, but most of the *wisdom* on the state of the nation that emerges from worldwide headquarters of narcissism and lame-brained moral satisfaction is not at all anonymous. In fact, based on their eagerness to share their views with the rest of us, the evidence seems overwhelming that Hollywood stars actually believe their *thoughts* are original, insightful, cutting-edge political commentary.

A few examples, randomly selected from several billion possibilities:

> *"Republican comes in the dictionary just after reptile*
> *and just above repugnant."*
>
> —POLITICAL SCIENTIST JULIA ROBERTS

"Bush is a f**king idiot."

—HISTORIAN JENNIFER ANISTON

Bush is "as bright as an egg timer."

—CONSTITUTIONAL SCHOLAR CHEVY CHASE

Bush is a "cheap thug."

—POLITICAL COMMENTATOR JOHN MELLENCAMP

So much for brilliant observations from people you normally read about at the supermarket checkout counter. How about a few Hollywood truisms: Bush is Hitler. Conservatives love war. Republicans are racists. Columbus was a bigot. Ashcroft is a fascist. Women are oppressed. Gays are oppressed. Blacks are oppressed. Liberals are compassionate. Ordinary Americans are idiots.

Oh, and my favorite: Liberals are not judgmental.

The simple fact is, there's more diversity inside the Taliban than there is inside the 90210 zip code. In Beverly Hills, comparing George Bush to Hitler isn't seen as outrageous; it's just a reasonable, civilized observation of the way things are.

"Hollywood is a society of liberal bigots," is the way L.A. journalist Jan Golab put it in a piece for *FrontPage Magazine*. "'Stupid' is their N-word, like 'coon' or 'jungle bunny.' They walk into a party or restaurant and say 'stupid Bush.' Somebody responds 'stupid cowboy' or 'drunken frat-boy,' and they know they are among Klansmen. If conservatives are offended—good—they want to drive them away. They don't want them around. . . . They surround themselves only with fellow 'Progressives,' lefties who hate Bush. Conservatives are people of a lesser mind who don't count. . . ."

So, why does it matter?

Because they're annoying, that's why it matters; because they never cease inflicting their inanity on the rest of us. If they would only keep their (pretty, often surgically enhanced) mouths shut,

9

we'd be happy to let them make their millions playing make-believe and screwing up their lives with their various excesses (drugs, sex, insecurity) and deficiencies (self-control, maturity, brains). But in this celebrity-obsessed culture, their problem becomes our problem. Because, unlike drunks in a bar, celebrities—even certified-moron celebrities—are given a very big megaphone. They're inescapable. There you are, enjoying a pleasant evening, and suddenly one of them appears on the tube, spouting the usual idiocy in that smug, self-assured, ignorant Hollywood way, and the next thing you know you're reaching for the Pepto-Bismol.

Oh yeah, one more Hollywood truism: Liberals are censored. They're not allowed to get their message out. This one is said mostly in front of television cameras with millions of people watching.

TV
SCHLOCKMEISTERS

I LOVED LUCY.

I'll never forget, sitting at home as a kid and watching one of the funniest episodes of her show—ever. It was the one where Lucy was trying to meet John Wayne after Ricky had *repeatedly* warned her not to get anywhere near the guy—so, as usual, Ricky was fuming. But now Lucy was trying to get back in good with him. I can still picture it: They were sitting on the couch in their little living room when Lucy smiled and said, "Ricky, you're going to get laid tonight."

That was a good one.

Then there was the episode on the old *Andy Griffith Show* where Aunt Bea went into town with little Opie to buy some blueberries to make a pie for the county fair, and while they were away, Andy took off his sheriff's badge—and his pants—and commenced humping his girlfriend Helen Crump beneath the covers.

I liked that one a lot, too.

Okay, admit it. It's impossible even to *imagine* anything like that really happening on television in the old days. And if anything like that, *somehow*, had gotten on the air, the uproar would have registered at least a fifteen on the ten-point cultural Richter scale. And it wouldn't just have been the prudes and bluenoses who would have been up in arms.

But turn on your television set today, to a prime-time sitcom called *Two and a Half Men* on CBS, the Tiffany Network, and you *can* hear a female character tell a guy, "You're going to get laid tonight."

Or turn on another CBS prime-time program, a reality show called *Big Brother*, and you *can* watch, as *TV Guide* put it, as "houseguests humped beneath the covers."

Or turn on *Will & Grace*, a huge prime-time hit for NBC.

One episode was about a sexpot named Tina, who tells Will how unhappy she is because she suspects that his philandering father, George, who is separated from Will's mother, is cheating on her.

"Every time we try to make love, he's tired," she complains. "And I'm sexual. I need it. I mean, *I really, really need it.*" (Remember, this is his father she's talking about.) Then she tells Will that she's only talking to him because "I have no one else to go to; I'd go to my girlfriends but I've slept with all their husbands."

Is Will shocked by this kind of talk? Get real. And when Will does some digging and tells her that it's true, that his dad is, in fact, cheating on her, Tina-the-sexpot whines, "When am I ever gonna find a married man who's faithful to me?" Seconds later, she regains her composure and says, "I hope he gets an STD from that whore." Oh yeah, "that whore"—the woman Will's dad is secretly having sex with—is none other than *Will's mother.* That's right: Will's dad is cheating on his mistress by secretly having sex with his estranged wife.

But wait, there's more. It turns out that Will's mother actually *likes* the fact that both she and Tina are having sex with Will's father, pretty much at the same time. Why? Because as this middle-aged, but oh-so-with-it woman charmingly puts it, "Cheating is fun."

How does it end? The two women work things out—behind Will's back. The ex-wife tells the mistress, "I'll take George Mondays, Wednesdays, and Fridays." Tina jumps in with, "And I'll keep him on the weekends. We'll give him Tuesdays and Thursdays to rest."

"And it's even more exciting," says Mom, "now that we're lying to Will."

Just so you know, in the world of network sitcoms—compared to all the other *drek* that's on—this is considered quality, smart, fairly highbrow stuff! And it's no coincidence that so many in what they like to call "the creative community"—so many who see themselves as sophisticated and progressive—perceive *Will & Grace* not just as a funny sitcom, but also as a force for what they regard as a social good. Part of that, obviously, is because of its message on gays; but also—as the show about Will's mother and his father's mistress makes clear—because, in general, the show's values are so consistently *hip* and *modern*. The attitude is: anyone who is offended by these *values* is, by definition, a square.

This is the same thinking that leads so many so-called progressives to look down with contempt on some of the most popular shows from television's past. It's why these *sophisticates* sneer at what they see as the idealized world of those old TV shows. And to people like that, nothing says "bad old days" more than *The Adventures of Ozzie and Harriet*, a show that pretty much has become code for the kind of empty, complacent, boring, white-bread 50s kind of TV that—in the view of those progressive and sophisticated Americans anyway—we thankfully have left behind.

And it's true that things were simple on *Ozzie and Harriet*. No divorces. No mistresses. No single mothers. No babies born out of wedlock. No drugs. No racial trouble at school. No racial anything, for that matter. No sadness. The parents never even argued. In fact,

I used to wonder why in the world they called the show *The* Adventures *of Ozzie and Harriet?* What *adventures?*

But let's be honest here: a lot of these people detest Ozzie and Harriet less for what *wasn't* there than for what *was.* They hate everything about Ozzie and Harriet's "phony" old-fashioned values, which weren't nearly progressive enough to please so many on the Left today. They hate the fact that Harriet was a stay-at-home mom; that she wanted to be in the house when her kids came home from school; that her kids didn't give her or Ozzie any smart-ass back talk; that they lived in a *mind-numbing* suburb; that they all found time to sit down and have dinner together; and that Ozzie was probably a damn Republican.

For the record, I'd be the first to agree that *Ozzie and Harriet,* and a few other shows of the day, were a tad lame at times. We should be able to deal honestly, and even irreverently, with subjects that once were off limits—like race and sex. Some of those old standards were so rigid they were suffocating. They needed to be loosened.

The good news is that over the years, they have been, and in some important and positive ways. But here's the bad news: while, reflecting the real world outside, TV was becoming less suffocating and less rigid, it was also becoming less decent, just like the real world. And because the standards came down just a little bit at a time, because the changes happened so slowly over so many years— a little more smut here, a little more contempt for the social niceties there—before you knew it, we were tolerating what used to be intolerable. We became conditioned to not only accept what used to be unacceptable, *but to not even notice it.* As any good cultural elitist will tell you, nobody but "prudes" and "reactionaries" is shocked by any of it these days. And the truth is, most of us just yawn.

That's why it might help to imagine if the slide into the muck had happened not slowly but overnight. Imagine that you were in the 50s or early 60s, watching Lucy and Ethel trying to keep up with the chocolates on the conveyor belt, or Wally and the Beaver hacking around with Eddie Haskell. Then a meteor crashes through the roof of your house, hits you on the head, and you go into a coma until . . . today. Suddenly you're hearing that "cheating is fun" on *Will & Grace* and you're watching Madonna and Britney Spears stick their tongues down each other's throats on one prime-time music awards show and hearing Bono say, "This is really, really f**king brilliant" on another. You'd think you had woken up not just in a different country but on a different planet.

The fact is, these days almost anything goes on TV. And on some shows, the cruder and more contemptuous of "old-fashioned" morality, the better. On an episode of CBS *Two and a Half Men*, for instance, when Charlie, the show's hard-partying bachelor (played by Charlie Sheen) gets together with an old girlfriend, he discovers that *she* is now a *he*—a man who (and this is where it supposedly gets even funnier) is soon having sex with . . . *Charlie's middle-aged mom*. Charlie dilemma: whether to tell his mother that "Bill" used to be "Jill." But after he does, Mom decides to keep seeing Bill anyway. After all, she says, "He knows what I like in bed." To which her exasperated son replies, "He knows what *I* like in bed."

Take away the glitzy production values and the star power of some of the actors and what you've got, smack in the middle of prime time, are shows that—both in content and values—are not that different from what most of us think of as TV's lowest life-form, the *Jerry Springer Show*.

So, what's next?

Well, will we really be surprised, say, in a year or two, to turn on the TV and hear a female character on a mainstream, prime-time network show tell some guy not merely "You're going to get laid tonight," but "I'm going to give you a blow job tonight"? And instead of couples just "humping beneath the covers" as they do now, maybe they'll hump right out there in the open.

If you're even vaguely tempted to say, "Come on, that's crazy;

that's way over the line; they'd never go that far"—remember that just a few years ago you would never have thought they'd go as far as they actually have!

And if you're also tempted to say, "Hey, *Will & Grace* and *Two and a Half Men* are *sitcoms*, lighten up, what's the big deal?"—then what do you say about a show called *The OC*, on Fox in prime time, about the lives of high school kids and their parents in ritzy Orange County, California? One story line has a boy named Luke having sex with his ex-girlfriend's mother after the mom just broke up with a buddy of Luke's grandfather. And what do you say about *Fear Factor*, the reality show where people hungry for their fifteen minutes of fame eat reindeer testicles and wash them down with fly and maggot shakes and do other stomach-turning things in order to amuse us? You think that stuff doesn't cheapen our culture?

Of course, there are those who will tell you with a straight face that crap on TV has *no* impact on society. As one liberal friend of mine puts it: "What's the big deal? If you don't like what's on, change the f**king channel."

And there it is, in all its charm and elegance, the liberal mantra: *What's the big deal? If you don't like what's on, change the f**king channel.*

Well, sure, go ahead and change the channel. But that's not going to make the problem go away. And just what *is* the big deal?

Just having to ask the question shows how far gone we are. For years now, we've understood that you truly are what you eat, that your diet has everything to do with your physical and even emotional health. Why then is it so hard to understand that inevitably you are also what you hear and see? I mean the same people who worry endlessly about the cleanliness of the environment—as they should—seem to have zero concern about the trashy environment promoted by TV.

A lot of cultural elites don't seem to notice—or don't seem to care—but in important ways, things have gone badly adrift in this country. We're less civil toward one another than we used to be—just like the characters on TV. We curse more and are more selfish, and cheat more—just like the characters on TV. No, of course that's not *all* the fault of television. But does anyone really doubt that there's an important connection between the "values" that are promoted on TV—the "values" that we and our kids stare at for hours and hours a day—and the way we behave in the rest of our lives? If messages on TV didn't matter, why in the world would advertisers spend billions year in and year out trying to sell us cars and computers and all sorts of other stuff? The fact is television doesn't simply *reflect* society's values. In important ways, it also legitimizes them. And more and more in recent decades it has made even the most dubious "values" and behaviors seem normal and routine. It's on TV, after all; what can be more mainstream than that?

I'm not saying people don't want to watch this stuff. They obviously do, or else a lot of these shows wouldn't be big hits. But if TV executives gave the American people free hardcore pornography on mainstream network TV, they'd watch that, too. As Max Headroom, the idealistic (and fictional) TV reporter, once put it: "In our business, morals are one thing, but ratings are everything."

So, *what's the big deal*? Most of us understand all too well what the big deal is—even if so many of those who should don't. And we also understand that changing the channel isn't even the beginning of a solution.

TV SCHLOCKMEISTERS—
NEWS DIVISION

ON FEBRUARY 15, 1966, Fred Friendly resigned as president of CBS News "as a matter of conscience," as he put it at the time.

A few days earlier, he had told his bosses at Black Rock, the CBS corporate headquarters in Manhattan, that he wanted to cover the Senate Foreign Relations Committee hearings on the war in Vietnam—live, at ten in the morning. America was getting deeper and deeper into the war—more and more young Americans were coming home in body bags—and this particular session that Fred Friendly wanted to cover live was seen as an especially important one.

But Friendly's bosses had a better idea. They figured that housewives would rather watch fun comedy shows than those boring hearings about the war. So they decided to air a fifth rerun of *I Love Lucy* and an eighth rerun of *The Real McCoys* instead of the Senate hearings.

Friendly, who was known to get emotional when things didn't go right, got plenty emotional. The way he saw it, his job—*and the job of television news*—wasn't ratings, but something a lot more important. Television news was supposed to keep the public informed about the important issues of the day, and nothing was more important in those days than Vietnam. So when the suits at Black Rock put on the *Lucy* and *Real McCoys* reruns, Fred Friendly quit.

Since news division presidents don't resign "as a matter of conscience" over anything anymore, there's a temptation to look at any comparison between Fred Friendly *then* and the men running television news divisions *now* as one between apples and oranges. But that would be unfair—to the fruit. Apples and oranges at least have a few things in common. Like, for instance, good taste. Comparing Friendly to the current presidents of CBS, NBC, and ABC News is more like comparing apples and lawn furniture.

Once, network news division presidents were men of great principle. These days, you don't get the top news job in the first place unless you're prepared to take off all your clothes and climb into bed with the network business guys who don't care about anything but the bottom line. These days, TV news executives not only understand but *embrace* the idea that job one, two, and three . . . is ratings. And if that means news shows like *20/20* and *Dateline* and *48 Hours*—that are watched by millions of Americans every week—have to be transformed into murder-of-the-week crime shows or vehicles for dumb celebrity ass-kissing interviews, if it means news has to become nothing more than any other show coming out of the TV set, hey, no problem—as long as I get to keep my fancy title, my big-salary job, my stock options, and my limo driver. And if Fred Friendly is spinning in his grave over all of this, that's his problem.

Forgive me if I put too fine a point on it, but these men are so cynical and so jaded, they don't even recognize how bad this is for their country. Journalists like Fred Friendly never had to be reminded that delivering the news wasn't the same as delivering a pepperoni pizza.

"This instrument can teach, it can illuminate; yes, and it can even inspire," as Friendly's CBS news partner, the legendary Edward R. Murrow, famously said of television in 1958. "But it can do so only to the extent that humans are determined to use it to those ends. Otherwise it is merely wires and lights in a box."

By now we all know about bias in the news and how destructive it has been to the credibility of network news divisions. By now we know about liberal agendas and how they worm their way into supposedly straight news. But bias isn't the only demon. The trivialization of news—the *corruption* of news by turning it into cheap entertainment—is, in its way, just as destructive a force.

Yes, it's true that despite the highbrow rhetoric, TV news people have always made compromises. It's the nature of their medium— "an incompatible combination of show business, advertising, and news" as Murrow also once said. In fact, back in the 50s, Ed Murrow himself not only did some of the most memorable broadcasts in television history—like his investigation of the tactics of Joseph McCarthy and the documentary *Harvest of Shame*, exposing the plight of migrant workers in America—but he also hosted *Person to Person*, a Friday-night ritual in America, which had Murrow sitting in New York, puffing away on a cigarette while interviewing stars like Marilyn Monroe and Elizabeth Taylor in their homes in faraway California.

But, unlike today's supposedly serious journalists, Ed Murrow never for a moment mistook his celebrity interviews for real news and, even on *Person to Person*, he never asked some starlet if she ever stuck her tongue down some other babe's throat or what she thought about masturbation. (If you're wondering what I'm raving about, just keep reading.) Besides, in those days Murrow was just the most renowned of a vast roster of journalists at CBS News of unquestioned skill and integrity, people like William L. Shirer, who had covered the rise and fall of Hitler in Germany, and Howard K. Smith, Charles Collingwood, Winston Burdett. One show alone,

Conversations with Eric Sevareid, a one-hour back-and-forth between the great CBS News correspondent and an equally intelligent guest, produced memorable conversations with heavyweights like Supreme Court Justice William O. Douglas, the blue-collar philosopher Eric Hoffer, and the brilliant commentator Walter Lippman.

Can you even imagine CBS putting on such a show today—in *prime time?* Can you imagine today's television news executives seeing it as part of their obligation to the American public? Sorry I even asked those questions. The very thought of one of today's "serious journalists" being asked to grapple with an actual idea beyond CONSERVATIVES = BAD, LIBERALS = GOOD would send them scurrying to their agents demanding an extra million in hardship pay.

Today, many of the most important journalists in the country are best known for sitting down with celebrities who have absolutely nothing important to say—and in the process, mangling the distinction between news and entertainment.

This is a business where the Queen of Crap herself, the one and only Barbara Walters, whom all the other news divas can only hope to imitate, feels completely at ease having the following charming exchange with Anne Heche, the actress and former lover of Ellen De Generes, the comedienne and talk show hostess.

WALTERS: Had you ever been with a woman before, sexually?
HECHE: No.
WALTERS: You went home with Ellen that night . . .
HECHE: That night.
WALTERS: . . . and you wrote in your book it was the best sex you ever had.
HECHE: No kidding. Up until that point that was the best sex— best sex I'd ever had.
WALTERS: Better than with any man?
HECHE: Yep.

And when it's all just too much, when Anne breaks down, as we all know she will, not to worry; she has her friend Babs nearby, who gently tells her, "Take your time. You all right? You want some water? . . . We'll do it together, OK?"

The only thing I'd like to see them do together is pull a Thelma and Louise and take a ride off a cliff into the Grand Freakin' Canyon.

Sure, this kind of stuff has always been around. Back in the 30s and 40s and 50s there were movie-fan magazines that peddled exactly the same kind of stuff to exactly the same kind of audience. And there are plenty of magazines around today that still do. Only no one back then confused celebrity fluff with real news.

How did it all happen? How did *Dateline* on NBC, to use one easy example, become such a journalistic embarrassment, shamelessly running hours and hours and hours of "news" reports on the network's own hit shows, like *The Apprentice* and *Friends* and *Frasier*? How did *48 Hours* on CBS, which used to run hour-long programs on the West Bank and South Africa, become a "mystery" magazine that now runs absolutely nothing but crime shows every week?

How did the once-sacrosanct realm of TV news get neck-deep in cheap exploitation in the name of ratings? Part of it, as Murrow said, is the nature of the medium. But there are also specific people who allowed and encouraged it to happen. Because while the people who used to run big important news divisions at big important television networks once had the right stuff, today's crowd doesn't come close. Because—and you'll excuse me for stating the obvious—Barbara Walters is no Ed Murrow, and even more so, the news division presidents who put this stuff on the air are no Fred Friendly.

But at least we still have Fred Friendly to remind us of how much we've lost. In his book *Due to Circumstances Beyond Our Control . . .* he wrote that by constantly playing to the lowest common denominator, the business people who run the networks have conditioned viewers to want only a certain kind of product coming out of their television sets.

"If you condition an audience to expect *The Real McCoys* . . . of course it will reject the Vietnam hearings," Fred Friendly wrote. "A Walter Lippmann interview in the weekly time period of *Petticoat Junction* would be greeted with just as much outrage as he would receive if you asked him to lecture between the double feature of any of the Forty-second Street movie houses. . . .

"Gresham's law—that the bad drives out the good—applies not only to the television schedules but to the television viewer."

News was always supposed to be the oasis in the vast wasteland of television. It would not only keep us informed about the most important events of the day, but also remind us of who we are, of our history and our values. The old gang understood that. The lawn furniture doesn't have a clue.

I'M YOUR PIMP, YOU MY BITCH
—and Other Great American Love Songs

I DON'T KNOW ABOUT YOU, but I'm just crazy about rap music. I especially like a certain kind of rap music known as gangsta rap. What I like most about gangsta rap are the lyrics. Something like this, for example, words which are as sweet and soothing as a sunny day in May.

> *I'm your pimp*
> *You my bitch*
> *Bring me my (dough)*

I admit it: I'm a sucker for a love song.

Then there's this one, a tune that calls to mind one of my favorites—Sinatra's uplifting "You Make Me Feel So Young":

> *Innie, minnie, mini, mo, pick the do' or the flo'*
> *Ho' you gotta go if you ain't takin off ya clothes*
> *All I really wanna do is stick a dick up in you*

Talk about heart-warming.

Another thing I so appreciate about gangsta rap is how it brings together people of all races and creeds. After all, who could articulate a message about brotherhood in America as well as the rapper Apache, on his album, charmingly titled *Apache Ain't Shit*?

> *Kill the white people,*
> *we gonna make them hurt,*
> *kill the white people,*
> *but buy my record first,*
> *ha, ha, ha*

I mean, who needs "God Bless America"?

And even though rap is mainly a black art form, there are some wonderful white rappers out there, led by that gentle soul Eminem, a favorite not only of children everywhere but also of distinguished critics at places like the *New York Times*. Remember how the sentimental singers of times gone by used to dedicate songs to their beloved mothers? Well, Eminem, whose real name is Marshall Mathers, has brought back this wonderful tradition, rapping this way about his mother in the extremely touching "Kill You":

> *Slut, you think I won't choke no whore*
> *till the vocal cords don't work in her throat no more?!*
> *Bitch I'ma kill you! Like a murder weapon, I'ma conceal*
>   *you*
> *in a closet with mildew, sheets, pillows and film you*

It almost makes you want to cry.

That part, I'm serious about. It really does.

Did I say I love gangsta rap? Sorry, slip of the tongue. What I meant to say is I hate gangsta rap. It is moronic, disgusting, inane, ignorant, and soul-deadening, not to mention—with its murderous lyrics that cheapen human life and glamorize perversity—dangerous and destructive. And that's the *best* I can say about it.

Of course, the lovers of rap—including legions of high-brow liberal critics—will tell you that rap artists are "just keepin' it real, just rappin' about the hard life in the 'hood, which beats that phony 'moon, June' garbage any day of the week." Besides, they'll tell you that pop music isn't *supposed* to be civil and polite, and that music aimed at kids has always been *edgy*. Remember Jerry Lee Lewis, Little Richard, and Elvis, and how all those straight-laced prudes and ignoramuses went after *them*? It's the same today, they'll tell you: smart, with-it people get it; hicks don't.

Then again, as one critic told me a few years back when I was reporting on the subject for CBS News, "There's a qualitative difference between 'I want you, I need you, I love you,' to, 'I'll slash you, I'll mutilate you, I'll kill you.'"

"What we are saying," he added, "is we don't think this is good. They say, 'We have a right to do this.' We say, 'We know. We know about your right to do it.' Now we're trying to run a society here. We're trying to raise children here."

But the man speaking this obvious common sense happened to be William Bennett, so don't expect any of the cultural elites to take any of what he said seriously. Or, for that matter, anything said on the subject by Herb London, a professor at New York University, because, on matters like these, he's also a conservative. Ask Professor London if rap signals the end of Western civilization, as some say.

"The end of Western civilization? Who knows. The end of civility? Without question."

"Try as they will, record executives contend that the lyrics do not lead to coarse behavior," London has written. "This is said with some disingenuousness since violence is manifest in the entire rap world."

And if there's a theme running through this so-called music, it's that women are worthless, nothing more than "bitches" and "ho's." Yet, as London writes, "What remains curious is the conspicuous silence of feminists. Here is so-called music that treats women as objects, that degrades and humiliates them. Yet very few feminists have come out against it.

"How can this be explained? Is there a fear that any criticism of rap will be interpreted as racism? Several feminist professors such as Catherine MacKinnon have called for speech codes at American universities in order to detect and remove language that might be offensive to women, words such as 'freshman.'

"When it comes to degradation in rap, even calls for unspeakably brutal acts, however, the feminists avert their gaze."

And with the degrading music come the grim videos and the other gangsta "entertainment" that typically portray black neighborhoods "as wastelands filled with pimps, addicts and prostitutes," as Errol Louis, a (black) columnist for the *New York Sun* has written. "Flip on any television or radio at virtually any hour of the day," he says, "and most of what purports to concern itself with black Americans is a long, stale parade of degrading caricatures.

"There are gun-toting men who boast of shooting their rivals to death in cold blood, and young women who brag about acting like money-crazed whores. Life is portrayed as horrifyingly violent and unendingly bleak—and this nightmare is sold to the global market as 'authentic' black culture."

And as John McWhorter, the scholar and author, has put, it: "If this idiom had been created by whites, it would have been gone a long time ago, because we [blacks] wouldn't have stood for it."

In a way, this tolerance —or avoidance—gets to the very heart of the problem, and to some of the names on the list of one hundred. There's always been ugliness in the world, and there have always been those who peddled it for profit. We live in a society that is free enough for even the demented to operate in the marketplace. But until very recently, those whom society regarded as "responsible people"—including leaders in the entertainment field and critics at important national publications—treated them with the contempt they deserved, thereby protecting the culture by holding the line on standards. No more. Today, too many of those who should be protecting the culture are too busy applauding those tearing it down.

"In the end there will be a price to be paid for this," says Herb London, the conservative professor and critic, "the price one always pays for ignoring evil. Some of the best potential minds will be decimated. Culture will be assaulted beyond repair and the nation will be undermined from within."

Or, as my friend, the journalist and author John Underwood, has so elegantly put it: "In a society where anything goes, everything, eventually, will. A society that stands for nothing will fall for anything—and then, of course, will just simply fall."

AMERICAN JACKALS

IT'S SUNDAY MORNING IN SPRINGFIELD, and Homer Simpson is on his way to church with his family, when he gets lucky. Not paying attention to what he's doing, as usual, Homer falls into a hole right outside the church.

And out of nowhere, a sleazy ambulance-chasing lawyer pops up. "Slip and fall?" he says, just like one of those real-life victim-trolling lawyers on TV. "Can't go back to work? I am Larry H. Lawyer Jr. and I will fight for YOU! (I also habla espanol.)"

It's like a light bulb goes off over Homer's head, and he exclaims, "I'll sue the church!"

"You have rights," Lawyer eggs him on. "You deserve compensation."

Suddenly the ever-sleazy Dr. Nick Riviera appears on the scene, in a neck brace, breathlessly telling Homer, "He got *me* $60,000! And I was driving drunk in a graveyard!"

"You're my first client who is actually injured," the lawyer says, holding up a big book labeled LAW. "According to this book, that's a big plus."

I guess so, because Homer takes the church to court, wins a million dollars, and when the church is unable to come up with the money, he is awarded the building and the church is forced to shut down.

Okay, *The Simpsons* is a fictional TV show. Homer is a cartoon character. The show's writers can be as ridiculous as they want just to get a laugh. Here's the problem: when it comes to outrageous lawsuits, no matter how hard they try, they can't top reality.

Need proof?

A woman from New York sues the city because she was hit by a subway train and seriously injured. Right before the train hit her, police say, she had been calmly lying on the tracks trying to commit suicide.

After lightning knocks out a Florida prison's TV satellite dish, a prisoner—convicted of brutally murdering five people—sues because now he can only watch *network* programs, which he says contain violence, profanity, and other objectionable material.

A man from Montana sues the media giant Viacom, charging that its MTV show *Jackass* has plagiarized his name and defamed his good character. The man doing the suing is named Jack Ass. It used to be Bob Craft, but he, Mr. Ass, legally changed it to raise awareness about the dangers of drunk driving.

A man from California sues two Las Vegas hotels, claiming their casinos were negligent in allowing him to gamble away more than a million dollars—while he was intoxicated.

A woman in Tennessee files a class-action lawsuit against Janet Jackson, Justin Timberlake, CBS, MTV, and Viacom because she and others suffered "outrage, anger, embarrassment and serious injury" when Janet Jackson flashed her breast during halftime of the 2004 Super Bowl. Less than a week later, she withdraws the lawsuit saying she believes she made her point.

And what exactly would that point be? That you don't have to officially be called Jack Ass to act like one? That in the United States of Litigation anybody can sue anybody for anything any time he or she feels like it?

The temptation to bring Shakespeare into this ("The first thing we do is kill all the lawyers") is overwhelming, but that would be too easy—and maybe just a bit unfair. Not *all* lawyers are jackals, after all. Some are good people who do good, honest work.

That's why we have to hold the others accountable, the ones who have systematically trashed one of the fundamental principles that has made America the great country that it is—*the principle of personal responsibility*. Thanks to a "lawsuit culture" the jackals helped create, a lot of Americans figure if something goes wrong in their lives, well, then "somebody's got to pay." Nothing could possibly be *our* fault. It's always the other guy who did us in. Somehow we think we're entitled to *perfect* lives. And if some imperfection intercedes, there will be no shortage of lawyers who will not only take the ridiculous case but also argue passionately that there is absolutely nothing ridiculous about it—no matter how inane it might be!

These days, we live in a country where people who manufacture car batteries have to put warnings on them, pretty much saying "Don't Drink the Battery Acid"—because either somebody already did or because they're afraid they'll get sued if somebody does. Over the years, I have collected a list of incredibly dopey warning labels, all aimed at heading off costly (and equally dopey) lawsuits:

On the packaging of an iron: "Do not iron clothes on body."

On a package of Nytol sleeping aid: "May cause drowsiness."

On a hair dryer: "Do not use while sleeping."

On a TV remote-control device: "Not dishwasher safe."

On a kid's scooter: "This product moves when used."

Okay, either we've become a nation of morons or something has gone drastically wrong in America. Not that long ago, no one would believe that some fat guy would actually sue the fast food industry for making him . . . fat. It sounded more like a joke. Let me know when you're through laughing, because a New Yorker, who weighs nearly three hundred pounds and has eaten junk food for decades, four or five times a week, even after suffering a heart attack, not only filed a class-action lawsuit against four fast-food chains but with a straight, fat face says, "They never explained to me what I was eating."

And here's the real bad news: Lawsuits like that don't shock us anymore. We're not even remotely surprised that, having moved on from cigarettes, the litigation industry now has its eye on fast-food chains as the next big cash cow. So expect more fat guys who eat fast food four or five times a week to claim they didn't know what they were shoving down their throats. And why *not* go after fast food? Especially since none other than the great consumer crusader Ralph Nader himself has called a McDonald's hamburger "a weapon of mass destruction."

But does a guy who eats like a horse and winds up looking like a pig really deserve a few million dollars—or a few cents, for that matter? Isn't he responsible for what he stuffs into his big mouth? To which his lawyer, if he were honest, would reply: *"What does responsibility have to do with anything—especially with so many dollars at stake?"*

The lawyers, of course, argue that they're just standing up for the "little guy"—and these days that may literally be true, at least when they're representing some twelve-year-old kid suing his parents. They'll tell you that ordinary people need protection against doctors who screw up and corporations that abuse their customers or their own employees—and they're absolutely right. Careless doctors should be pounded when they make stupid mistakes and hurt patients who trusted them. Corporations should have to pay up, too, if they make products that are so badly designed that they cause needless injury. Businesses should be penalized if they violate the labor laws at the expense of their own workers. That's all good with me.

But there's also another truth that a lot of lawyers don't like to talk about, a larger truth, about how trial lawyers have changed the American landscape, and not in a good way, routinely going after individuals and companies not always because they've done wrong, but simply because they can. As an exhaustive report by the Center for Legal Policy at the Manhattan Institute, a conservative think tank, sums it up, today's "kingpins of the lawsuit industry have pursued mass tort and class action suits and turned litigation into a multi-billion-dollar business. . . . The impact of predatory litigation is staggering. Asbestos litigation alone has driven 67 companies bankrupt, including many that never made or installed asbestos, costing tens of thousands of jobs and soaking up billions of dollars in potential investment capital. . . . The lawsuit industry even has its own venture capitalists—investors who back firms filing enormous, speculative class action suits with the hope that there will be rich rewards somewhere down the road."

If you're starting to think this sounds like what goes on in a casino, you're not alone. "We're waiting for the nation's judges to raise an alarm over what's happening to their hallowed courts," as an editorial in the *Wall Street Journal* put it. "If they won't, then maybe we should think about exchanging those black robes for tuxes and pink ties and replacing the gavel with a croupier's stick."

And as we know by now, jackpot-seeking lawsuits have had an especially devastating impact on the medical field. The Manhattan Institute study points out that in 2002, "a dozen states experienced medical emergencies because doctors and hospitals could no longer afford malpractice insurance. Women scrambled for doctors to deliver their babies, seriously injured patients had to be airlifted out of some locations because there were no practicing emergency-room physicians available and hospitals closed maternity wards to protect themselves.

"And thanks to [the trial lawyers] the babies that do get delivered are vulnerable to deadly and thoroughly preventable diseases. Why? The litigation industry has used specious theories lacking scientific support to sue vaccine manufacturers for alleged harmful effects caused by vaccines and vaccine preservatives."

The fact is the legal industry has become hazardous not only to our individual health but also to our national well-being. "Doctors, teachers, ministers, even Little League coaches find their daily decisions hampered by legal fear," according to Philip Howard, who runs a nonprofit organization called Common Good. "Our system of justice is now considered a tool for extortion, not balance."

Philip Howard, by the way, is a lawyer himself!

And to make sure the casino never closes, the trial lawyers have even set up numerous Web sites to troll for class-action victims online. "Justice is now a click away," according to one of those Web sites, where, for $8.95 a month, you can find hundreds of class-action "opportunities" and sign up to get "the money that you may be due."

Speaking of "the money that you may be due" . . . remember that woman who sued New York City because she got hit by a subway train after, according to the cops, she apparently decided to lie down on the tracks and wait for the train to run over her? A jury awarded her $14.1 million. The court, however, said that was too much, since she did, after all, voluntarily put herself in the path of the train. So it cut her award . . . down to a measly $9.9 million.

I told you this stuff is a riot. It makes you laugh and laugh and laugh . . . right up until the time you want to cry.

I'M OFFENDED,
THEREFORE I AM

I READ SOMEPLACE that about 70 percent of all Americans have a special advantage: they're *disadvantaged.*

In other words, they're black, Hispanic, Indian, female, gay, disabled, fat, blind, deaf, mute, depressed, angry, perfume-sensitive, unable to pay attention in class, *won't* pay attention in class, non-English-speaking, or . . . hell, just fill in the blank.

The great thing about being disadvantaged is that you get all sorts of advantages. You get affirmative action points and government contracts and special consideration at diversity-obsessed colleges and corporations.

"White males are the only growth area for the modern victim movement," says John Leo, in his *U.S. News and World Report* column. "Everybody else is already covered." Good thing. I mean if they start counting white guys as victims there won't be anyone left to blame for all the *other* victims.

Welcome to the not-so-wonderful world of identity politics, where the whole marvelous idea of this nation, captured in its original motto "*e pluribus unum*"—"out of many, one"—has been turned on its head. Instead of celebrating the things that unite us as a people, in today's America we dwell endlessly on the things that divide us, then figure out how we can profit from those differences— and who cares if it's at the expense of someone else?

E pluribus unum? Forget about it. Our new national motto might as well be "What's in it for me?"

Of course, there's nothing wrong with a healthy dose of self-interest. But this is different. Identity politics is fundamentally whiny and debilitating. And as no less a liberal than blue-collar journalist Pete Hamill has put it, "at the core of identity politics" is "wormy self-pity."

"The genius of the American experience," as Hamill has eloquently written, "has been its great leveling power. Human beings from a great variety of cultures arrived here, collided, went to schools or wars together, married each other, and built an amazing country. Most of them were too busy to feel sorry for themselves. Much of that healthy attitude has eroded. Today, we too often find Americans whose essential slogan is, 'I'm offended, therefore I am.'"

Why does it matter? Because "that oh-woe-is-me attitude is paralyzing," as Hamill puts it. "If you believe the deck is stacked from birth, then why bother struggling? If you think that you will never have a real chance at a full life because you are a woman, a homosexual, short, bald, or fat, or if your ancestors came from Africa or spoke Spanish, you will never have that real chance because you will not take it. If you reduce yourself to some sociological category instead of being fully human, you will also be building your own little psychic jail."

Which, sadly, is where too many "victims" feel most comfortable.

When did we start to see that being a victim had its rewards? According to James Piereson, in the *Weekly Standard*, it was during the 70s, when "an impressive network of interest groups was developed to promote and take advantage of this sense of historical guilt.

These included various feminist and civil rights groups who pressed for affirmative action, quotas, and other policies to compensate women and minorities for past mistreatment; the welfare rights organizations who claimed that welfare and various poverty programs were entitlements or, even better, reparations that were owed to the poor as compensation for similar mistreatment.

"If one asked whether it was really fair to impose employment quotas for women and minorities, one often heard the answer, 'White men imposed quotas on us, and now we're going to do the same to them!' Was busing of school children really an effective means of improving educational opportunities for blacks? A parallel answer was often given: 'Whites bused blacks to enforce segregation, and now they deserve to get a taste of their own medicine!'"

And that's what identity politics, and its first cousin, multiculturalism, are largely about—dividing Americans into groups, then cataloging all the injustices you can dig up. Open up a junior high school history book sometime and you'll have a tough time finding references to even the greatest American achievements—because they've been pushed out by all the stuff about the cruelty and oppression our forefathers heaped on ethnic minorities. Even our cherished National Museum of American History in Washington has become "a museum of multicultural grievances," as David Brooks once called it in a piece on that venerable institution.

"Six times more space is devoted to the interment of and prejudice against Japanese Americans," he wrote, "than to the entire rest of World War II. There is no mention of Eisenhower, Patton, Marshall, or MacArthur, leaders who weren't exactly incidental to American conduct of the war. Similarly, there is but one showcase devoted to World War I. And that showcase is devoted to the role of women in the war. Nor would you have any idea why World War I was fought, who was on which side, or how America came to be involved."

Then again, as far as the most dedicated multiculturalists are concerned, why *should* America be celebrated? What's so special about us? One of their core beliefs, after all, is that all cultures are equal. Help me out: How exactly is a nation that cherishes "inalienable rights" and codifies its most sacred beliefs about government and its people in a "Bill of Rights" *in any way* "equal" to cultures that are built on brutality and intolerance? To the true believers, Western civilization is no better than any other civilization in the world. Earth to Palo Alto: Yes it is.

In multicultural America, everything is relative—even (make that *especially*) matters of right and wrong. In multicultural America, being sensitive carries more weight than being thoughtful. Consider this little gem from the National Education Association, the largest teachers union in the country and one of multiculturalism's biggest cheerleaders: Right after September 11, 2001, the NEA came up with some "tips for parents and teachers," which included a piece of advice on what we should all learn from the terrorist attacks against the United States: "Appreciating and getting along with people of diverse backgrounds and cultures, the importance of anger management and global awareness."

As the columnist George Will put it: "Let's see. Some seriously angry people murder almost 3,000 people in America and *Americans* need to work on managing *their* anger?"

This nonsense would be a lot easier to laugh at if it weren't so potentially dangerous. The fact is, for a long time, in other places, they've been pushing this idea of people focusing on their own group's grievances instead of the common good, and we've seen the results: places like Northern Ireland and Rwanda and the former Yugoslavia. No one says that the multiculturalists don't have good intentions. But you know the old saying about how the road to hell is paved with good intentions. Well, I'm afraid that the radio commentator Dennis Prager got it right: "If we continue to teach about tolerance and intolerance instead of good and evil, we will end up with tolerance of evil."

RACIAL ENFORCERS

CHRIS ROCK USED TO DO A BIT he called "Niggas vs. Black People." In the routine, black people are decent folks who work hard to feed their families and pay the bills. Niggas are something else altogether. Black people play by the rules. Niggas think they should get a medal just for taking care of their own babies. Black people go to the movies to watch the movie. Niggas go to shoot up the place. "There's like a civil war going on with black people," Chris Rock said. "There are two sides: there's black people and there's niggas. *And the niggas got to go.*"

The routine always got a great reaction—because, like all the best comedy, it was honest, and the audience knew it. It was the kind of material that transforms a mere stand-up comic into an important social commentator, which is exactly what Chris Rock has become (his performance at the 2005 Academy Awards notwithstanding).

And even though, according to the unwritten rules, there are certain things black people aren't supposed to say in front of white people, Chris Rock gets away with stuff like "Niggas vs. Black People" not just because he's black (an absolute prerequisite), but also because he's doing it as comedy. Say the same thing without

39

the laughs, say it straight-faced and serious, say it with America's black civil rights establishment listening, and heaven help you— even if you're black *and* a comedian.

Just ask Bill Cosby.

In May 2004, Cosby was the keynote speaker at an NAACP-sponsored gala in Washington, D.C., and, as you might expect, he talked about civil rights, about the long, hard struggles black people had to endure in this country. But then he veered way off the usual course and did the unthinkable. On the stage of Constitution Hall, speaking from his heart to a multiracial audience, he told some of the same truths Chris Rock had told in his comedy act. Too many black kids, Cosby said, were squandering the many opportunities that some very brave people in the civil rights movement had made possible for them.

It was a watershed moment, one that might actually launch a brutally honest, long-overdue national conversation about the devastating problems that are crippling too many black communities in this country: a 70 percent out-of-wedlock birth rate that puts black children behind the eight ball from the day they're born, a 50 percent high school dropout rate for inner-city black males (which Cosby correctly characterized as an "epidemic"), the senseless violence that destroys not only individual lives but also entire communities.

"I can't even talk the way these people talk," Cosby said, referring to the "black English" that is so common in inner-city neighborhoods. "'Why you ain't, where you is?' . . . They're standing on the corner and they can't speak English. . . . I don't know who these people are. And I blamed the kid until I heard the mother talk. And then I heard the father talk. It's all in the house. You used to talk a certain way on the corner and when you got in the house you switched to English. Everybody knows that at some point you switch to English, except these knuckleheads. . . . You can't be a doctor with that kind of crap coming out of your mouth."

Then, a few politically incorrect words on black crime: "I'm talking about these people who cry when their son is standing there in an orange [prison jump] suit. Where were you when he was two? Where were you when he was twelve? Where were you when he was eighteen and how come you don't know he had a pistol?"

And on the single biggest cause of black poverty in America—kids having kids out of wedlock—Cosby had this to say: "Grandmother, mother, and great-grandmother in the same place raising children, and the child knows nothing about love or respect from any one of the three of them. All the child knows is give me, give me, give me.'"

If Chris Rock had said this, walking back and forth, up and down the stage, belting it out in his signature-style, he would have brought the house down. But not Bill Cosby. Because he wasn't joking.

How did *his* audience, the civil rights establishment that had invited him to speak, respond to the speech? Not too well. When he was done, several of his hosts walked up to the podium, "looking stone-faced" as the *Washington Post* put it. One of them, Theodore Shaw, the head of the NAACP Legal Defense Fund, even took the microphone to (in his view, anyway) set the record straight, telling the crowd that the problems "in the black community were not self-inflicted."

Why such a reaction to Cosby's remarks about dysfunctional behavior when every sensible person knows that what Bill Cosby said was true? Partly because he said it out loud. Mainly because white people heard what he said. "Bill Cosby broke the unwritten rule of keeping black dirty laundry in black washing machines," as *Time* magazine columnist Christopher John Farley neatly put it.

Maybe, but if anyone should have been able to break the rule, it's Bill Cosby, who not only has dedicated much of his life to the fight for civil rights, but—more than almost anyone—has put his money where his mouth is, donating tens of millions of dollars to black colleges. But none of that mattered, not after Cosby spoke the truth about race—out loud, without joking.

Because when it comes to the issue of race in America—without question, the single most important domestic issue we face in this country—there are those who will fight tooth and nail to prevent the telling of certain truths, enforcing what the brilliant black academic Shelby Steele calls "racial etiquette."

Who are the enforcers on race? Start with the leaders of the black civil rights establishment. To them, the very idea that in the twenty-first century, the problems that continue to beset the black community might have less to do with racism than with *values* and *behaviors* in that community is a dangerous idea; dangerous because decades after numerous laws were passed to ban discrimination, many black leaders continue to derive their moral authority—and much of their funding—by pushing the idea of black victimhood, by blaming white "society" for what ails black America, no matter how unproductive that may be.

There's no question that many problems black Americans face today stem from slavery and segregation. No question at all! But the slaveholders and the segregationists can't fix the problem. The government can help, but it can't fix it, either. As Amy Wax, a professor at the University of Pennsylvania Law School, has written, "short of coercion, it is literally impossible for the government or outsiders to change dysfunctional behavior or make good choices for individuals. No one can force a person to obey the law, study hard, develop useful skills, be well-mannered, speak and write well, work steadily, marry and stay married, be a devoted husband and father, and refrain from bearing children he cannot or will not support."

Maybe the black civil rights establishment would see that more clearly if it were not for the coconspirators who are at work here— white liberals. They are at least as guilty, if not more so, because in the name of compassion and decency and "racial etiquette" they have become enablers. The liberal establishment has a cozy deal with the black establishment: liberals don't bring up uncomfortable realities about black Americans and, together, black leaders and white liberals get to blame racism and heartless conservatives for the black community's ills. As Shelby Steele points out, the payoff for liberals is they get to parade their "racial virtue" and "show themselves free of racism." Never mind that this willingness to hold blacks to a lower standard in everything from speech to educational achievement itself smacks of racism. What else does such condescension signify, if not the assumption of inferiority? Still, in their moral smugness, this never seems to occur to well-meaning liberals. Like so much else, it's ultimately about them, and their own sense of virtue.

Indeed, when black conservatives like Shelby Steele, Clarence Thomas, or Ward Connerly try to address some of these issues in a serious and responsible way—questioning affirmative action, for instance, or supporting vouchers to give poor blacks a chance to attend the kind of schools middle- and upper-class whites take for granted—it is white liberals who are usually the first to start throwing around terms like "sellout" or "Uncle Tom."

In fact, when it comes to mealy-mouthed terror at the thought of saying what needs to be said, the further left the liberal is, the mealier the mouth. Which is why my favorite moment of the 2004 campaign season was also one of the most telling. Just before the Iowa caucuses—when liberal firebrand Howard Dean was still riding high as the front-runner for the nomination, admired by his party's left wing for his supposedly courageous willingness to speak out—he came under attack from fellow candidate Al Sharpton. The charge? Dean had appointed no blacks to his cabinet as governor of Vermont.

"Do you have a senior member of your cabinet that was black or brown?" Sharpton demanded to know.

Watching Sharpton do what he does best—play the race card—Dean could have gone a number of ways. He might have said,

"Brush up on America, Reverend Sharpton, it's a ridiculous question. According to the last census, only one-half of one percent of Vermont's population is black. One-half of one percent! What was I supposed to do, turn down qualified local people and start looking for black people from other states?"

Or even better, he could have gotten angry—something, in other situations, he famously had done so well—and demanded: *"Reverend Sharpton, how dare you, of all people, lecture me on the subject of race relations."*

He could have thrown in Sharpton's associations with Tawana Brawley—whose very name can't even be mentioned anymore unless you also throw in the word "hoax" someplace close by. He could have brought up the matter of the Jewish shop owner in Harlem whom Sharpton had called "white interloper," shortly before the man's store was set on fire, a fire that left eight people dead.

Instead Dean looked like a deer in the headlights, and as he fumbled for an answer, you could almost see the wheels turning: *"This isn't fair, only conservatives are supposed to be attacked this way!"* "We had a senior member of my staff," he finally mumbled.

"No, your cabinet!" Sharpton persisted.

"No," said Dean, badly shaken, "we did not."

But just imagine if Dean had spoken the truth. If he had done that, most of the country would have cheered. If he had done that, he might even be President Howard Dean today.

But, of course, that's impossible, because if he had done that, he wouldn't be what he is: a white liberal, who will *never* speak honestly about race.

WHITE-COLLAR THUGS

JON STEWART, the host of the *Daily Show*, is a pretty smart guy, and one night he asked a pretty smart question. After showing his audience a videotape of executives from Enron and its crooked accounting firm Arthur Andersen, he turned to the camera and shouted: "Why aren't all of you in jail? And not like white-guy jail. *Jail* jail. With people by the weight room going, 'Mmmmmm.'"

Or as a pal of mine wondered: "Why don't they take the bastards out and hang 'em?"

Of course, it's not just Enron or Arthur Andersen. A lot of people have been asking that very same question about the cretins at companies like WorldCom and Global Crossing and Tyco and a few other Fortune 500 giants whose very names have become synonymous with shameless greed and the exploitation of ordinary people. These are companies, in many cases, that no longer exist, because they were driven into bankruptcy by well-educated crooks in pinstripe suits who were unhappy making a crummy 20 million or so a year. These were people who just had to have more, so they could live even more ostentatiously—buy even bigger houses, drive even flashier cars, take even more lavish vacations to even more exotic places in their private jets. So they cooked the books and screwed everybody—from some of their biggest stockholders down to the janitor.

These are white-collar thugs who cost tens of thousands of good, decent Americans their jobs. Many lost their pensions. Many saw their life savings vanish in an instant. Some were too old to start over again. And while the crooks were trying to figure out new and exciting ways to spend their money, the ones who came to work every day and played by the rules—the ones who *trusted* the people they worked for—were trying to figure out more mundane things, like how to keep paying the mortgage and send their kids to college.

To call what they did obscene is an understatement.

Remember that upbeat dog-and-pony show that Enron executives put on for their own employees? How they reassured them that business was terrific? How they enticed them to buy even more Enron stock for their 401(k) pension accounts—and how those workers lost their life savings when the company went bankrupt? And, by the way, while Enron employees were buying, top Enron executives and directors were selling—over a billion dollars worth of their own Enron stock, which, I'm sure, was just a coincidence.

Remember the *secret* audiotapes of those *private* telephone conversations between Enron energy traders on the West Coast that became *public* in mid-2004? In case anyone wanted to hear what pure, shameless greed sounds like, here it was, in tape after tape after tape.

After a forest fire shut down a transmission line into California—which cut power supplies and raised prices—Enron traders were jubilant.

"Burn, baby, burn. That's a beautiful thing," we hear a happy trader telling one of his colleagues.

When a power company near Seattle charged Enron with illegally jacking up energy prices and tried to get its money back, the traders laughed at the *suckers* they had swindled.

TRADER #1: They're (expletive) takin' all the money back from
you guys? All that money you guys stole from those poor
grandmothers in California?

TRADER #2: Yeah, Grandma Millie, man.

TRADER #1: Yeah, now she wants her (expletive) money back
for all the power you've charged right up—jammed right up
her ass for (expletive) $250 a megawatt-hour.

During California's rolling blackouts—when people were trapped
in elevators and sat in dark houses without air-conditioning—the
tapes reveal Enron's traders scheming about shutting down power
plants and talking about shipping electricity *out of the state*—to drive
prices up even higher.

TRADER #1: What we need to do is to help in the cause of a
downfall of California. You guys need to pull your megawatts
out of California on a daily basis.

TRADER #2: They're on the ropes today. I exported like (expletive) 400 megs.

TRADER #3: Wow, (expletive) them, right?

These are the kind of people that make their role models—the
robber barons of the late nineteenth century—look like Mother
Teresa by comparison.

If some black kid in Harlem mugged an old lady and was caught
on tape laughing about it, they'd lock his ass up in Attica, or someplace like it. Which is exactly what they ought to do with the
white-collar thugs who ruined so many lives.

Or, better yet, "take the bastards out and hang 'em."

SEX WARRIORS

A FEW YEARS AGO, I was the keynote speaker at the annual meeting of the National Organization for Women in Washington, D.C. Every important feminist this side of Venus was there. I got a standing ovation as I walked to the podium, and my speech was interrupted too many times to count by enthusiastic applause.

I started out by saying, "I'm going to take this opportunity to speak truth to power." I pointed out that there was just too much anger coming from the entrenched feminist camp, too much hostility that often showed its ugly face in the form of male-bashing. I told them I thought Gloria Steinem's line about how "a woman needs a man like a fish needs a bicycle" was juvenile, and that over the years, there had been too much of the same from feminist leaders. In conclusion, I told them to back off, to knock off the sexual-warrior crap, that men were not the enemy, and that their constant whining about being "victims" made them look not like strong women but like little schoolgirls.

Then, two incredible things happened: First, every woman in the room rose as one and gave me a roaring second standing ovation, which went on even longer than the first. Then my alarm clock went off.

Yes, I would have to be dreaming to think anything like that could really happen, because the second you open your mouth to say anything even mildly critical of feminism—or, more accurately, the excesses of feminism—you're immediately called either anti-woman, right-wing, reactionary, or, if you're female, a traitor to your gender. And that's just for openers.

Look, let me gladly acknowledge the many good things feminists have accomplished for women in this country: Women can vote, thanks to feminists. Women can work in whatever field interests them, thanks to feminists. Women can be sexually liberated if they choose, thanks to feminists. Women can compete in school sports and even pro sports, thanks to feminists. Women can blah, blah blah, blah blah, blah, blah blah . . .

A personal note: I have a daughter, as well as a son, so I couldn't be happier that she's got many more opportunities than her grandmother had. And if that were all that feminism was about—leveling the playing field—I'd not only have a picture of Molly Yard hanging over my bed, I'd kiss it every now and then.

But that's not what feminism in America is about. Too much of the time it's about the never-ending saga of women as "victims" and men as "oppressors."

Let's look at what some of the leaders of modern feminism have said since the revolution began:

- Catherine Commins, when she was an assistant dean of students at Vassar College, told *Time* magazine that "Men who are unjustly accused of rape can gain from the experience."

- Marilyn French, a best-selling feminist author, has written that "The entire system of female oppression rests on ordinary men, who maintain it with a fervor and dedication to duty that any secret police force might envy. What other system can depend on almost half the population to enforce a policy daily, publicly and privately, with utter reliability. . . . As long as some men use physical force to subjugate females, all men need not."

- Mary Daly, an important feminist academic, when asked what she thought of the idea (put forth by another feminist) that the male population should be reduced, to cut down on violence, responded: "I think it's not a bad idea at all. If life is to survive on this planet, there must be a decontamination of the Earth. I think this will be accompanied by an evolutionary process that will result in a drastic reduction of the population of males. People are afraid to say that kind of stuff anymore."

Gee, I wonder why. But instead of being shunned as radicals spouting screwball feminist theology, these women, and many more like them, have actually been embraced—and not just by other radical feminists, but also by the mainstream media, who portray them as visionaries and latter-day heroines. And with that kind of respectability bestowed on them, they have pushed programs and legislative agendas that have driven us apart, defining women as victims perpetually in need of special treatment; worse, they've been allowed to rewrite textbooks and alter school curricula in an effort to indoctrinate our children, pushing their tired notions about victims and oppressors.

Like so many other activists, who are less interested in the facts than in stoking anger on behalf of their own agenda, radical feminists refuse to acknowledge a basic reality: Times have changed. They've changed a lot and they've changed for the better. The evidence is so obvious and so overwhelming, it takes a lot of work and a kind of willful blindness to deny it.

- In America today, women earn the majority of bachelor's degrees and master's degrees, and are projected to earn the majority of doctoral degrees within a generation.

• For all the attention paid to the "wage gap," when allowances are made for experience and voluntary absences to have and raise children, such a gap ceases to exist.

And as Cathy Young, who describes herself as a "dissident feminist," has pointed out, the feminist rhetoric of women-as-victims has almost nothing to do with today's reality. "Girls are not silenced or ignored in the classroom," she writes in her book *Ceasefire!* "Medicine has not neglected women's health. Abuse by men is not the leading cause of injury to American women. . . . Gender disparities in pay and job status are not merely a consequence of sex discrimination . . ."

Ms. Young is right. It is time for a ceasefire. Better yet, it's time to finally end the gender wars altogether. Because the radical feminists who have been trying to create a brave new world in their own image only speak for themselves. They sure don't speak for most men in America and—you know what?—they don't speak for most women, either.

And they never did.

READING, WRITING,
AND RADICALS

ON NOVEMBER 18, 2004, I saw this headline in the *New York Times*: REPUBLICANS OUTNUMBERED IN ACADEMIA, STUDIES FIND.

What's next? SUN RISES IN THE EAST, STUDIES FIND.

It's not exactly news that most professors these days are liberals. But the numbers are probably more lopsided than you thought. According to the *Times*, one study of more than 1,000 academics nationwide showed that Democrat professors outnumbered Republicans by at least 7 to 1 in the humanities and social sciences.

Studies like this come out all the time. One poll found that in eight academic departments at Cornell, 166 professors were registered Democrat (or another party on the Left), and just 6 were registered Republican (or another party on the Right).

At the University of Colorado at Boulder it was 116 on the Left, 5 on the Right.

At Brown, 54 professors were on the Left, 3 on the Right.

Talk to any liberal on a college campus and you get a lecture about how *essential* diversity is to campus life. Of course, they don't mean the ideological kind of diversity. These are people who support things like free speech—except when free speech gets in the way of something they hold even more sacred. And that would be the sensibilities of the "oppressed"—a group that includes just about everyone except white guys who aren't disabled. As Wendy Kaminer, the author and journalist, has put it: "Never mind that you're at Harvard; if you're non-Caucasian or female, then like a woman in Afghanistan, you can claim to be oppressed."

We'd have to cut down an entire forest to make enough paper to document all the cases of liberals running amok on American college campuses over the past twenty-five years or so—in the name of virtue, of course. Sadly, they're all about the same thing: banning anything—speech, behavior, whatever—that might offend some sensitive soul on campus.

Here are just a few examples:

- The University of Connecticut once put into effect a policy that banned "inappropriately directed laughter" and the "conspicuous exclusion of students from conversations" to make sure nobody's feelings got hurt.

- Brown has had rules against "verbal behavior" that produces "feelings of impotence or anger," whether "intentional or unintentional."

- Colby College in Maine has restricted speech that causes loss of "self-esteem (or) a vague sense of danger."

- Lots of schools have shut down bake sales that poke fun at affirmative action policies—where students sell identical cookies for different prices depending on the buyer's race or gender. White guys get charged a dollar for a cookie; white women, seventy-five cents; Latinos, fifty cents; and blacks, twenty-five cents.

Let's see if we have this right: burning the American flag is allowed because that's "free speech." Bake sales that make fun of affirmative action are not allowed because they offend the liberal sensibilities of some students. Makes sense to me. Why would anyone want the free exchange of controversial ideas—on a college campus of all places?

"What is the future of civil liberties," Wendy Kaminer asks, "when 'progressive' students at elite colleges and universities display an ignorance of basic American values that you might expect from junior high school kids who've never had a civics course?"

"It's the Bill of Rights," she says, "not a Code of Etiquette."

There wasn't always this suffocating ideological sameness on campus. In the 1950s and early 1960s, as John Leo, the columnist, says, "Professors were routinely hired by department chairmen who opposed their principles—because the candidates were sound scholars and students needed divergent views." But today, he says, "Professors know they are unlikely to get hired or promoted unless they embrace the expected package of campus *isms*—radical feminism, multiculturalism, postmodernism, identity politics, gender politics. . . . Remaining conservatives and moderates can survive if they keep their heads down and their mouths shut. . . . A single expressed doubt about affirmative action or a kind word about school vouchers may be enough to derail a career."

So what's liberal about any of this? "The real liberals today are *conservatives*," David Horowitz, the radical leftist-turned-conservative told me. "*We're* the ones who are taking on the speech codes, not the so-called liberals."

Yes, David, you're right. But remember . . . they're doing it in the name of virtue.

The LIST

Rick *and* Kathy Hilton

OKAY, PARIS HILTON has an excuse. She's a moron. But her parents can't be let off so easily.

If they gave Nobel Prizes for the mom and dad who raised the most vapid, empty-headed, inane, hollow, vain, tasteless, self-centered, useless twerp in the entire country—maybe in the entire world—Rick and Kathy Hilton would be on their way to Stockholm to pick up the medal.

Paris wears designer T-shirts with slogans like "Got Blow?" and has said, "Wal-Mart? What's that? Do they, like, make walls there?" She's made headlines for shoving her way to the head of a washroom line, and when upbraided for her rudeness, said she just wanted to look at herself in the mirror. And, as everyone knows, she's a big movie star—if you count having sex in a home video that has made its way around the world on the Internet as being a movie star.

But Rick and Kathy's little celebutante insists she's misunderstood. The bad press "sucks," she pouts, and she thinks that "people are mean."

Congratulations, Rick and Kathy. You did a fine job. People *are* mean—especially to heir-heads like your daughter.

Matthew Lesko

MATTHEW LESKO.

Name doesn't ring a bell, you say. Maybe this will help: You're watching cable television, probably late at night, a commercial comes on, and there's a "grown-up" man wearing big eyeglasses, a black suit emblazoned with lime green question marks, and a lime green bow-tie emblazoned with lime green question marks, and while he's prancing around in front of the Capitol building in Washington, he's shouting in a high-pitched voice about all the "free money" the government has . . . just for you!

Want $100,000 to start a business in your own house? Lesko tells you how to get it. How about $75,000 to remodel that house? You say you always wanted to open a bookstore? The government's got $140,000 for you, and Matthew Lesko will help you get your grubby little hands on it. And, of course, there's all that "free money to pay your bills."

Right, *that* Matthew Lesko! The sort of embarrassing doofus you *pray* your daughter will never bring home and introduce as her fiancé. So, no, as evil goes, he's not exactly in the same league as Osama bin Laden.

Yet this character, who has devoted what passes for his adult life to peddling his books and CDs on how to get "free college money" and "free stuff for moms" and "free money to change your life" does stand for something disheartening that's happened to this country in recent years. Once, it was understood by almost everyone that there is no free lunch and that you got yours, as the old commercial had it, "the old-fashioned way"—you *earned* it! But now, this joker

56

caters to a mindset that believes there's not only free lunch, but free dinner, and free midnight snacks, and a takeout bag if you're still hungry later on. Matthew Lesko is the Pied Piper for way too many Americans who are interested only in themselves.

Because, of course, the "free money" Lesko is talking about isn't really free at all. It's "tax money," which, in his way of thinking, is "everybody's money," otherwise known as "nobody's money."

A lot of us would argue that it's bad enough that slimy politicians take our money in the first place so they can hand it out as "free money" to somebody who wants to open a pizza parlor in Akron. But do we really need Matthew Lesko making himself the go-between, the conduit, between *our* money and the pizzeria?

And then, in December 2004, the New York State Consumer Protection Board issued a report suggesting that Mr. Lesko may have been—oh, let's be generous—exaggerating in his commercials.

For example: Lesko once claimed that a researcher was given $500,000 by the government "to travel the world." Turns out, the researcher was a physicist from Georgetown who won a grant from the National Science Foundation.

For another example: Lesko has said his books tell you how to get free car repairs. Actually he was talking about an automobile recall by the manufacturer.

And then there was the pitch about how you could get $400 a week if you were out of work. True enough. It's called "unemployment insurance."

"Lesko is now promoting a new book . . . by claiming that the federal government has more than $350 billion in hidden money that ordinary people can use to pay their credit-card bills and get out of debt," said Teresa Santiago, the chairwoman of the Consumer Protection Board. "That claim is simply not true."

On his Web site, Lesko shot back: "I provide my customers with legitimate sources of government money for business, education, housing and, yes, to pay bills."

Okay, so here's an idea, Matthew: Take some of that "free" money from "legitimate sources of government," buy a plane ticket to Outer Mongolia—and stay there.

98 ☞

Sheila Jackson Lee

SHEILA JACKSON LEE is a black Democratic congresswoman from Texas who has put her finger on one of the great problems facing African-Americans in these United States of America.

There aren't any hurricanes named after black people.

I guess that means there aren't enough hurricanes named Keisha, Jamal, DeShawn, or LaToya. I mean, black people also have names like (such well-known recent hurricanes as) Charley and Frances, but I'm pretty sure that's not what she's talking about.

Congresswoman Lee believes hurricane names shortchange black kids, according to a story in the July 9, 2003, edition of *The Hill*, "the newspaper for and about the U.S. Congress," as it proclaims on its masthead. "All racial groups should be represented," Lee said, according to *The Hill*. She hoped federal weather officials "would try to be inclusive of African-American names."

That's right. Hurricane names like Andrew and Bonnie and Ivan are just too darn white. This is not fair to all those black children who are left out. We need affirmative action when it comes to naming catastrophic storms. Right on, sister!

I can hear Dan Rather now, called out of semiretirement to

chase one more hurricane, in his yellow slicker, blowing around in 135-mile-an-hour winds, hanging on to a telephone pole for dear life, microphone in hand, Dan parallel to the ground several feet below: "This vicious, killer storm—Shaniqua—is barreling through Pensacola at this very moment, destroying everything in sight. I'll bet you a ten-pound bag of unsalted goobers to a sack of horse feathers that no one in his right mind wants this big bad girl Shaniqua anywhere near where they live."

Or Brian Williams, in his blazer, calmly sitting in the NBC studio in New York, comes on and says, "Last month's hurricane Bruce didn't cause much damage at all, but this one, this hurricane Dexter X is something else altogether, responsible for more mayhem and destruction that any in recent memory. This one is causing even more misery than Shaniqua did back in August, and Shaniqua, you may recall, was one big bad girl."

Oh yeah, I'm sure that would make black people throughout the United States pleased as Punch, forgive the lily-white cliché. "We're finally getting our due in this white racist culture," the affirmative-action-for-hurricane-names crowd would say. "Now we have hurricanes named after our black children, too. Why should whitey get all the glory?"

Here's a news flash for the congresswoman: Hurricanes are bad. They're deadly. People don't like them. If I were you, I'd try to pass a law *mandating* that all hurricane names—*without exception*—be restricted to Biff and Skip and Muffy, as a kind of reparation for all the bad stuff that has happened to black people over the years in this country.

"What could she have been thinking?" as La Shawn Barber (a black woman) asks on *America's Voices*, a conservative Web site. "That black children watching 'Hurricane Denzel' wreak havoc in their neighborhoods would gain higher self-esteem? That seeing a family member lost in a flood brought on by 'Tropical Storm Tanisha' would fill them with racial pride?"

Here's a suggestion for the congresswoman that comes from the philosopher William James, who said about a hundred years ago, "The art of being wise is the art of knowing what to overlook." Like the names they give hurricanes, Congresswoman.

97

Todd Goldman

HIS NAME IS TODD GOLDMAN, but I like to think of him as the T-shirt Genius.

Why? Well, because Todd Goldman is the "brains" behind a line of boy-bashing T-shirts emblazoned with slogans like these:

"Boys Are Stupid. Throw Rocks at Them!" (The image on the shirt shows a bunch of rocks flying through the air toward a stick-figure boy's head.)

"Lobotomy—How to Train Boys."

"Boys Cheat . . . Cut Off Their Feet." (The T-shirt shows a girl holding a bloody butcher knife while the footless boy "stands" in a pool of blood.)

"Boys Are Stupid . . . Run Them Over."

"Boys Are Smelly . . . Kick Them in the Belly!" (The girl in this one, as you might imagine, is doing just what the T-shirt says.)

"Boys Make Good Pets, Everyone Should Own One."

"Stupid Factory—Where Boys Are Made."

"The reason we have boys [on the shirts] is that our customers are teenage girls," Goldman says. On a TV show, he was asked if he had an "obligation to consider the impact" of the products on young boys. "No" was his answer. In fact, when people raise objections to his boy-bashing T-shirts, it makes him laugh—all the way to the bank. "I couldn't pay for this press," as he put it.

You see, it's nothing personal, just business.

The fact is we live in a time when it's become okay to belittle not only men, but also future men. Never mind that in almost every negative statistical category—from failure in school to suicide—boys today are in worse shape than girls, and the gap is only increasing. Feminism has made it okay for women—and a certain kind of man—to laugh at boys.

And these days there are all sorts of entrepreneurs out there cashing in on the boy-bashing craze. One of them is a guy named Jim Benton, an artist and children's author who puts his put-downs on all sorts of things you can buy, like stickers and notebooks and air fresheners and clothing and who knows what else. His main character is a happy bunny icon that says things like "You suck big time" and "Hi, scumbag." But Jim also sells stuff that says, "Boys lie and kind of stink." Would he do a line of girl-bashing shirts or stickers or air fresheners that say, "Little Girls Are Nasty and Mean And Grow Up To Be Angry Feminists"? Surely you jest.

"I don't find misogyny funny," as the oh-so-politically-correct Mr. Benton puts it. "I *do* find girls' contempt of men funny."

He may have a point. Maybe I'm taking this stuff too seriously. Maybe these T-shirts really are funny. Maybe they're so funny that Benton and Goldman should expand their product lines so they can make even more money. So here are a few suggestions, which I offer to them free of charge:

"Black Folks Are Stupid. Throw Rocks at Them."
"Jews Are Smelly . . . Kick Them in the Belly."
"Stupid Factory—Where Mexicans Are Made."
"Homos Make Good Pets, Everyone Should Own One."

Hilarious, don't you think? And besides, it's nothing personal, just business.

96 ☞

Eve Ensler

YOU KNOW THE GRINCH WHO STOLE CHRISTMAS? Think of Eve Ensler as the Loon Trying to Steal Valentine's Day!

That's not how Ensler thinks of herself, of course. She thinks of herself as a wise and compassionate freethinker and social activist. And most important—trust me, folks, this is not a joke—she thinks of herself as the Vagina Woman. In fact, Ensler is so proud of the vagina—her own and that of every other woman—that she wrote a very important play about it, called *The Vagina Monologues.*

The Vagina Monologues is basically a bunch of sketches featuring women talking about—guess!—right, their vaginas. The *New York Times* says the show is Ensler's "crusade to wipe out the shame and embarrassment that many women still associate with their bodies or their sexuality." Ensler's chosen method for wiping out shame and embarrassment is shouting out the word "vagina" from the proverbial rooftops—in the play, more than a hundred times, though not all in a row (thank God).

But that's just part of her agenda. The other part has to do with men and—take another guess!—right again, all the rotten things they do. In fact, all this free and easy vagina talk is also supposed to be a way to empower women to fight what Ensler—who tosses around the discredited, vastly overblown statistics on the subject with the best of them—sees as an epidemic of male violence. As David Brooks wrote in the *Weekly Standard* after seeing the show, "I just don't get it. But maybe that's just because women are from Venus, men are from Hell."

What happens in *The Vagina Monologues*? Well, there's stuff about childbirth, and stuff about sex, and *lots* of stuff about violence and rape. In one scene that's gotten particular attention, a twenty-four-year-old woman gets a thirteen-year-old girl (later changed to sixteen) drunk and has sex with her. But, as far as Eve Ensler is concerned, this is not a bad thing. To the contrary, afterward, the girl says, "If it was rape, it was a good rape. I'll never need to rely on a man."

If you think this sort of thing might get Ensler attacked, well that just shows what a hick you are. What, in fact, it has gotten her are international recognition and a boatload of awards. At last count, the play has been done in forty-eight countries, as well as on HBO—and Hollywood actresses stand in line to appear in it. Hillary Clinton had Ensler to the White House when Bill was president, and Ensler is sometimes at Hillary's side at political events. At one rally, in August 2004, outside New York's City Hall, Ensler took the microphone and exhorted: "It is really important for us to get our vaginas to the polls!"

Vagina? Polls? Stop me before I write something I'll regret.

And that thing about Valentine's Day? Well, back in 1998, Ensler set out on a campaign to do away with all the silly stuff like romance and love—especially the heterosexual kind!—and rename it V-Day, dedicated to stopping rape, incest, and domestic violence.

Sound to you like a crackpot notion? You're even less hip than I thought. In the years since, V-Day has grown exponentially. Indeed, February 14 performances of *The Vagina Monologues* have become an annual ritual on literally hundreds of college campuses. And at just one V-Day event, in 2001, Ensler rounded up enough vaginas to fill Madison Square Garden. Among those who agreed to appear at the Garden on V-Day 2001 were Oprah Winfrey, Jane Fonda, Glenn Close, Gloria Steinem, Marlo Thomas, Winona Ryder, Rosie Perez, Lily Tomlin, Calista Flockhart, Ricki Lake, Kathy Najimy, Brooke Shields, Ali McGraw, Marisa Tomei, Edie Falco, Melissa Joan Hart, Teri Hatcher, Julie Kavner, Claire Danes, Sharon Gless, Cynthia Nixon, Julia Stiles, Linda Ellerbee, Julianna Margulies, and the "Vulva Choir," to name the better-known vagina activists in attendance.

But have no fear. Ensler assures us V-Day will come to an end as soon as the oppression of women is over. Not, of course, that we'll get back Valentine's Day. Perish the thought, you silly romantic. At that point, V-Day will be renamed Victory over Violence Day.

95 ☞

Courtney Love

HO.

Guy Velella

FOR YEARS, Bronx Republican chairman and state senator Guy Velella was one tough *hombre*—especially when it came to crime. And if you didn't believe it, all you had to do was ask him.

Most politicians wouldn't think twice about punks who commit mere misdemeanors, right? Velella wasn't most politicians. He rammed a bill through the New York State Senate ensuring that anyone convicted of three misdemeanors in ten years would be treated as a felon and have to do hard time. Enough coddling of these guys, he said; no longer would "criminals have a blank check when it comes to their number of misdemeanor convictions."

This was in February 2004.

Three months later, Senator Velella got an even better chance to show how he felt about crime and punishment—his own. Facing up to fifteen years in prison after being indicted for taking $137,000 in bribes from contractors to steer state business to him and a couple of his partners, he leapt at a plea bargain that put him in jail for only a year; then paid his hundreds of thousands of dollars in legal bills from his campaign fund, all while managing to hang on to his tax-free $80,000 pension.

As his campaign commercials used to say: One Special Guy!

Led off to do his time on Riker's Island with the other bad-asses, sixty-year-old Guy Velella behaved exactly as you might guess. Like a man.

A girlie man.

When he entered the prison, he was "shaking like a leaf," according to the *New York Post*, and afterward he kept sobbing and vomiting in his cell. I hate when that happens. Then he started writing letters to his influential pals. "You can't believe how horrible Riker's Island is," he wrote one. "Sometimes the food is so bad most of the inmates just tell the wagon to keep going so the smell doesn't get them sick."

His influential pals were touched. They were filled with kindness and humanity. And they arranged, as Clyde Haberman put it in the *New York Times*, "for the best Get Out of Jail Free card since Monopoly was invented." You see, Mr. Velella's pals were high-octane types, indeed. They included former New York mayor Ed Koch and big shots in the Catholic Church—and they wrote letters to something called the Local Conditional Release Commission, a body that until then almost nobody even knew existed.

But figuring the letters may not be enough to get him sprung, Velella called the chairman of the commission himself, to plead for his freedom. According to news accounts, the chairman said Velella was whimpering and crying. And guess what? After serving only three months of his one-year sentence, Velella was magically set free. As the unembarrassed former mayor Koch put it, "What are friends for, only the good times?"

Then, just a few days before Christmas 2004, an appellate court took away Velella's Get Out of Jail Free card and sent him back to the slammer to serve the rest of his sentence, saying the Local Conditional Release Commission—the one just about nobody even knew existed until it let Velella out early—had "run amok." The lawyer who represented Velella and the others convicted in the bribery scheme, in the finest tradition of people in his line of work, commented: "It will not be a pleasant holiday for our clients."

Richard Timmons

SPEAKING OF WHINERS . . .

You know the old joke about the guy who killed his parents and expects sympathy because he's an orphan? Think Richard Timmons.

If you're looking for a poster boy for victimhood gone wild, Richard Timmons is your man! Timmons didn't kill his parents. He went one better. On June 8, 1997, in New York City, he took an ax and brutally murdered *three* people: his wife (whom he beheaded), his seven-year-old son (whom he also beheaded), and his thirteen-year-old stepson (whom he stabbed to death). Then, in March 2004, while he was serving three life sentences, Richard Timmons decided he was a victim, too. So he sued New York City in federal court for $80 million, claiming that he was beaten by the police while they were interrogating him.

There were just a few small problems with his case. First, he admitted that his memory was "hazy" that night. Why? Well, because of all the alcohol, crack, PCP, heroin, and whatever else he had been taking before he killed everybody in the house. He even testified: "I don't know exactly what happened." But he said he was sure of one thing: that he was beaten. Except nobody at the hospital, where one of the beatings supposedly took place, heard anything *at all* indicating someone was being roughed up.

"This case is about a man who has no shame," as the lawyer for the city put it in one of the great understatements of all time.

The good news is that it took the jury less than an hour to reach its verdict: The jurors told Richard Timmons—who acted as his own attorney—to take a hike right back to his prison cell. He didn't get one cent in damages.

On the other hand, you've really got to wonder about what's going on when a guy like Timmons gets to have a case like this heard at all. I know, in this country even monsters have rights. But you look at Richard Timmons and you have to wonder if we've lost our minds.

Because there's way too much of this going on these days. In fact, on the very day Timmons's case was being heard, on another floor in the same building, a guy named William Kanyi was having *his* day in court. He only wanted $5 million—from the hospital that saved his life after the heroin-stuffed condoms he was trying to sneak into the country started leaking into his stomach. You see, according to Kanyi, he never *consented* to the operation—and his lawyer claimed the surgery left his poor client emotionally and physically scarred.

Boo-hoo!

"Leave it to a drug mule to file a jackass of a lawsuit," is how one New York tabloid began its story. The jury didn't buy Kanyi's sob story, either. He got nothing.

As for Timmons, the longer his trial went on, the more ridiculous it became. Remember, he was serving as his own lawyer and playing the part like a third-rate Perry Mason. Perry Mason, as we all know, was always coming up with a great witness or piece of evidence that turned the case around. With Richard Timmons, it was the exact opposite. In his trial, the evidence kept piling up *against him*—proving that not only did he have no case, but that he was an "attorney" with a fool for a client.

It turned out that the night he was arrested, far from being beaten, Timmons actually got along well with the cops. On the way to the police station he told them he was hungry, so they stopped at Burger King.

"He ordered two Whoppers, two hamburgers, ketchup only," the city's lawyer told the jury. And "he ate all of it."

Timmons's gall would be hilarious if it weren't such a colossal waste of the courts' time and taxpayers' money—and if it weren't so morally repugnant. Among the details jurors did not hear, because the judge thought it was too horrible, was the 911 tape from the night of the murder, the one that caught his young son Aaron crying, "Stop, Daddy, stop," just before Timmons cut off his head.

"It was horrible," said one of the cops who testified about the crime scene, "the worst I've seen in twenty-five years. . . . I can't believe [his lawsuit] went this far in federal court."

☞ *92*

Kerri Dunn

KERRI DUNN is one of those marginal figures that pop up every now and then to show just how far the world has spun off its axis.

Think of Dunn as higher education's (white, middle-class) version of Tawana Brawley: a self-dramatizing phony caught crying wolf, revealing for everyone to see the stomach-turning role of victimhood—and PC idiocy in general—on today's college campus.

On August 18, 2004, Dunn, until recently a visiting professor of psychology at Claremont-McKenna College, was convicted in a Pomona, California, courtroom of attempted insurance fraud and later sentenced to one year in state prison. But that doesn't even begin to tell the story.

The charge stemmed from an episode that occurred during the previous spring term, on March 9, when Dunn—"a passionate and outspoken advocate against human hate, especially racism, anti-Semitism, and homophobia," as one of her supporters described her, deeply involved in issues of "diversity and women's rights"—reported that she had returned from addressing a forum on racial intolerance to find her 1990 Honda Civic vandalized. She said the car's tires had been slashed, its windows smashed, and, most alarmingly, its exterior spray-painted with the words "nigger lover," "kike whore," and "bitch," as well as an unfinished swastika. In addition, more than $1,700 worth of personal property had been stolen from the car, she said, including a $500 Coach briefcase and a $600 Palm Pilot.

The reaction on campus was all too predictable: not just understandable outrage at what appeared to be a vicious, isolated incident, but fury at American society in general. Because—and so goes the thinking on many college campuses these days—wasn't what happened to Professor Dunn just more proof (as if any were needed) that just below the surface, life in these United States seethes with violence and hate?

Claremont-McKenna is one of five undergraduate colleges collectively known as the Claremont Colleges, and in the days that followed the "hate crime" they were all seized by righteous indignation. In what Pomona College's dean of students termed "a day of solidarity and teaching," all five schools canceled classes, as thousands of students massed at rallies to hear speakers denounce hate and chant antihate slogans. "Everyone was dehumanized by the act of violence that occurred," one student told the crowd. "What we need to do is push back with ferocious love." And Kerri Dunn, a bigger star than ever, denounced the incident as "a well-planned-out act of terrorism" and shouted "hate needs to go back underground where it belongs."

Meanwhile, Claremont-McKenna offered a $10,000 reward for information leading to the capture of whoever was responsible for the heinous crime, and the Claremont police, aided by the FBI, began investigating.

As in the case of Tawana Brawley, it didn't take long for Dunn's story to begin unraveling. Within days, the Claremont Police Department issued a statement saying Dunn's version of events was full of inconsistencies—and two eyewitnesses had positively identified the alleged *victim* as none other than the person who'd vandalized her own car—Kerri Dunn.

Later, it came to light that Dunn had been down a similar road before. According to the district attorney who prosecuted her, four years earlier in Nebraska, she claimed police had roughed her up during a shoplifting arrest. What got in the way of that allegation, he said, was an eyewitness who reported seeing her inflict bruises on her own arm and tear the buttons off her own shirt. On another occasion, the DA said, Dunn posed as a nurse to obtain prescription drugs from a pharmacy. And in this latest case, Kerri Dunn, true to form, tried, without success, to play victim, accusing the Claremont officers who had investigated her of falsifying their reports.

But, of course, the real issue here is not Kerri Dunn, who clearly has serious problems, but the colleges themselves. After all, any reasonable observer following the case has to wonder how much checking up they had done before putting this person in a classroom to instruct impressionable students. And however wacky she may be, Kerri Dunn surely understood as well as anyone how to get ahead on today's campus—just as she knew full well the reaction her inflammatory concocted charges would provoke.

But here's the worst part of the whole crummy story: Even after Kerri Dunn was exposed as a fraud, the college administrators were still at it. Pomona College president David Oxtoby said, although "some members of our community may feel disillusioned by yesterday's revelations, and perhaps may even feel that their idealism was misplaced . . . [the antihate] discussions, marches, and speeches were a wonderful example of the best of education, even though all of our classrooms were closed."

"I can only emphasize that, irrespective of whether the incident was real or a hoax," Claremont-McKenna president Pamela Gann chimed in, "the tremendous response of our students and faculty in coming together on Wednesday, March 10, was very positive and should not be forgotten. Their actions exemplified the leadership skills and sense of civic responsibility that we seek to develop in our students . . ."

It's hopeless.

91 ☞

Barbra Streisand

I LOVE BARBRA STREISAND. She is, without doubt, one of the great singers of our time. And as a political commentator, she is, without doubt, one of the great singers of our time.

Look, I don't really want to put her on this list. But, come on, she's *Barbra Streisand*. How could she *not* be on The List?

I admit it. I never really believed that people who need people are the luckiest people in the world. Personally, I found them annoying. But, hey, that's me. And besides, that's not why she has to be on The List.

She's here because someone with such a beautiful voice shouldn't use it to say so many ugly things. I mean, she says, George Bush "stole the presidency." She says that "not only is he poisoning our air and water—he's poisoning our political system as well." And then, when she's not denigrating W and knocking him down, she says, "I don't know why it is that we need to denigrate, to knock down. It's so unhealthy for the culture. It's so sick."

I'm tempted to say, "You're not funny, girl," but I won't.

Babs detests W so much that at a Democratic fund-raiser in Hollywood she went so far as to show off her literary erudition by throwing William Shakespeare into a speech, the sole purpose of which was to bash George Bush.

"You know," she said, "really good artists have a way of being relevant in their time—but great artists are relevant at any time. So, in the words of William Shakespeare, 'Beware the leader who bangs the drums of war in order to whip the citizenry into a patriotic fervor, for patriotism is indeed a double-edged sword. It both emboldens the blood, just as it narrows the mind. . . . The citizenry, infused with fear and blinded with patriotism, will offer up all of their rights unto the leader, and gladly so. How do I know? For this is what I have done. And I am Caesar.'"

Just one teeny-weeny problem: Shakespeare never wrote it. The quote came right off the Internet and is a fake (not unlike those 60 *Minutes* documents)—"just a very clumsy piece of writing," in the words of Georgetown University Shakespeare scholar Lindsay Kaplan. Big deal! Who cares who said it? The Democrats loved it, and that's all that counts. They kicked in $6 million that night.

You want to make fun of her because she got the "Shakespeare thing" wrong? Be her guest. "I don't care what you say about me. Just be sure to spell my name wrong," Barbara once said.

Now, that is funny, girl.

Michael Jackson

IF I HAVE TO EXPLAIN it to you, you shouldn't be reading this book!

Jane Smiley

JANE SMILEY IS AN AUTHOR of many novels and essays. She's a true-blue liberal and proud of it. She's also a first-class bigot.

Right after Election Day 2004, she wrote a piece for *Slate*, graciously titled, "The Unteachable Ignorance of the Red States." Basically it's about how everyone who voted for George W. Bush is a moron and a bigot, not to mention dishonest, arrogant, and filled with hate.

Actually, since Smiley is one of those sensitive types who claims to love humankind, it's kind of fun to read her essay. Aside from the staggering hypocrisy, you can't wait to find out when she's going to use the word "ignorance" next.

Trust me, you never have to wait long.

"The election results reflect the decision of the right wing to cultivate and exploit ignorance in the citizenry," she writes. "I suppose the good news is that 55 million Americans have evaded the ignorance-inducing machine. But 58 million have not."

"Ignorance and bloodlust have a long tradition in the United States, especially in the red states."

"The error that progressives have consistently committed over the years is to underestimate the vitality of ignorance in America."

"The history of the last four years shows that red state types, above all, do not want to be told what to do—they prefer to be ignorant. As a result, they are virtually unteachable."

Why are Red State Americans so ignorant? You must be kidding. "Listen to what the red state citizens say about themselves, the songs they write, and the sermons they flock to. They know who they are—they are full of original sin and they have a taste for violence."

Then there's the part where she says that politicians, preachers, and pundits "encourage you to cling to your ignorance" . . . and the part where she says, "by this time you don't need much encouragement— you've put all your eggs into the ignorance basket" . . . and the part about how "the ignorant always have plenty of enemies" . . . and the line about how "if you are sufficiently ignorant, you won't even know how dangerous your policies are until they have destroyed you, and then you can always blame others" . . . and the stuff about how "lots of Americans like and admire [Bush and Cheney] because lots of Americans . . . don't know which end is up"—which is another way of saying . . . they're *ignorant*!

So, for all you ignoramuses who live in Red State America, let's review. Conservatives are bloodthirsty, they're unteachable, they love to cheat, they love to intimidate, they're arrogant, and, oh yeah, they're ignorant.

In other words, they're just like Jane Smiley.

88 ☞

Aaron McGruder

AARON MCGRUDER IS THE CREATOR of a comic strip called *The Boondocks*, whose hero is a black kid named Huey Freeman. As the *New Yorker* put it in a profile of McGruder, Huey "has been treating readers of the funnies page to an unhealthy dose of indignation, paranoia, and hatred" and "has roughly equal contempt for Dick Cheney, Cuba Gooding, Jr., and Santa Claus."

Sounds a lot like Aaron McGruder himself, who is also black, and also indignant, and like a lot of liberals these days, black and white, is also angry. The thing is, McGruder gets to spread his sunshine in over 250 papers every day. Michael Moore says *The Boondocks* is his favorite strip. Surprise!

Here, for example, is what McGruder had to say on *America's Black Forum*, a nationally syndicated TV show, about Condoleezza Rice, and her role in what McGruder calls the "illegal" war in Iraq:

"I don't like Condoleezza Rice because of her politics. I don't like Condoleezza Rice because she's part of this oil cabal that's now in the White House. I don't like her because she's a murderer. You know, I'm not bound by the rules of a politician or journalist. So, you know, when I say, 'She's a murderer,' it's because she's a murderer, and that's all that's necessary for me to make those statements."

That riled Armstrong Williams, the black conservative cohost of the show. "That is totally out of line, to say she's a murderer."

Being confronted with that, McGruder had second thoughts—which were exactly the same as his first thoughts! And so he repeated the accusation, except this time he stretched out the words

just to make sure Armstrong Williams, and everybody else, understood that he really meant it:

"S-h-e'-s . . . a . . . m-u-r-d-e-r-e-r."

He's not crazy about Colin Powell, either. At Emory University
in Atlanta, McGruder called Powell a killer, too.

"Let's just say, he's directly killed, not by hand, but he's been the
guy who says, 'Those people over there, that whole ethnic group,
they gotta go—kill them.' And they just disappear . . ."

And at the 138th anniversary dinner for the left-wing magazine
The Nation, a $500-a-plate Manhattan affair that drew liberals from
all over the place, McGruder, one of the featured guest speakers,
told the crowd what he thought about conservatives in general.

"One thing that you have to respect about the right wing is that
they will steal, lie, cheat, and murder to maintain power."

Once, in America, this was the language of the Loony Left. But
liberals don't run from Aaron McGruder. Quite the opposite. They
embrace him. He is, after all, one of them, a *mainstream* liberal. They
invite him to speak. They give him awards. The Green Party asks
him to run for president (he couldn't, because he's too young). The
New Yorker calls him "a talented young black man who is outspoken
in his political beliefs."

"Outspoken" is an interesting way to describe his corrosive rhetoric, which doesn't seem to register with so many of the cultural elites
who see conservatives the same way Aaron McGruder does—not
simply as wrong or misguided, but as lying, cheating, morally bankrupt killers.

Sheldon Hackney

WHEN POLITICAL CORRECTNESS first began running amok on the nation's campuses, there were many lily-livered namby-pamby college presidents to help it along. But there probably was no one so pathetically cowardly as Sheldon Hackney of the University of Pennsylvania. That's why columnist John Leo, one of the nation's staunchest defenders of free speech on campus, named his annual award, which he symbolically gives to the college administrator who has done the most to stifle that right, "the Sheldon."

"The Sheldon is a statuette that looks something like the Oscar," Leo explains, "except that the Oscar shows a man with no face looking straight ahead, whereas the Sheldon shows a man with no spine looking the other way."

There were many examples of Hackney's willingness to cave in to campus militants, from his avid support of radical feminists in the university's women's studies department to his embarrassing reaction following the theft by black students of the entire press run of a campus newspaper in 1993—because the paper printed something they didn't like. Of this last episode, Leo writes: "Hackney refused to discipline the thieves. But the guard who pursued them was reprimanded, a nice touch."

Under Hackney's watch, there was one case that came to show him for the poltroon he is. The story begins on the night of January 13, 1993.

Eden Jacobowitz, a freshman, had been in his dorm room that night writing a paper for an English class when about fifteen young women students stopped beneath his window and began a celebration to mark their sorority's Founder's Day. They sang and chanted and stomped their feet and were generally making so much noise that Jacobowitz yelled out to them to "Please be quiet." Twenty minutes later, the ruckus was not only still going strong, but had gotten even louder. This time Jacobowitz stuck his head out the window and shouted, "Shut up, you water buffalo."

Jacobowitz is white; the sorority sisters black. And before you could say "bigot," five of the women said they were victims of racism, and after a preliminary investigation, Sheldon Hackney's "judicial inquiry officer" filed charges against Eden Jacobowitz—for violating Penn's speech code, which prohibited racial harassment.

Racial harassment? What did "water buffalo" have to do with racial harassment? A judicial hearing was convened and experts were interviewed. Had any of them ever heard the term used as some kind of racial slur? None did. It didn't matter. This was the politically correct University of Pennsylvania, after all, and Sheldon Hackney was its president.

Still, it was odd that Eden Jacobowitz—or any other Penn student for that matter—would be charged with harassment, no matter what he meant by his "water buffalo" remark. You see, just a few years earlier, in 1988, none other than Louis Farrakhan spoke at Penn—over the protests of several Jewish organizations. At the time, President Hackney issued a statement acknowledging that Farrakhan's views were "racist, and anti-Semitic," but concluded: "In an academic community, open expression is the most important value. We can't have free speech only some of the time, for only some people. Either we have it, or we don't. At Penn, we have it."

Hackney's shameful hypocrisy aside, Eden Jacobowitz adamantly denied his comment had anything at all to do with race. He was just trying to tell a bunch of noisy students to pipe down, he said.

But this was not nearly enough to end the matter.

What followed was what the *Wall Street Journal* termed "one of the more Kafkaesque chapters in the ongoing campus follies," as the young man was dragged through months of hell. Was he, demanded the judicial officer hearing the case, "*having racist thoughts*" at the time. No, he insisted. But that wasn't enough, either. Because even if Jacobowitz didn't *intend* his remarks as a racial slur—*that's how they were taken by the black students*. And that was enough to keep the case going!

And then the case took on a twist that no one on either side could have seen coming. A world-renowned Israeli scholar, whose field was African folklore, was asked about the term "water buffalo." Was the student who used it an Israeli, or did he speak Hebrew, the scholar wanted to know. It turned out that Eden's parents were both Israelis and that he went to a Hebrew-language high school. So? Well, the scholar explained, "water buffalo" in Hebrew is "*behema*"—which is also slang for a thoughtless or rowdy person! He said the term had no racial connotation whatsoever.

With this information, Eden's lawyer went to his client and asked, "What's the first thing that comes into your mind if I say '*behema*'?" A light went off in Jacobowitz's head. "That's amazing," he said; in his high school "we called each other *behema* all the time, and the teachers and rabbi would call us that if we misbehaved." In other words, this was a case of a student thinking in Hebrew and speaking in English. Case closed, right? No way!

By now, the "water buffalo" affair was becoming front-page news around the country and on network television newscasts and was even a lead editorial in the *Wall Street Journal*. And there was one especially juicy quote that got picked up and put on the news, which came from one of Jacobowitz's pro bono lawyers, Arnie Silverstein, who told reporters: "I can't wait to get off Penn's campus and get back to the United States of America."

Sheldon Hackney and his university were looking dumber by

the minute. Maybe it was just a coincidence, but the university finally dropped its charges against Jacobowitz just around the time Bill Clinton nominated Hackney to be the new chairman of the National Endowment for the Humanities. During his confirmation hearings, Hackney was asked about the "water buffalo" episode and said it had been a mistake to bring charges against Eden Jacobowitz. A different answer and there's a good chance Hackney would never have been confirmed.

In his new job, Hackney soon showed that he hadn't lost his touch for relating to young people—especially those with a chip on their shoulder. Announcing his intention to launch a "National Conversation" on campus, Hackney steered $559,500 in taxpayer funds to a project posing the question, "What Is an American?"

The answer he was looking for had nothing to do with shared values, let alone such silly, outmoded concepts as love of country. As the agency's announcement put it, "The focus of this new initiative is on ethnic, racial and cultural differences, with other important differentiating and unifying factors such as class, gender, religion and region interwoven where appropriate." (I'm nauseous.)

Soon after, Hackney elaborated on this point, describing a speech he had recently given to the American Studies Association. He recalled that "a young Latino activist was recognized, looked steadily around the big table, and said in a voice full of challenge, 'I am not an American. There is nothing about me that is American. I don't want to be an American, and I have just as much right to be here as any of you.'"

I know you'll be shocked (not really!), but Sheldon Hackney thought this was one of the greatest things he'd ever heard. "What an American thing to say," he noted enthusiastically, "squarely in the great tradition of American dissent. He was affirming his American identity even as he was denying it. I think he was also launching a preemptive strike against the threat of exclusion by declaring that he did not want to be included, and he was announcing that his pre-American identity was very important to him and he did not want America to deprive him of it."

A water buffalo makes more sense.

86 ☞

Chris Ofili

IN EARLY 1999, Chris Ofili was a young artist, pretty much unknown outside of his native Great Britain. Then one of his works appeared in a show called *Sensations* at New York's Brooklyn Museum. Overnight, Chris Ofili was a sensation himself, hailed in trendy, liberal circles not only as tremendously gifted, but (to his fans, even more important) as a courageous, principled fighter for artistic freedom.

Why? Well, he painted a picture of the Virgin Mary and because he's so *cutting-edge,* don't you know, he also painted a bunch of female asses on the canvas, then sprinkled the whole thing with that well-known artistic material . . . *elephant crap.* Only among the effete elites in the world of art is something like this considered an act of bravery!

To regular folks, especially regular folks of faith, the picture was understandably offensive. Mayor Rudolph Giuliani said it was "sick" and "disgusting" and called for an end to public funding for the museum that presented it. Why, he asked, should taxpayers be forced to pay for "art," the whole point of which was to trample on their most cherished beliefs and values?

To the "artistic community," this was a declaration of war against art, and was more than enough to turn Ofili into a cause célèbre, an antiestablishment hero, a victim of the unenlightened heathens. The New York City Arts Coalition sent Giuliani a petition, signed by over two hundred representatives of the city's arts institutions, condemning his "flagrant disregard of the Museum's First Amendment rights." The case went to federal court, and a group called Volunteer Lawyers for the Arts weighed in with a brief in support of the beleaguered artist.

In the end, the judge ruled that "There is no federal constitutional issue more grave than the effort by governmental officials to censor works of expression and to threaten the vitality of a major cultural institution."

Ofili was bigger than ever. And the price of his art went through the roof. So let's give him credit: He may work in the medium of ass and crap, but he certainly knows what it takes to make it in today's art world.

Of course, Ofili is not unique among contemporary artists in his eagerness to shock and offend with in-your-face art. As one critic observes, citing assorted other artists who've worked with the same material, "human and animal excretions have gotten a real workout from the contemporary art crowd." But Ofili is certainly the most celebrated of the bunch, a winner of numerous awards and prizes, and that makes him a fitting symbol of the whole rotten system. One angry English lover of traditional art pretty much said it all when, after dumping a wheelbarrow of cow manure on the sidewalk outside an Ofili exhibit, he explained: "Modern art is a load of bullshit."

And not just any old bullshit—but self-righteous, highly ideological, aggressively antitraditionalist bullshit. In today's art world, almost anything aimed at offending the ordinary middle-class observer is celebrated as cutting edge—as long as the targets are those "backward" types who believe in religion and love their country. As Karl Zinsmeister of the American Enterprise Institute says, while it's become common for artists to spread American flags on the floor and have gallery patrons walk on them, "the art smarties never lay out Cuban flags for gallery visitors to trample on, or decorate Martin Luther King's picture with elephant dung."

"Many of today's avant-garde artists," Zinsmeister adds, "have modeled themselves on that well-known societal fixture, the snot-nosed teenager. Since the 1960s, the hippest modern art has aspired to exactly what every garden-variety 13-year-old brat aims for: maximum opportunities to shock, flout, insult, and otherwise chuck rocks at polite society. . . . Images of presidents and religious leaders have been defiled . . . It ridicules, it desecrates, it celebrates vileness, it rejects all rules, conventions, and decencies."

"Antiart" is what the legendary critic Jacques Barzun calls it, noting "it attacks everything by dislocating everything. . . . The cruel, the perverse, the obscene, the 'sick' [are] increasingly taken for granted as natural and normal . . . unless a piece of art is 'disturbing,' 'cruel,' 'perverse,' it is written off as not merely uninteresting but contemptible."

The late sculptor Frederick Hart, who did the moving statue of the three soldiers at the Vietnam Memorial, may have said it best of all: "Deliberate destruction of the ideals of Grace and Beauty characterize much of the art of the twentieth century. . . . The current philosophy and practice of art thrives on deliberate contempt for the public. An offended public is a critical necessity for the attainment of credentials. . . . Once, under the banner of beauty and order, art was a rich and meaningful embellishment of life, embracing—not desecrating—its ideals, its aspirations, and its values. Not so today."

The Dumb Celebrity

CAMERON DIAZ: "Women have so much to lose. I mean, we could lose the right to our bodies. If you think that rape should be legal, then don't vote. But if you think that you have a right to your body, then you should vote."

FRED DURST (of the band Limp Bizkit, presenting an award at the Grammys): "I hope we are all in agreeance [sic] that this war should go away as soon as possible."

KATE HUDSON: "Thoughts" on filming the movie *Le Divorce* in Paris: "Sometimes I'll be walking down the street and I'll hear some American and I'll just go, 'Of course they hate us, of course they can't stand us. We're the most annoying, boisterous creatures in the world.' I mean we come in and we eat mounds of food, and we're like, 'Where's the ketchup for our French fries?' I'm like, 'Shut up.'"

MARGARET CHO: "There is such a weird stranglehold on the liberal community where we're so afraid to speak." (Speaking on national television.)

JANEANE GAROFALO: "The Republican Party, their message and their politics of exclusion and the tilted playing field appeals to the dumb and the mean. There is no shortage of dumb and mean people in this culture. So therefore . . . the dumb and the mean find a nice home in the GOP."

The Vicious Celebrity

ALEC BALDWIN: "If we were in other countries, we would all right now, all of us together would go down to Washington and we would stone [Congressman] Henry Hyde to death! We would stone Henry Hyde to death and we would go to their homes and we'd kill their wives and their children. We would kill their families. What is happening in this country? What is happening? UGHHH!" (Playfully exaggerating, I think, on *Late Night with Conan O'Brien*, how "we" would deal with Hyde and other congressmen involved in the Clinton impeachment.)

WALLACE SHAWN (playwright, actor, and darling of the New York intelligentsia, writing in the left-wing magazine *The Nation*): "Why are we being so ridiculously polite? It's as if there were some sort of gentleman's agreement that prevents people from stating the obvious truth that Bush and his colleagues are exhilarated and thrilled by the thought of war, by the scale, the massiveness of the bombing they're planning, the violence, the killing, the blood, the deaths. . . .

"Why do they want this war so much? Maybe we can never fully know the answer to that question. . . . Why do some people want so desperately to have sex with children that they can't prevent themselves from raping them, even though they know what they're doing is wrong? Why did Hitler want to kill the Jews?"

SEAN PENN: "I am not disturbed by Ronald Reagan's Alzheimer's. You know, there's not a lot of cleaner pictures of karma in the world. I mean, it's not a very Christian way of thinking. I do stray sometimes. But I go right from him mocking the farm workers and eating grapes on television during the boycott to him dribbling today. And I feel a sense of justice."

JANEANE GAROFALO: "What you have now is people that are closet racists, misogynists, homophobes and people who love tilted playing fields and the politics of exclusion identifying as conservative."

☛ *83*

The Dumb *and* Vicious Celebrity

LINDA RONSTADT: "I worry that some people are entertained by the idea of this war. They don't know anything about the Iraqis, but they're angry and frustrated in their own lives. It's like Germany, before Hitler took over. The economy was bad and people felt kicked around. They looked for a scapegoat. Now we've got a new bunch of Hitlers."

MARTIN SHEEN: "George W. Bush is like a bad comic working the crowd, a moron, if you'll pardon the expression."

DAVID CLENNON (star of the CBS program *The Agency*): "I'm not comparing Bush to Adolf Hitler—because George Bush, for one thing, is not as smart as Adolf Hitler."

JANEANE GAROFALO: "Our country is founded on a sham: our forefathers were slave-owning rich white guys who wanted it their way. So when I see the American flag, I go, 'Oh my God, you're *insulting* me.' That you can have a gay parade on Christopher Street in New York, with naked men and women on a float cheering, 'We're here, we're queer!'—*that's* what makes my heart swell. Not the *flag*, but a gay naked man or woman *burning* the flag. I get choked up with pride."

82 👉

Laurie David

LAURIE DAVID IS A PAIN in the ass. She's the wife of Larry David, the comedy writer and actor who created *Seinfeld* and stars in the HBO hit *Curb Your Enthusiasm*. She's also an environmental crusader and a Hollywood heavy-hitter when it comes to raising money for liberal causes. But mostly, she's a pain in the ass.

At an environmental fund-raiser not long ago, Larry David got up to tell the group about his wife. "Thirteen years ago I met a materialistic, narcissistic, superficial, bosomy woman from Long Island," he said. "She was the girl of my dreams. She read *People* magazine, watched hours of mindless television, and shopped like there was no tomorrow. Finally I'd met someone as shallow as me. I was hopelessly in love. We got married in a touching ceremony in Las Vegas. The cab driver who witnessed it was deeply moved. But then, after a few short months, I began to sense that something had changed. She started peppering her conversation with words like 'ozone layer,' 'sustainable forestry,' and 'toxic runoff.' The very mention of the word 'diesel' would bring on back spasms. I began to notice new people hanging around the house, people who were not in show business and wore a lot of tweed. Clearly something was amiss. She was growing. How hideous. But what was now all too painfully obvious was that I, Larry David, the shallowest man in the world, had married an environmentalist."

But not just any eco-chic Hollywood environmentalist—the kind who simply recycles and tells her kids, "Don't run the water when you're brushing your teeth," and leaves it at that. No, she's way beyond the baby stuff. Laurie David is a true believer, the kind of activist who gets in the face of perfect strangers and reviles them as "terrorist enablers" for committing the unforgivable sin of—driving an SUV.

"I've heard that you pull alongside Hummer drivers on the highway and yell at them," an interviewer once said to her.

"I'm very confrontational," she'd proudly replied. "It's gotten to the point where my kids in the back seat of my car see an SUV coming and they say, 'Mommy, please! No! Don't say anything!' They're horrified. But I believe in peer pressure. . . . We have to spread the message that it isn't cool [to drive gas-guzzlers] anymore."

And there was this exchange with Paula Zahn on CNN:

ZAHN: You have been known to use some pretty aggressive tactics to try to get SUV drivers to change their habits. You've ticketed people, right?
DAVID: Right.
ZAHN: Put tickets on the windshield . . .
DAVID: I have done that.
ZAHN: Which is more of a joke than anything else.

DAVID: It kind of is.

ZAHN: But what is the greatest length you've gone to get somebody to quit their SUV?

DAVID: Well, I actually confront people personally one-on-one.

ZAHN: And what do you say to them?

DAVID: I say, how many miles per gallon does your car get? And
wouldn't you rather be driving a car that had a higher fuel ef-
ficiency? . . . And most people, you know, in the past haven't
really thought that much about it. . . . I mean, we have serious problems in this country. We have a global warming
problem, and we have an insane dependence on foreign oil
that we have to confront. And people really need to start
thinking about what they're doing and what they're driving.

Yes, people do need to start thinking about what they're doing.
So let's start with you, Laurie!

While it is indeed true that Ms. David drives one of those
fuel-efficient little hybrids, an article in the September 2004
Atlantic Monthly reveals she's not always so concerned about the
environment—not when her own personal comfort is involved,
anyway. The article calls Laurie David a "Gulfstream liberal"—
because it seems that Ms. Finger-Pointing Environmentalist
doesn't like to fly commercial, where she'd have to sit next to ordinary people, even the kind who fly in first class. So instead she
flies in *private* jets, the ones that guzzle enough fuel to poke big
holes in the ozone layer.

Gregg Easterbrook, in the *New Republic Online*, picks up where
the *Atlantic* leaves off. "I did a few quick calculations," he writes.
"The mid-sized Gulfstream G200 model can carry about 2,100 gallons of jet fuel, which is made from petroleum, and would burn
around 1,200 to 1,500 gallons flying from New York to Los Angeles,
depending on wind speed and how many passengers were aboard. A
Hummer driven 15,000 miles, the average put on a car per year,

would burn around 1,250 gallons of gasoline. So for Laurie David to take one cross-country flight in a Gulfstream is the same, in terms of Persian Gulf dependence and greenhouse-gas emissions, as if she drove a Hummer for an entire year. But then, conservation is what other people should do."

It's fun to imagine one of those "other people"—some total stranger who knows Ms. David only by reputation—getting in *her* face, the way she does with SUV drivers, getting "confrontational" with *her*, calling *her* "a terrorist enabler" for tooling around in a private airplane without regard to the well-being of the planet. Or imagine if some stranger stopped *her* on Rodeo Drive and began scolding *her* for living in a huge Beverly Hills mansion that consumes enough energy to keep China lit up for a couple of years. Doesn't she realize that people who live in glass mansions shouldn't throw stones?

Well, no, actually, she doesn't. Because when a reporter asked why she doesn't live in a smaller place, Laurie David replied, "Everybody has to strike their own balance between how they want to live and how they can reduce their impact [on energy consumption]. If the environmental movement wants to be mainstream, it has to lose its purer-than-thou, all-or-nothing attitude."

This doesn't even come close to passing the "Are You Kidding" test—which, as far as I'm concerned, proves my point: Laurie David may be a true-believing environmental activist, a major-league crusader and Hollywood heavy-hitter who raises millions for liberal causes—but mostly she's a pain in the ass. So here's a memo, Earth to Laurie: When it comes to lecturing us heathens about our evil ways . . . Curb Your Damn Enthusiasm!

81 ☞

Tim Robbins

I PLUGGED THE KEYWORDS "arrogant, know-it-all, whining, windbag" into one of those online search engines, and it spit out "Tim Robbins."

Robbins reminds me of those middle-aged peace guys you see holding signs on the side of the road that say WAR IS NEVER THE ANSWER and HONK FOR PEACE. They mean well. But they're not too deep.

Robbins, of course, doesn't need to hold up signs on the side of the road, because, as a Renaissance man of Hollywood left-wing politics, as a triple threat—movie star, writer, and director—he carries a big megaphone around with him, which he shouts into whenever he's got something to say.

For example: On October 6, 2002, he told a peace rally in New York's Central Park that when al Qaeda hit us on September 11, he was angry, "very angry." And he wondered: "Why New York? New York more than any other city in the world encourages diversity of faith."

Are you kidding, Tim? Maybe you missed it, but Muslim fanatic killers aren't all that keen on diversity. In fact, Tim, *there is no diversity inside al Qaeda. At all. None!* As for the "Why New York" question: Because—and this is just between the two of us—*that's where the towers of the World Trade Center were. That's why New York!*

Robbins had a better grip on the underlying problem, which, he told the crowd was fundamentalism. "Let us find a way to resist fun-

92

damentalism that leads to violence," he said, " fundamentalism of all kinds, in al Qaeda and within our own government."

My guess is that I'm not the only one who has had enough of this moral-equivalence crap. In Tim's world, on the one hand, there are the fundamentalists in al Qaeda who kill innocent civilians. They're bad. And on the other hand, there's the fundamentalism within the United States government. And that's bad, too.

Really, Tim? While we're on the subject, exactly what "fundamentalism within our own government" are you talking about?

"Cloaked in patriotism and our doctrine of spreading democracy throughout the world, our fundamentalism is business, the unfettered spread of our economic interests throughout the globe," Robbins said.

Oh, now I get it. The bad guys are businessmen. What businessmen? Oilmen! Who else?

"In the name of fear and fighting terror, we are giving the reins of power to oilmen looking for distraction from their disastrous economic performance, oilmen more interested in a financial bottom line than a moral bottom line, oilmen ready to expand their influence with new contracts on the soil our bombers have plowed, new contracts forged with governments that do not allow democracy on their soil for fear of losing control over the oil that governs their lives, that governs our lives."

And then Tim Robbins leaves the Central Park crowd with these deep thoughts, which the guys holding HONK FOR PEACE signs on the side of the road would be real proud of: "Let us hate war in all its forms, whether its weapon is a U.S. missile or its weapon is a domestic airplane."

Okay, by now it's clear that whatever else Tim Robbins is—words "shallow" and "smug" immediately come to mind—he is a man of peace, a man who hates violence "in all its forms," right?

Well, not really!

Thanks to a March 25, 2003, column by Lloyd Grove in the *Washington Post*, we learn about *the other Tim Robbins*, the one who flashes the peace sign one minute and threatens to kick your ass the next.

Here's the story:

Lloyd Grove bumps into Robbins and his longtime girlfriend Susan Sarandon at a late-night post–Academy Awards party in L.A. Grove says hello to Robbins and Sarandon, and things start out peacefully enough. But, Grove reports, as soon as he mentions that he'd "had the pleasure of talking recently with 79-year-old Lenora Tomalin—conservative Republican, George W. Bush supporter and wry observer of *her daughter Susan Sarandon*—his expression turned cold." (Emphasis added.)

"Wait. You're the one who wrote about Susan's mother?" Robbins demanded as he "narrowed his eyes and pursed his lips. 'You wanted to be divisive and you caused trouble in my family.'"

At this point, Grove tells us, Robbins "moved within inches and said, 'If you ever write about my family again, I will [bleeping] find you and I will [bleeping] hurt you.'"

Tim Robbins was great in a movie called *The Player*. He'd be a natural if they ever made one called *The Hypocrite*.

80 ☞

Kitty Kelley

WE KNEW ALL WE REALLY NEEDED to know about Kitty Kelley, sleaze merchant extraordinaire, a long time ago.

To be specific: way back in 1991, Kelley published a book that claimed to expose the sordid truth about Nancy Reagan. Kelley said that Mrs. Reagan was not her husband's beloved partner and help-mate, as the gullible American public had been led to believe, but a conscienceless user. In the book's most sensational revelation, Kelley claimed that Nancy had actually cheated on the president in the White House—with Frank Sinatra!

As you might guess, the liberal press ate it up. Kelley's book, Maureen Dowd breathlessly announced in a *front-page story* in the *New York Times*, "could forever shatter" the Reagan myth "and add allegations of scandalous sexual behavior to the folklore of the Reagan era."

It was, of course, the trashiest of lies. Even Max Frankel, executive editor of the *Times*, was finally forced to acknowledge that repeating it on page one of his newspaper was a "mistake."

No, she hasn't been called the Queen of Innuendo for nothing. Her books are filled with gossip and rumors, often backed up (if that's the right way to put it) by unnamed sources—and she's been accused of misquoting sources she does identify. So why are we even still hearing this low-rent hack's name?

The answer, alas, has everything to do with how things have changed for the worse in this country. Not very long ago, someone like Kitty Kelley, far from getting $4 million book advances and extended sit-downs on the *Today Show* would have been consigned to the sleaziest of gossip sheets—if she could even get published *there*. In a world where journalism had a lot more self-respect, there was simply no place for someone like her.

But in today's journalism, she serves a purpose. It's a nice quid pro quo: she gets to make her millions, and the "respectable" press gets to spread her scurrilous poison in the guise of "reporting." It also doesn't hurt that so many of Kelley's smears are aimed at conservative Republicans.

Thus it is that, in her most recent hit job, she gets wide exposure, in the middle of an election campaign, for her claims that George W.

Bush snorted cocaine during his father's presidency (denied by her own "source") and Laura Bush dealt marijuana in college (again, denied by her "source"), and still gets treated with respect—even celebrated—in elite liberal circles.

So, it's useful to be reminded of how someone like Kitty Kelley *should* be treated. When his wife was so viciously trashed, former president Reagan, soon to be diagnosed with Alzheimer's, issued a very brief statement. "While I am accustomed to reports that stray from the truth," it began, "the flagrant and absurd falsehoods cited in a recently published book clearly exceed the bounds of decency. They are patently untrue—everything from the allegation of marijuana use [by Nancy and me] to marital infidelity to my failure to be present at the birth of my daughter Patti. Many of my friends have urged me to issue a point-by-point denial of the book's many outrages. To do so would, I feel, provide legitimacy to a book that has no basis in fact and serves no decent purpose."

That's called "dignity," a word Kitty Kelley might want to look up sometime.

79 ☞

Harry Belafonte

AS FAR AS HARRY BELAFONTE IS CONCERNED, Colin Powell is an Uncle Tom, maybe even "a house nigger." You decide. This is what Belafonte said about Powell in an interview that aired on a San Diego radio station:

"There is an old saying, in the days of slavery. There were those slaves who lived on the plantation, and there were those slaves who lived in the house. You got the privilege of living in the house if you served the master, do exactly the way the master intended to have you serve him. That gave you privilege. Colin Powell is committed to come into the house of the master, as long as he would serve the master, according to the master's purpose. And when Colin Powell dares to suggest something other than what the master wants to hear, he will be turned back out to pasture. And you don't hear much from those who live in the pasture."

This raises a few questions: Why do so many who apparently see themselves as "authentically black" get so angry when a fellow black man strays from the liberal plantation? Why are they so afraid of diversity of opinion? Why is it okay for white people to have diversity of thought, but not for black people?

Maybe the man who made "Day-O" famous has a few thoughts on that, which he'd like to share with America.

☞ *78*

Norman Mailer

"THIS GUY ISN'T A MURDERER, he's an artist," Norman Mailer said in 1981, pleading for the release from prison of convicted murderer-turned-writer Jack Henry Abbott. "Not only the worst of the young are sent to prison, but also the best—that is, the proudest, the bravest, the most daring, the most enterprising and the most undefeated of the poor."

Mailer, the Pulitzer Prize–winning intellectual, lobbied to get

Abbott paroled. He convinced friends from around the world to do the same. Abbott was such a good writer, Mailer said, that to ignore his talent would be a crime. And besides, he said, "Culture is worth a little risk."

Mailer's campaign succeeded. Abbott was released and went to New York, where, thanks to Norman Mailer, he became the darling of Manhattan literary society and a prize guest at many fancy dinner parties thrown by the city's radical-chic crowd.

Then, six weeks after he got out, Norman Mailer and everybody else learned the real meaning of "Culture is worth a little risk." Six weeks after he got out, Jack Henry Abbott got into an argument with a twenty-two-year-old waiter and stabbed him to death.

Mailer told reporters he hoped Abbott would not get a life sentence if convicted, because "it would destroy him." At his trial, the prosecutor read from Abbott's best-seller *Belly of the Beast* a short paragraph about how you stab a man to death. "You move your left foot to the side to step across his right side, body length. A light pivot toward him with your right shoulder and the world turns upside down. You have sunk the knife to its hilt. . . . Slowly he begins to struggle for his life . . . You can feel his life trembling through the knife . . ."

When he finished reading, the prosecutor asked Abbott, "Did you write that?" With a smirk, Abbott replied, "It's good, isn't it?"

After Abbott was found guilty, Norman Mailer said that he felt "a very large responsibility" for what happened. He also said, "I am willing to gamble with certain elements in society to save this man's talent!"

Despite the fact that he was a convicted murderer, Jack Henry Abbott remained a star among at least some of the glitterati. Shortly after the trial, Susan Sarandon had a baby. She and the father, actor Tim Robbins, named him Jack Henry.

Abbott was sent back to prison, where he killed yet again, this time, thankfully, himself. A newspaper began its story about his death, saying, "If Jack Henry Abbott did nothing else in his life, he put an end to the budding romance between public intellectuals and murderers."

Sadly, that was not true. Today, Norman Mailer is among the many intellectuals and celebrities pleading for the release of Mumia Abu-Jamal, who was convicted of killing Philadelphia police officer Danny Faulkner. Mailer apparently doesn't believe Abu-Jamal really is a "murderer," either.

☛ 77

Linda Hirshman

LINDA HIRSHMAN is not the best-known feminist in America, but she just may be the most self-important, smug, condescending one in the whole bunch, and that's no small accomplishment.

I had never heard of Linda Hirshman until I saw her on *60 Minutes,* in October 2004, in a story by Lesley Stahl about young, well-educated women who were choosing to leave their high-paying, high-powered, prestigious jobs in order to stay at home with their young kids.

To many Americans, of course, this is great news. I mean, what could be more important than taking care of your own little children? Which is just what the young moms interviewed in the piece thought. Before they had kids, one was a clerk for a Supreme Court justice, another a TV news producer, a third an analyst with the Congressional Budget Office! Now they were saying things like "I wanted to experience getting to know my children, being there in a consistent way" . . . "I'm very glad that I'm staying at home" . . . "I enjoy seeing and being with my children."

But to Linda Hirshman—lawyer, philosophy professor, and author—women like these are hopelessly misguided, at best. After all, she informs us in that self-important tone so common to those of the feminist Left, we're talking about *smart* women, *powerful* women. "These are the women that would have gone into the jobs that run our world. These are the women who would eventually have become senators, governors. These women would have been in the pipeline to be CEOs of Fortune 500 companies."

Yet—talk about sacrilege!—now they were staying at home, changing diapers, and singing "The Itsy Bitsy Spider." *How could these pathetic morons throw their lives away like this?*

Never mind that being with their young children is what they *wanted* to do! Never mind that many of us regard that as a job more important than working in some law firm or shuffling papers around at some big investment bank! Never mind even that feminism was supposed to be all about *choice*! To Linda Hirshman, such a choice simply is not acceptable!

Hearing this, even Lesley Stahl seemed taken aback. "But how can you tell them what the right decision is?" she asked.

"Well, I mean, I'm a philosopher, of course I can tell them what the right decision is," Linda Hirshman shot back, adding, "As Mark Twain said, 'A man who chooses not to read is just as ignorant as a man who cannot read.'"

"But that's so judgmental," Stahl said.

"You know, that's such a loaded word," the philosopher responded. "These women are choosing lives in which they do not use their capacity for very complicated work, they're choosing lives in which they do not use their capacity to deal with very powerful other adults in the world, which takes a lot of skill. I think there are better lives and worse lives."

There are better lives and worse lives—and thank God for Linda Hirshman, because she's right there, ready to tell all of us dummies which is which.

If you ever wondered why old-fashioned radical feminism has become the butt of so many jokes and the target of so much hostility, if you ever wondered why it is becoming more irrelevant by the day, now you know.

☞ 76

Barbara Foley

"WHAT IS IT about higher education that encourages political idiocy?"

It's a very good question, succinctly asked by the *New Criterion*, a journal that speaks up for common sense—one of the casualties, along with common decency, in our culture these days.

In fact, I had been wondering the very same thing for years. How can so many professors with such lofty titles and high IQs be so damn stupid?

"Consider the case of Barbara Foley, a Marxist professor of English at Rutgers University in New Jersey," an essay in the magazine's "Notes & Comments" column begins just one month after September 11, 2001.

Yes, let's consider it, *not* because Barbara Foley is especially notable, but precisely because she's not, and because the views she espouses are so typical on campuses across America.

"In the wake of the deadly assaults on New York and Washington," the *New Criterion* article continues, "Foley posted a message on the internet for her students. It dealt partly with readings for the class, partly with the terrorist attacks. '[W]e should,' Foley wrote, 'be aware that, whatever its proximate cause, its ultimate cause is the fascism of u.s. [sic] foreign policy over the past many decades.'"

Translation: It was our fault. We brought the mayhem of 9/11 down on ourselves. And, by implication, we deserve what we got.

"Foley's pontificating did not end there," the essay continued. "She went on to advise her students that, 'we should be well aware of the ways in which this event will supply the ruling elite with a pretext for massive repression and control. airport surveillance will be, truly, only the tip of that iceberg.' (We preserve Foley's avoidance of capitals since it is probably by design: capital letters being a linguistic sign of unwarranted hierarchy, you see.)"

Thanks to 9/11, the "ruling elite" now has a "pretext" for "massive repression and control" of the American people? That's the good news. The bad news is that people like Barbara Foley—countless thousands of people exactly like Barbara Foley—*are teaching our kids!*

If you somehow can get beyond that, then consider, as the *New Criterion* does, the simple matter of plain old common decency. "Such behavior by an 'on-duty' college professor is completely inappropriate, of course," the essay points out. "There is, first of all, the matter of gross insensitivity. What if some of her students lost a parent, a spouse, a sibling in those attacks? How would they like being told that the cause was the 'fascist' foreign policy of the United States? There is also the larger issue of what an English professor is doing using official communications with her class as a soapbox for political proselytizing. Since when did memoranda about readings for a class in American literature become occasions for expatiating on the supposed evils of American foreign policy?"

I was wondering the exact same thing. I mean what does any of this have to do with *English?* Shouldn't America's "fascist" foreign policy be left to, well, the left-wing radical profs in the *poli-sci de-*

partment? Shouldn't Professor Foley (who, I'm embarrassed to say, teaches at my alma mater) stick to *The Great Gatsby* (oops, that one was written by a Dead White Male and I'm sure she wouldn't go anywhere near it)—or something even *vaguely* connected to the subject she teaches?

These are all good questions, if I do say so myself. But not as good as the one we began with: "What is it about higher education that encourages political idiocy?"

☞ 75

Eric Foner

ERIC FONER, PROFESSOR OF HISTORY at Columbia University, isn't just another run-of-the-mill left-wing academic. He's a major-league player in his field, a past president of the American Historical Association. Foner's many books are used in high school and college classrooms throughout America, helping shape the perceptions of countless students about their country and its role in the world.

Which is why what he had to say after September 11, 2001, matters a lot; and why it's so depressing. "I'm not sure which is more frightening," he said, "the horror that engulfed New York City or the apocalyptic rhetoric emanating daily from the White House."

If the good professor truly isn't sure which is more frightening, then a reasonable person can draw only one conclusion: that Eric Foner, despite his Ph.D., is a fool.

As William Bennett put it, "I haven't heard any apocalyptic rhetoric, but if Foner is unsure of which is worse, I suggest he leave his Ivory Tower for a moment and take a walk to where the Twin Towers used to stand. Or ask the widow or orphan of a firefighter."

Can you imagine, if someone on the Right had said, "I'm not sure which is more frightening: the horror that engulfed New York City or the moronic drivel that routinely emanates from the mouths of professors at some of our most elite universities and is poisoning both the mind and the soul of so many impressionable young students."

Actually, that's not a bad question.

74

Katha Pollitt

JUST DAYS AFTER September 11, 2001, a journalist named Katha Pollitt, a columnist for the left-wing magazine *The Nation*, who also writes regularly for the *New Yorker* and the *New York Times*, did a piece for *The Nation* called "Put Out No Flags."

"My daughter, who goes to Stuyvesant High School only blocks from the World Trade Center," she wrote, "thinks we should fly an American flag out our window. Definitely not, I say: The flag stands for jingoism and vengeance and war."

After a bit of give and take, during which Ms. Pollitt half-heartedly acknowledges that her daughter may have a point about how the flag can also mean "standing together and honoring the dead," they reach a compromise. "I tell her she can buy a flag with her own money and fly it out her bedroom window, because that's hers, but the living room is off-limits."

It's heartwarming, isn't it? Just a few days after three thousand of her fellow Americans were murdered—most in her own New York City neighborhood—Katha Pollitt felt the need to go public with her view that old-fashioned patriotism is a sentiment for blood-thirsty fools, a sentiment that is "off-limits" in her own living room. But it was just the right time, she figured, for one of those mother-daughter talks on the never-ending sins of America. If instead of flying the flag, her daughter had suggested they sing "God Bless America" together, Ms. Pollitt might have disowned the poor girl.

I wonder if Ms. Pollitt really understands that if either one of those hijackers who had taken aim at the Twin Towers had been just a little off-target, she might never have had that discussion with her daughter about the American flag. Her daughter might very well have been buried under a pile of rubble on September 11, murdered as she sat in history or English class at her school just a few blocks from the World Trade Center.

I understand that the world is a complicated place; that issues are complex and are rarely all black or all white. I understand that the good guys don't always do the right thing. But I also understand that it takes a certain kind of American—*in the days right after September 11, 2001*—to tell her young daughter that the American flag "stands for jingoism and vengeance and war." In normal times, this would be bad enough. But in times of crisis, it really is repulsive.

73 ☞

Barbara Kingsolver

"MY DAUGHTER CAME HOME from kindergarten and announced, 'Tomorrow we all have to wear red, white and blue.'"

This is how the novelist and left-wing social critic Barbara Kingsolver begins an op-ed right after September 11, 2001.

"Why?" She wants to know.

"For all the people that died when the airplanes hit the buildings," the little girl explains.

For most Americans, this would seem like a nice, loving gesture. Not to Barbara Kingsolver.

"I fear the sound of saber-rattling, dread that not just my taxes but even my children are being dragged to the cause of death in the wake of death," she writes, exhibiting a kind of knee-jerk paranoia about a dark and dangerous America that is way too common among her kind.

She asks her daughter why she can't simply wear black. Why does she have to wear the colors of the flag? What does that mean, she wants to know.

"It means we're a country. Just all people together," the young girl innocently replies.

When a little girl in kindergarten sounds—no, make that *is*—smarter than her mother, you know there's a problem.

The next day, Kingsolver tells us, she sent her daughter to school in red, white, and blue. She also tells us that, "my wise husband put a hand on my arm and said, 'You can't let hateful people steal the flag from us.'"

As I got to this part in the op-ed, I said: Finally, someone in the house, beside the kid, with some common sense. Of course you can't let those hateful bastards who killed so many Americans that day steal the flag from us.

Stupid me.

"He didn't mean terrorists," Barbara Kingsolver explains, "he meant Americans."

Americans? What Americans? "Like the man in a city near us," she writes, "who went on a rampage crying 'I'm an American' as he shot at foreign-born neighbors."

You see, one jerk—maybe even *several* jerks—in a nation of nearly 300 million people goes on a rampage and this is all the proof she needs: that the *real* enemy of this country, the enemy we all need to fear, is . . . *patriotism.*

No kidding. Patriotism! Here is Barbara Kingsolver in her own words:

"Patriotism threatens free speech with death. . . . It despises people of foreign birth . . . In other words, the American flag stands for intimidation, censorship, violence, bigotry, sexism, homophobia and shoving the Constitution through a paper shredder? Who are we calling terrorists here?"

There is a temptation to feel at least a moment's pity for this woman with such dark fantasies about her own country. But the one I really feel sorry for is her poor defenseless daughter.

72 ☞

Ward Churchill

ON SEPTEMBER 11, 2001, 1,600 very long miles from the nightmarish devastation in New York City, a college professor named Ward Churchill, who teaches ethnic studies at the University of Colorado, sat down to write about what had happened to America that day.

After looking at the same horrors the rest of us looked at, Professor Churchill, scholar that he is, decided that the United States of America had brought it all on itself, the day's carnage being nothing more than payback for what, in his view, were America's own murderous actions around the world. In other words, we deserved what we got.

"The most that can honestly be said of those involved on Sept. 11," he wrote, "is that they finally responded in kind to some of what this country has dispensed to their people as a matter of course." Of the innocent civilians who perished in the Twin Towers, Professor Churchill had this to say: "Well, really, let's get a grip here shall we? True enough, they were civilians of a sort. But innocent? Gimme a break."

But even that wasn't quite enough to sum up his feelings on the events of the day. Ward Churchill proceeded to compare the people who were killed in the World Trade Center to Adolf Eichmann, the architect of the Holocaust who masterminded the slaughter of six million Jews. "If there was a better, more effective, or in fact any other way of visiting some penalty befitting their participation upon the little Eichmanns inhabiting the sterile sanctuary of the twin towers," he wrote, "I'd really be interested in hearing about it."

Churchill's vile little essay, which initially appeared only on the Internet and later became part of a book, didn't make a ripple back in 2001 in what they like to call the "scholarly community"—or anyplace else for that matter. But in early 2005, when he was about to speak at Hamilton College in upstate New York, the whole sorry mess came to light—and prompted Churchill to *clarify* his position. "If we want an end to violence," he clarified, "especially that perpetrated against civilians, we must take the responsibility for halting the slaughter perpetrated by the United States around the world."

As for those comments comparing the victims in the Twin Towers to Nazis, an exasperated Ward Churchill now explained that not *every* person killed in the Twin Towers was a "little Eichmann." How dumb of us to jump to that conclusion. The janitors weren't Nazis and neither were the food-service workers. Or even the firemen. Just the "technocrats," as he put it—the men and women who were keeping the American economy going by engaging in business—only they were the "little Eichmanns" who just got what they had coming.

And when given the opportunity to apologize, Churchill not only was unrepentant, he was downright hostile. He had nothing to apologize for, he said, and besides, the politicians and other yahoos calling for his dismissal, he suggested, ought to mind their damn business and let him teach—at the taxpayers' expense, of course.

Actually, I'm of the school that believes Ward Churchill should be allowed to keep his job. Generally speaking, I don't think anyone should be fired for his opinions, no matter how loathsome they are. Colleges, especially, are places where the free exchange of ideas must be the paramount value. Indeed, this is one of the things that make America great.

Perhaps we shouldn't be shocked, or even surprised by all we have learned about Ward Churchill. After all, he is a left-wing college professor with tenure who operates out of the People's Republic of Boulder. The real questions are: How did a guy like this get to be a tenured professor in the first place? Would the University of Colorado grant a lifetime job to a crackpot on the far, far Right— someone who wrote an essay, say, about how murdered civil rights workers deserved what they got?

The good news is that in the end, Ward Churchill is of little significance, a lightweight who happened to have the misfortune of catching our attention. The bad news is, there are many, many Ward Churchills on American college campuses today, unapologetic America-bashers who every day abuse their important positions to undermine the very free exchange of ideas universities are supposed to encourage. As another scholar—a legitimate one— Diane Ravitch of the Brookings Institution put it: Long after Ward Churchill disappears from view, "what will remain as a problem for our society is the political atmosphere on many American campuses, where zealots like Mr. Churchill are hired and tenured, ever after free to inflict their one-sided rants on their hapless students."

Phil Donahue

NO NEED TO BE CRUEL to Phil Donahue, a man whose time has come and gone. As Matt Drudge put it when Donahue's last, little-watched talk show was mercifully cancelled by MSNBC in 2003: "How can you tell?"

But that doesn't mean we should go easy on him, either. Because Phil Donahue is one of those pioneers who has had a huge effect on the most popular medium in human history, and by extension, on how we all live and think. You can make a case that more than any other individual Donahue has made the world safe for emotion masquerading as thought.

And when Phil launched TV's first modern television talk show in 1967, on WLWD-TV in Dayton, Ohio (with atheist Madalyn Murray O'Hair as his first guest), this was a very different America. While much of the country was still trying to hang on to its old values, the times were rapidly changing. There was the turmoil of Vietnam; and there was the racial violence, not to mention the casual sex and drugs. There was enough going on in the country to make Phil Donahue a rising star. In show biz talk, his timing couldn't have been better.

Within a few years, he was national, a bona fide phenomenon, creating a whole new kind of daytime TV, not merely interviewing people, but dashing with his mike from the stage into the studio audience like a wide-eyed choir boy to include ordinary people in the discussion about some of the most important issues of the day. Donahue's show was so new and so fresh that we hardly even stopped to realize how far, even for a liberal, his ideas were from the mainstream.

Of course, there were hints right from the beginning. When bar codes were introduced in 1974, for example, Phil denounced them as a corporate plot against consumers. *Bar codes?* For all I know, he *still* believes that.

But mainly what he did, in show after show, year after year—nearly seven thousand, before he finally quit—was give tremendous exposure, and his own strong support, to the forces challenging traditional beliefs and behavior. Donahue was not merely a feminist, but a cheerleader for feminism's most radical wing. He was constantly infuriated that any mere man (especially any mere white one) would dare so much as question a woman's right to have an abortion.

And during the height of the AIDS epidemic in America, Phil endlessly parroted the gay activist line, in defiance of the facts, that AIDS was "everyone's disease" rather than one overwhelmingly confined to gay men and junkies, and that how one got it "doesn't matter." Except that how one got it mattered a lot. It was a matter of life and death!

Then again, this was just in keeping with Donahue's longtime advice to viewers on personal responsibility, which was, basically, if at all possible, avoid it! Violent crime? Homelessness? Rotten parenting? Whatever the issue, on Phil's show there was always someone or something to blame—"society" or "the government" or "the legal system"—and always a psychiatrist or social worker right there on the stage to lend weight to the "it's not your fault, you're a victim" mentality.

Then, of course, when he wasn't dealing with the secret lives of lesbian nuns (he actually did a show on the subject), there was Donahue on the weighty matters of foreign affairs. Who can forget his famous satellite "spacebridge" telecasts between the United States and the old Soviet Union in the mid-80s, which he cohosted with the silver-tongued, English-speaking Russian "journalist" Vladimir Pozner? During those shows, Phil just couldn't come up with any really meaningful differences between the United States and the iron-fisted dictatorship that enslaved nearly half the world. As Mona Charen observed in her book *Useful Idiots* (a term Lenin might have coined with Donahue in mind), "while Pozner served as an indefatigable apologist for the Soviet Union, Donahue maintained a fine impartiality . . . Donahue was moral equivalence personified. 'The trouble between the superpowers,' he explained, was 'a small percentage of people in both countries—yours and mine—who remain hard-line and militaristic.'"

No Phil, that was not the trouble between the superpowers. The trouble was that one country believed in freedom and the other believed in throwing domestic dissidents into the gulag and building an iron curtain to keep everyone else in line.

Enough. Let's leave Phil with his twenty Emmys and his Peabody for "sensitive, yet probing interviews on issues relevant to today's society," with his Media Person of the Year Award from the Gay and Lesbian Alliance Against Defamation, and his President's Award from the National Women's Political Caucus, with his lovely wife Marlo Thomas, and with his memories.

All we ask in return is that he continues to leave *us* alone.

70 ☞

Jimmy Swaggart

THERE ARE THOSE—okay, let's go ahead and call them "liberals"—who see "intolerance" everywhere, including all kinds of places where it is not. They see it in anyone who thinks it makes more sense for airline security personnel to pay more attention to young Arab men than to eighty-two-year-old grandmas from Dubuque. They see it in those who believe that kids should get into college on the basis of merit, not skin color. And they see it, too, in those who, on the basis of religious belief, object to aspects of the gay agenda that would overturn thousands of years of Western moral tradition.

People who see "intolerance" everywhere are so aggressive in pushing their views, both in the media and through the courts, that lots of us have come to regard the very word "intolerance" as a red flag. We hear the word and we think: *Here they go again, the militant forces of tolerance, trying to shut up everyone who dares to disagree with them.*

The fact is, for some of us that feeling is so strong that we sometimes forget something important: that there really is such a thing as genuine intolerance, and it can be as ugly now as it ever was. There can be genuine racism, and genuine sexism, and genuine gay-bashing—and if we're intellectually honest, and morally consistent, when it rears its ugly head, we should call it what it is.

Which brings us to TV evangelist Jimmy Swaggart.

"I've never seen a man in my life I wanted to marry," said Swaggart during a church sermon on September 12, 2004. "And I'm gonna be blunt and plain: if one ever looks at me like that, I'm gonna kill him and tell God he died."

When this came to light, Swaggart eventually issued an "apology." He said he was only joking, but that if he offended anyone he said he would kill, he was sorry.

☞ 69

Matt Kunitz

MATT KUNITZ IS THE EXECUTIVE PRODUCER of *Fear Factor*, the NBC prime-time TV reality show that has featured the following stunts where contestants (the female ones often wearing very little) . . .

1. . . . Had to eat a pizza with a crust made of cow bile, a sauce made of coagulated blood paste, cheese that was rancid, and toppings that included red worms—live ones.
2. . . . Were covered with four hundred rats.
3. . . . Were put in a body bag, in a drawer in a morgue; the bag was filled with giant, hissing cockroaches.
4. . . . Had to eat African cave-dwelling spiders—again, live ones.
5. . . . Had to stick their faces in a jar full of cow eyeballs, pick them up without using their hands, and puncture them with their teeth.
6. . . . Had to eat *Fear Factor* spaghetti—a concoction of night crawlers and coagulated blood balls.
7. . . . Were covered in hundreds of pounds of cow intestines, which they had to puncture with their mouths, suck out the liquid, fill a glass with it—then drink the "juice."

8. . . . Had to eat two large bull testicles in four minutes.

9. . . . Had to eat a horse's rectum.

10. . . . Had to eat ten fat, slimy slugs and wash them down with a shot of cow bile.

Here's a reality show the geniuses in Hollywood might want to do: It's called *Lunatics Run the Asylum*. It's all about them.

68 ☞

Katherine Hanson

CHRISTINA HOFF SOMMERS, the brave ex-philosophy professor who took on the radical feminist crazies in *Who Stole Feminism* and *The War Against Boys*, has seen a lot of ugly, politically motivated misinformation in her day peddled by left-wing feminist ideologues. So when she says that "Katherine Hanson's 'facts' are the most outrageously distorted I have yet come across," it's time to sit up and listen.

Hanson is a self-styled expert in "the culture of violence." She believes that in this country we "socialize males to be aggressive, powerful, unemotional and controlling," and that such activities as Little League baseball "encourage aggressive, violent behavior . . ."

Two of Hanson's more provocative "facts," cited by Sommers, are these:

- Every year nearly 4 million women are beaten to death in the United States.

- Violence is the leading cause of death among women.

Geez, that sounds pretty serious to me! *4 million women beaten to death in this country every year?* Yes, Katherine Hanson actually wrote that, in a work called *Gender and Violence*. It's the sort of statistic that even the most vicious man-hater, if she used her brain even a little, would recognize as laughable.

Let's see, that would mean 11 thousand women are beaten to death in this country *every single day of the year*; that would come to 40 million women beaten to death in ten years; 160 million in forty years. Why, in a couple of generations, *there'd be no women left!*

As Sommers points out, the total number of female deaths annually in the United States from *all* causes is approximately *1* million— and the total number murdered is around *4,000*. Just for the record, the real leading cause of death for women is heart disease (370,000 deaths per year), followed by cancer (250,000).

All of which would be bad enough if Katherine Hanson were just another in the legion of ideologically driven women's studies profs on the nation's campuses, ranting to a couple of classes of students, mostly female, who are more than willing to believe anything she tells them.

We should be so lucky. You see, Katherine Hanson is one of those angry radical feminists who have helped set the agenda in classrooms *all across the country*. Indeed, in the 90s, the organization she headed, the Women's Educational Equity Act Publishing Center, became the national clearinghouse for so-called "gender-fair" educational material bound for American teachers and schoolchildren. Under the auspices of Bill Clinton's Department of Education, Hanson's outfit produced more than 350 publications and distributed material to hundreds of educational conferences. Sommers reports that by 2000, Hanson's organization had received more than $75 million in federal funds—otherwise known as *your* tax dollars!

How was the money spent? Well, one typical publication Hanson's group helped fund was an antiharassment and antiviolence guide for teachers, grades K to 3, called "Quit It!," which instructed teachers on how to socialize little boys away from typical little-boy behavior. For example: "Before going outside to play, talk about how students feel about playing a game of tag. Do they like to be chased? Do they like to do the chasing? How does it feel to be tagged out? Get their ideas about other ways the game might be played."

Here's an idea: How about if radical feminists took a long walk on a short pier and just let kids be kids?

Hanson has now moved on to start up something called the Gender and Diversities Institute. Don't ask! The name says it all. And in this capacity, as her Web site puts it, "Ms. Hanson is Principal Investigator of five major National Science Foundation (NSF) projects, including two large scale national research projects on learning and technology."

"Principal investigator." "National research projects on learning and technology." "*Four million dead from beating.*" Is it just me or is something way out of whack here?

Randall Robinson

AS IF THERE'S NOT ALREADY ENOUGH BITTERNESS and misunderstanding in this country on the subject of race, along comes Randall Robinson with a bright idea: Reparations!

Robinson is a Harvard Law grad as well as founder and former president of a group called TransAfrica, which seeks to influence American policy toward African and Caribbean countries. He's also a longtime favorite of liberal-media types.

"Randall Robinson has dedicated his life to fighting racism and injustice," Matt Lauer said in his introduction of Robinson on the *Today Show* in 1998. Two years later, Robinson's book on reparations, *The Debt: What America Owes to Blacks*, came out, and the debate was on.

"The United States is obliged to come to terms with its past and to make the victims whole," Robinson has written. "This means compensation, restitution, reparations." After all, he argues, Germany has paid billions to survivors of the Holocaust. And in 1988, the United States compensated Japanese-Americans interned during World War II. And besides, he says, America was largely built by centuries of free labor. "An apology is not the end of the matter," Robinson says. "An apology is the beginning of the matter."

It's a passionate, heartfelt argument that makes you think. The problem is that when you do, you're hit by the obvious: that as immoral as slavery was, it ended more than 140 years ago. And unlike those who survived the Holocaust and those Japanese-Americans who were kept in camps against their will, slavery's actual victims are long gone—as are the people who kept the whole nasty system going. In fact, millions upon millions of our ancestors weren't even in this country back in the days of slavery, and, among those who were, hundreds of thousands died at Gettysburg and on a lot of other battlefields to *end* slavery.

Still, it's true that the vestiges of slavery—segregation, violence, and everyday humiliation—lingered long after the Emancipation Proclamation. So, if we as a people decide to pay reparations to black Americans, how much would be enough? How much do we give someone whose ancestors were slaves? Is $10,000 per person enough? How about $100,000? And does anybody really think— whatever number we theoretically would agree on—that this would end the matter? I guarantee you that many white Americans— probably most—would say, "Okay now that you have your repara- tions, no more racial preferences, no more affirmative action, no more *anything* like that!" And that, my friends, far from putting the matter to rest, would only open up more wounds, when blacks re- spond, as they surely would, with the inevitable, "You think your blood money—you think a measly (fill in any amount you want here)—can make up for what my people went through?"

Maybe an apology, as Robinson says, "is not the end of the matter." But rest assured, neither are reparations.

And do we really think that reparations would fix what ails black America? Do we think that the horrendous out-of-wedlock birth rate among blacks in the country would drop because of this one- time payment of reparations? Do we think that black kids who disproportionately are failing in school would somehow do better because of reparations?

But Randall Robinson's case for reparations is misguided in still another, even more important way: It casts black Americans as per- petual victims, unable to make it in this country on their own merits. "In singing the song of racist persecution, Robinson demeans the sacrifices and successes of so many great black men and women from the past and present—rebels, intellectuals, activists, judges, and public officials . . ." as the historian Anders G. Lewis observes in *FrontPage Magazine*. "Robinson inexcusably denies the simple, obvious truth that black Americans (Robinson included) have benefited from a racial revolution that has profoundly transformed American society. The 1964 Civil Rights Act, the 1965 Voting Rights Act, the growth of the black middle class and the presence of blacks in positions of political, legal and intellectual power are all testaments to these remarkable changes. For Robinson, these changes have never occurred, and America is a bastion of closet Klansmen and lynching parties."

And throwing political correctness to the wind, economist Walter Williams, who is black, adds, "Almost every black American's income is higher as a result of his being born in the United States than any country in Africa . . . Could you tell me how Oprah Winfrey is a victim? Bill Cosby? Walter Williams?"

"Certainly, more progress is needed," Lewis acknowledges, "particularly for blacks trapped in failing schools—not by segregation but by their own leaders' fealty to unaccountable public school officials. Further progress, however, will never come if blacks listen to Randall Robinson."

And the more you do, in fact, listen to Randall Robinson the more you begin to realize that he's not nearly as noble as Matt Lauer and other liberals may think. For one thing, he doesn't seem to have much use for white people, who, according to Robinson, "once well inside the place of another's different, less pugnacious, more welcoming culture, destroy it, root and branch. For inexplicable reasons, they are seemingly constrained by some aberrant force of nature to disparage all culture, all history, all religion, all memory, all faces, all life not theirs." This is the reason he believes that "only white countries are capable of killing so many [people] at one time." Never mind that the Hutu slaughtered nearly a million Tutsi in Rwanda.

In 2004, Robinson said, "Whites don't give a sh-t what we think. Never did. Never will." So, Randall Robinson, as Anders G. Lewis informs us, took "his criticism of this country to its logical conclusion: he has moved out of the United States." Yes, indeed, Randall Robinson packed his bags and moved to the Caribbean island of St. Kitts.

I hope the godfather of reparations is happy there, and with all due respect, that he stays there.

66 ☞

David Duke

REMEMBER THAT OLD GAME, Dead or Alive? I say a name, and you have to guess if the person is dead or alive.

David Duke: dead or alive?

If you said alive, I'm afraid . . . you're right.

David Duke, who just might be America's most famous bigot with good hair, has been off the radar screen for the past few years, because he was in federal prison, for tax and mail fraud, and before that he was living in Russia, where (no kidding) he wrote an article called "Is Russia the Key to White Survival?"

If it is, maybe David Duke will settle down in the old Soviet Union and stay there until "dead" becomes the right answer to the question "dead or alive?" But for now, David Duke is still with us and still proof that you can take the boy out of the neo-Nazi brown shirt, but you can't take the neo-Nazi out of the boy.

David Duke wasn't the kind of imperial wizard to rest on his laurels. In recent years, he's been a busy little bigot. He wrote a couple of books about his "racial consciousness" from childhood to what passes for adulthood, and about the worldwide "Jewish threat." He also talks from time to time about the "so-called Holocaust" and about how it's been blown way out of proportion—"exaggerated" as he puts it. He's also quoted as telling an interviewer, "You know, they had a soccer field at Auschwitz. They had an orchestra at Auschwitz, and the band was for the prisoner's enjoyment—pleasure." And he speaks to other Jew Haters in all sorts of exotic places.

But on September 11, 2001, David Duke hit the crackpot jackpot. From that day on, he had a brand-new opportunity to do what he does best: Blame the Jews for Everything Bad in the World!

A year after 9/11, Duke went on the World Wide Web to share his "thoughts" about how the Jews did us in yet again. He called his essay "The Big Lie: The True Reason Behind the Attack of September 11."

In it, he promises his readers that he will give them "only the truth, the whole truth, and nothing but the truth. Nothing less than the whole truth can help us build a secure and prosperous future for our nation."

And what exactly is this truth? That if it weren't for U.S. support of Israel, none of this would have ever happened to us. "Many traitors in our government have supported Zionism's criminal activities rather than the true interests of the American people," he wrote. "They have spawned the hatred against America that drove on these terrible acts. They are as much responsible for the carnage of September 11 as if they themselves piloted these planes that were turned into bombs."

Why don't more of us know about the treachery of the Jews? Because of the Jews in the media, silly, that's why. "Many Americans suspect that Jews have disproportionate influence in the press, but their actual power is more than most people imagine," Duke informs us in "The Big Lie."

Stuff like this has made David Duke a popular guy in certain circles. A news item of November 12, 2002, out of Dubai, begins with this: "A former U.S. Senator is to arrive today in Bahrain to lecture on 'behind the scene influence of the Zionist lobby on U.S. politics,' at the invitation of a local religious centre, a spokesman told *Gulf News* yesterday."

Indeed, this is why David Duke cannot be ignored. That he never was a U.S. senator doesn't stop those in the Arab world (and heaven knows where else) from identifying him as a "mainstream politician," and in these places he gets a serious hearing.

Discredited as he is in his homeland, David Duke is nonetheless a pestilence that refuses to go away. Let's face it, if anyone belongs on a list like this, *he* does. Because if they gave out awards for bigotry, David Duke would pick up a plaque for "lifetime achievement."

I wonder if he'd attend the ceremony in his white robe or brown shirt.

65 ☞

Oliver Stone

IN 2004, OLIVER STONE'S MOVIE *Alexander* bombed at the box office and was greeted with reviews like this one by John Podhoretz: "Oliver Stone's *Alexander*, which opens today, isn't just bad. It's *Springtime for Hitler* bad."

But there's no need to shed tears for Oliver Stone. He's had a long, successful run in Hollywood—and he hasn't deserved much of it.

The problem with Oliver Stone is not really that he's a leftist with paranoid fantasies about sinister forces running America. People have a right to their delusions. Besides, in Hollywood having fashionably leftist delusions is always an excellent career move.

The problem isn't even that Stone lies about history and unloads his fantasies on the rest of us in his movies. It's his right as an "artist"—the word they like to use in the "creative community" to describe themselves—to put whatever he wants on film, as long as he can get someone to pay for it.

No, the problem is that, even as he plays fast and loose with facts, distorting things in the most unscrupulous and heavy-handed way, Oliver Stone cavalierly goes out of his way to present his warped take on events . . . *as real, authentic history.*

This would be bad enough at any time—how we see our past, after all, has everything to do with how we see ourselves as a people; with whether we view our country and its leaders as basically decent and well intentioned, or fundamentally indecent and corrupt. But it's more appalling than ever right now, in an era when fewer and fewer Americans, especially young ones, know very much about history. A lot of kids actually think that if they see it in a movie and if it *look*s real . . . then it must *be* real!

"So, you want to know who killed the President and connived in the cover-up?" *Time* magazine asked, in a piece about Stone's 1991 movie *JFK.* "Everybody! High officials in the CIA, the FBI, the Dallas constabulary, all three armed services, Big Business and the White House. Everybody done it—everybody but Lee Harvey Oswald."

Stone's case, based in part on the wild-eyed conspiratorial theories of New Orleans District Attorney Jim Garrison, was so ludicrous that a comprehensive review of the film by attorney Mark Zaid for a course on the Kennedy Assassination at New York's Hudson Valley Community College documented literally hundreds of factual errors, many of which completely distorted *well-established* fact. It's as if Stone cleared his script with Dan Rather and Mary Mapes for accuracy before he started shooting the movie.

And then there are the two big-league academics—Tulane political science professor Robert S. Robins and George Washington University psychiatry professor Jerrold M. Post, M.D.—who collaborated on a paper they called "Political Paranoia as Cinematic Motif: Stone's *JFK.*" It begins with a clinical definition of paranoia—a "mental disorder characterized by systematized delusions and the projection of personal conflicts, which are ascribed to the supposed hostility of others"—and goes on to show precisely how the movie is a reflection of just such paranoia. But their most interesting observation had to do with the movie's impact on the public. "[JFK viewers] reported emotional changes, [became] significantly more angry and less hopeful. . . . Those who had seen the movie were significantly more likely to believe [the various conspiracies depicted in the film]."

Then there was Stone's 1995 film, *Nixon*, where he tried to inoculate himself against such criticism by releasing a massive file of "documentation" along with the movie itself.

"This scholarly blitz impressed reporters and reviewers, but it is fraudulent," wrote the historian Stephen Ambrose, whose biography of Nixon was one of the sources quoted—or *mis*quoted—by Stone in his movie. "Stone's peacock-like display of his scholarship is too thin to cover his basic contempt for real scholarship. . . . He feels free not merely to conjecture but also to invent scenes that never happened, to give one man's words to another . . ."

Ambrose goes on to detail how Stone twists the research just so he can make whatever points he feels like making in his movie. "Examples of Stone's inventions include Nixon's saying about John

Kennedy: 'We were like brothers, for Christ's sake'; Pat Nixon's demanding a divorce; Mao's telling Nixon 'You're as evil as I am. . . . Others pay to feed the hunger in us. In my case, millions of reactionaries. In your case, millions of Vietnamese.'

"Can anyone imagine Mao's talking to Nixon like that?" Ambrose asks. And then, answering his own question, he says: "In fact, yes. Here, as elsewhere, Stone counts on his audience's believing that it is possible that Dick and Jack were friends, that the Nixon marriage was always on the verge of breaking apart, and that Mao would say such things to Nixon.

"The first canon of history is that you cannot put words into people's mouths. Stone not only does that, but he regularly takes lines he likes from the actual speakers and puts them into the mouths of others."

But here's the real point about Oliver Stone, and Ambrose sums it up as well as anyone: "This is sophomoric Marxism circa 1950. . . . Stone thinks that the United States is rotten because of the sinister forces that rule. He used both Kennedy and Nixon to prove it. He wants to change the country and points to the Kennedy assassination and the Nixon presidency as proof of the need for radical political action. In that sense, it matters greatly that he has distorted the past."

64 ☞

James Wolcott

JAMES WOLCOTT IS A RESPECTED COLUMNIST for the ultra-chic *Vanity Fair* magazine. On Election Day 2004, he posted the following message on his Web site: "I am preparing myself for either outcome today. Should Kerry win, I will post an important statement called 'A Time for Healing,' or something equally noble-sounding. Should Bush win, I shall post a statement of philosophical resignation tentatively titled 'Good, Go Ahead, America, Choke on Your Own Vomit, You Deserve to Die.' The latter will probably require a little more tweaking."

This is what is known as sophisticated wit in such sophisticated witty places as Manhattan. Except you just know he's not kidding—not even a little!

So, there is simply no other way to say this: America will never come back together—liberals/conservatives, Democrats/Republicans, Blue States/Red States—as long as journalists like James Wolcott hold important positions at big mainstream media outlets. Intelligent and urbane as Wolcott may be, his entire take on his country and its people requires a *lot* of tweaking.

Amy Richards

HERE'S A LITTLE QUIZ. Assume you're a feminist who is pregnant with triplets. What does Hell look like?

Give up?

Answer: Costco. On Staten Island. The mayonnaise aisle, to be precise.

This is pretty much how Amy Richards sees it, if her guest column in the July 18, 2004, *Sunday New York Times Magazine* is any indication. And it's also pretty much the least of her problems.

Rarely have I read anything so chilling as Ms. Richards's essay titled "When One Is Enough"—on the subject of what is euphemistically called "selective reduction."

Who is Amy Richards? Well, to judge from the piece, she's simply an average citizen, sharing her firsthand experiences with abortion. Only later, prompted by revelations on the Internet, does the *New York Times* bother informing its readers that Amy Richards is, in fact, a longtime abortion-rights activist, a little piece of information that might have, as the *Times* put it, "shed light on her mind-set."

In her essay, Ms. Richards tells us that she is thirty-four years old, lives in Manhattan, went off the Pill because it made her "moody," and became pregnant. Her boyfriend, Peter, whom she's been with for three years, is the father. At the doctor's office, she gets the unexpected news that she's carrying *three* fetuses.

"My immediate response was, I cannot have triplets," Ms. Richards tells us. "I was not married; I lived in a five-story walk-up in the East Village; I worked freelance; and I would have to go on bed rest in March. I lecture at colleges, and my biggest months are March and April. I would have to give up my main income for the rest of the year. There was a part of me that was sure I could work around that. But it was a matter of, Do I want to?"

What do *you* think?

"I looked at Peter and asked the doctor: 'Is it possible to get rid of one of them? Or two of them?' The obstetrician wasn't an expert in selective reduction, but she knew that with a shot of potassium chloride you could eliminate one or more."

Which is just what Ms. Richards decides to do—*"get rid of"* one or two of them. After all, she writes, if she kept all three . . . this is where the mayo at Costco on Staten Island comes in.

"I'd have to give up my life. . . . I'm going to have to move to Staten Island. I'll never leave my house because I'll have to care for these children. I'll have to start shopping only at Costco and buying big jars of mayonnaise."

She would have to move to Staten Island and shop at Costco and buy big jars of mayonnaise! Oh, the humanity!

The point is not that Amy Richards is in favor of abortion, an issue as complicated and contentious as any in our public life. The point is that this woman is the poster child for all those who so easily reduce the procedure simply to a matter of personal convenience. Amy Richards is not even embarrassed to let the world know she would rather croak than leave her five-story walk-up in Manhattan . . . *for a place like Staten Island;* that she'd rather green-light a couple of shots of chloride to the hearts of the twins . . . *than give up her biggest income months on the college-lecture circuit.* This is a woman, despite her matter-of-fact tone, who is dripping with contempt—not for the twins, of course, for whom she apparently feels nothing at all—but for basic decency, not to mention for all those *pathetic,* ordinary Americans who don't think it's so terrible to live in the suburbs and who actually like shopping at Costco and who have lives that include Little League and Girl Scouts; the ones who would feel *something* (other than relief) if they had to *get rid of* a set of twins they were carrying.

"When we saw the specialist," Richards goes on, "we found out that I was carrying identical twins and a stand alone. My doctors thought the stand alone was three days older. There was something psychologically comforting about that, since I wanted to have just one."

Psychologically comforting? Well, yes. Because, armed with this new information, the choice was easy: The twins go, the stand alone stays, "a shot of potassium chloride to the heart of the fetus" takes care of the whole thing, she writes without a hint of emotion.

So, how does the Amy Richards saga end? She tells us that she had a boy "and everything is fine."

Really? I think the jury is still out on that one. Who knows what her son will think when he grows up and finds out about the siblings that his mom "got rid of," the ones who were so efficiently "eliminated"? Who knows what he will think if he ever reads her frightening essay in the *New York Times*. If he has a shred of humanity his mother so proudly lacks, he'll be sick.

☞ *62*

Howard Stern

I HAVE FRIENDS WHOM I ADMIRE and whose opinions I respect, who tell me they like Howard Stern.

They tell me they like his honesty. How he's not afraid to go against the grain and take the un-PC position. They liked it, for example, when he said the cops in Los Angeles who beat Rodney

King "didn't beat this idiot enough." No, my friends are *not* bigots. They just liked the fact that Stern was saying what a lot of people with common sense wanted to say about a moron, high on PCP, who led the cops on a late-night high-speed chase all over town, but didn't have the guts to say themselves.

But come on! Who are we kidding? The "honesty" most of his fans really like is the same "honesty" that kids have, the uncontrollable compulsion to say whatever comes into their undeveloped little minds, like, "Boy, you make stinky farts." They tune to Howard for the adolescent, look-how-naughty-I-can-be stuff.

For instance, they like the way Howard makes fun of retarded people. Once, when he took his radio show to Las Vegas, in front of a live audience, Stern hosted a segment he called "Retarded Card Sharks," and asked contestants questions like, "What does t-o-o-t-h spell?" Answer: "Seven." Everybody howled at how stupid the retarded guy was.

They like the way he exploits people with cleft palates, people who stutter, and people like "Vomit Man," whose claim to fame is that he stinks, to get cheap laughs.

They like the fact that in Howard's world, nothing is sacred—not even tragedy. After almost eighty men, women, and children were killed at the Branch Davidian Church in Waco, Texas, Stern opened the show to his callers—for about an hour of Branch Davidian jokes.

But mostly, of course, they like the sex. The nonstop, never-ending sex.

On one show, Stern told a female guest: "I need you to nude-model for me and my penis. I'm swollen bigger than Rosie O'Donnell's head."

On another, a nineteen-year-old woman came into the studio and asked Stern to shave her. Guess where.

On still another, a female guest blew out a candle and tossed a ping-pong ball. Guess with which part of her body.

Once, he gave a guy a lie-detector test to find out if he got aroused watching tapes of a certain porn star—who was his step-daughter.

Once, he asked a bikini-clad model to play a game with him: ". . . If you get [a question] wrong you have to have sex with me . . . [we] make out, I touch your cans and you grab my ass."

Another time, when a female guest offered to be his slave, Stern told her, "First of all, I'm gonna need you to pee in a diaper . . . I want you to bend over . . . while I throw eggs at your buttocks . . . you're lucky I'm not asking you for sex."

As a consolation prize to a grandfather and grandson who lost out in a "dating game" contest, Stern fixed them up with a prostitute who had offered to sleep with both of them.

And then there's the lesbian sex, the endless parade of women who strip so Howard can evaluate their asses, and all sorts of other assorted losers who routinely come on to do almost anything, just so they can bask in the glow of their Sun God, Howard Stern.

None of this means that I think Howard Stern should be taken off the air for indecency. That's not what this is about—*at all!* This is a very big, very free country, and people should be allowed to say almost anything, even on the radio, even (I'm afraid) in the morning.

No, this is about something else entirely. It's about Howard Stern as a form of pollution, as a kind of sludge that runs through our culture today.

Once upon a time in America, it would have been impossible for someone like Howard Stern to become a star on radio, TV, or even in a flea circus. Not so long ago, if a radio personality got caught *thinking* "you're making me hard, come over here and sit on my lap," he'd be finished. Today, in our more *open,* more *honest* America, he becomes "the king of all media."

Leave Howard Stern on the air. Let him have his soon-to-be satellite radio show. But *please,* don't turn him into a First Amendment poster boy. Howard is what he is—a smart man with some interesting thoughts on some important issues who plays a fifty-something-year-old junior high school kid who loves to see how far he can push it, how much he can shock us.

And this, in the end, is Howard Stern's most significant, lasting, and saddest legacy: that the king of all "shock" jocks no longer shocks us. Not even a little. We've become used to all of it—the fart jokes, the humiliation of easy targets, the all-sex-all-the-time humor . . . it simply washes over us, like sludge in a polluted river—just part of our daily environment.

61

Michael Savage

LET'S SAY YOU CALL IN to Michael Savage's immensely popular nationally syndicated radio talk show, and let's say he doesn't like what you just told him about gays or abortion or immigration or anything else. There's a good chance the next words you're going to hear—aimed right at you, you pathetic loser—will be something like "You are a Commie pinko pervert." And that's only if he's feeling generous that day. It's not for nothing that Michael Savage has been called "America's angriest, most vicious conservative radio host."

At a time when we can use a lot more civility in our national discourse, you can count on Michael Savage to tell you to take your pansy-ass civility and drop dead, "you little hateful nothings," you "stinking rat hiding in the sewers."

A few years back, in the summer of 2003, Savage had a weekend talk show on MSNBC, when someone called in with something he didn't like. "So you're one of those sodomites. Are you a sodomite?" Savage demanded.

The caller replied: "Yes, I am."

"Oh, you're one of the sodomites. You should only get AIDS and die, you pig. How's that?"

How's that? MSNBC fired him, that's how that is.

A year later, when Bill Clinton had heart surgery and was on the road to recovery, Savage told his listeners, "We heard, of course, that hell was full and therefore Mr. Clinton will be with us for a while longer."

This is a guy who makes Ann Coulter sound like Mary Tyler Moore. Besides—and this is a vital distinction—Coulter always has that twinkle in her eye when she calls some liberal "pond scum." With Michael Savage, it's all venom all the time, without so much as a hint of humor.

And even worse, Savage's brand of over-the-top bile—which puts him right in there with the angriest haters on the Left—plays right into the hands of liberals, who use him as a bludgeon against even mainstream conservatives. To them, Michael Savage is not simply someone who "gives voice to the right wing's darkest fantasies," as one profile put it, *but that he's typical of all conservatives!*

There are those who say it's all an act, that when Savage calls someone "latrine scum," he's just giving the audience that made him a radio star and best-selling author what it wants. Frankly, I don't care if it is "total opportunism" as an ex-friend of his puts it, in order to make a fast buck. All I know is that Savage is doing as much harm to this country as those he claims to despise.

As his listeners know, Savage has a catchphrase, that he usually shouts at full volume, when he confronts someone or something he finds monumentally stupid: *"I can't take this anymore!"*

Small world. A lot of us can't take this anymore, either.

60 ☞

Ludacris

IF A BUNCH OF WHITE RACISTS got together and tried to come up with a way to make young black guys look really dumb—like demented caricatures of real black men—first they'd invent gangsta rap, and then they'd invent somebody just like Ludacris.

Ludacris, in case you're not familiar with the name, is a giant in the dingy world of gangsta rap. His songs are about the usual stuff—bitches, ho's, niggas, and . . . well, that pretty much sums it up. He's very big with kids, (too) many of whom get their "values" from the pop culture and the street and guys like Ludacris—instead of from a mother and a father at home.

But to really understand this artistic giant, it's best that you experience Ludacris in his own words. So, here is a sampler from a number of his hits, including several from his big CD *Word of Mouf*.

> *The game got switched on some Ludacris shit*
> *So all y'all can suck my dick, BEOTCH!!*
>
> *I make niggas eat dirt and fart dust*
> *Then give you a eighty-dollar gift certificate to Pussies*
>   *'RUs*
>
> *I've got ho's in different area codes (area, area codes . . . codes)*

Okay, enough! You get the idea.

Is Ludacris the *worst* of the bunch? Of course not! They're *all* the worst! When it comes to gangsta rap and the glorification of ignorance, it's one big giant tie for last place! Still, given his popularity, and all the support he enjoys from the ho's in different area codes, Ludacris certainly merits recognition on The List.

☞ *59*

Shirley Franklin

AS BAD AS SOME of the gangsta rappers are, the ones who try to give them an aura of respectability are worse.

Take Atlanta mayor Shirley Franklin.

On June 7, 2004, Mayor Franklin and the Atlanta City Council honored Chris Bridges—Ludacris's real name—with an official proclamation citing his good works.

No kidding.

You see, Ludacris, having made a lot of money over the years calling people niggas and ho's, has given some of it away to charities in the Atlanta area. This is a surefire, time-tested way to get in good with local politicians. And sure enough, it worked: Atlanta gave him what he craves most—legitimacy and respect.

Mayor Franklin's justification for honoring the rapper—"While there may be those who dislike or have personal differences with Ludacris, his contributions to young people through the work of his foundation . . . blah, blah, blah"—rightly infuriated decent people who saw right through it. As Juan Williams, the Fox News and NPR commentator, put it on *The O'Reilly Factor*, "It's outrageous! To me, what you've got here is a situation where the mayor, Shirley

Franklin, says, hey, look, you know what, there is some good that this man does with his charities. But how ridiculous! Would you say that about a drug dealer? Would you say that about someone who was a gangster, who was killing people? No!"

That Juan Williams is black and liberal is not beside the point. Like Bill Cosby, he has had enough. And like Bill Cosby, he's not afraid to say what a lot of the black establishment won't say.

"So a lot of these people are trying to put a nice face on what is a very ugly situation," Williams added, "which is basically they say to young black people, if you want to be authentically black, you have got to dress like you are just out of prison, got your pants hanging off your butt and your hat turned around, and calling people horrible names, the kind of abuse of women that I just think has no place in the black community, especially in the community where we see so much family break up.

"And yet somehow the mayor and the city council are willing to embrace this under the facade, the fake face of saying, 'Oh, there are all kinds of music that deserve attention.' This is not about that. It's about the *content* of this music. It's what it says to young people. It's how it allows them to interpret authentic blackness in this very negative way."

Hey, lighten up, Juan. You can't expect the mayor of a big city like Atlanta, Georgia, to care about high-minded stuff like that, not when some guy is handing out free money to poor people in town—that is, when he's not rapping about "niggas [who] eat dirt and fart dust."

Come on, Juan. That would be ludicrous.

Eminem

GO TO GOOGLE AND PUNCH IN "EMINEM," the white rap artist who gives depravity a bad name. You get over 13 million hits. That's more than for Queen Elizabeth, Winston Churchill, Albert Einstein, Michelangelo, Leonardo da Vinci, Jonas Salk, Elvis Presley, Frank Sinatra, Adolf Hitler, Osama bin Laden, Christopher Columbus, Abraham Lincoln, or even Princess Diana. There are more hits for Jesus Christ than Eminem, but not much more.

Which is another way of saying that Eminem can't be ignored; no matter how hard we may try. It's not that he's more vulgar than a million other gangsta rappers; it's that, at least in part because he's white, he appeals to so many more kids than other rappers. He not only sells millions and millions of CDs, he also starred in a hit movie about his own life. Eminem is such a cultural icon, in fact, that it's not just teenagers who think he's hot. Apparently, so does a certain type of well-educated, sophisticated, middle-aged woman.

Like, for instance, *New York Times* resident girlish adolescent, Maureen Dowd.

"A gaggle of my girlfriends are surreptitiously smitten with Eminem," Maureen Dowd wrote in her *New York Times* column. "They buy his posters on eBay. They play him on their Walkmen at the gym."

Yes, of course, these are sad women trying to hang on to their youth at the expense of their dignity. Yet what is troubling is that they and others in the "progressive" elite have lent Eminem respectability—even cachet. And that gives him all the more power to spread his destructive messages. As Bob Herbert, another *New York Times* columnist has put it, Eminem "is a white rapper who has burrowed his way to the nauseating depths of degradation and self-loathing pioneered by gangsta-rapping blacks. No image is too vile. In Eminem's world, all women are 'whores,' and he is eager to rape and murder them. He dares us to question whether he would choke a woman 'til the vocal cords don't work in her throat no more . . .'"

Or how about this lovely line from a song appropriately called "No One's Iller Than Me":

> *"Ripped this old lady, hung her neck by a hook*
> *Didn't realize it was my grandmother 'til I checked her*
> *pocketbook."*

Maybe we never were the Norman Rockwell's America of our imagination, the one of apple pie, patriotism, and church suppers, but not too many years ago, a guy this vile could never have come close to becoming so mainstream—let alone an idol to millions. But like so many other things that have cheapened our culture, this shift in our standards crept up on us a little at a time, so gradually we hardly noticed. And now, as Bob Herbert writes, "This stuff is readily available to 10-year-olds, which should make any serious person both angry and sad. A steady diet of this ugliness is poisonous, the equivalent of developing one's self-image by looking in a toilet."

Frankly, I don't give a damn about whether Maureen Dowd's ditzy girlfriends are smitten or not with Eminem. But we should all be worried about all those kids staring into the toilet.

Ted Field

TED FIELD IS RICH. Sure, it's possible that Bill Gates or some Saudi oil sheik might not think he's loaded, but Ted is doing okay—if you consider having a net worth of about $1.2 billion as doing okay.

Field, who was born Frederick Woodruff Field on June 1, 1953, got his money the old-fashioned way: he inherited it from his family. The Fields owned Chicago's legendary Marshall Field Department Store. So when he was old enough to take the silver spoon out of his mouth, young Ted could have done just about anything he wanted with his money. He could have stayed in Chicago and gone into the family business. Or he could have spent his life windsurfing off of some island he could easily have bought for himself.

But Ted Field wanted to do something important. Like so many other guys born rich—FDR and JFK come to mind—he wanted to have an impact on American life, which he indeed has had, and which is precisely why he's on this list.

Here's what Field did with his money: the young man went West, all the way to Hollywood, where he donned leather jackets and sunglasses and contributed to American culture by producing movies and raising cash for Democrats. He was good at the latter, but regarding the former, an executive at Disney once told *Vanity Fair*: "Ted Field knows no more about day to day producing than you do."

In any case, Ted Field's real claim to fame has nothing to do with the movies—or with politics, either. His lasting contribution to the culture is that he's the white guy who took his fortune and started up a record company called Interscope, an act that made Ted Field a true American pioneer—the man who helped make mostly black gangsta rap the malignant force it has become in American life.

Nice going, my Caucasian!

Field may not have been the brains behind the operation—that would be his partner Jimmy Iovine, an otherwise accomplished producer-executive. But without Ted Field's deep pockets, there would have been no Interscope, the company that gave the world, among others, Eminem, Snoop Dogg, and (through the infamous Death Row, which joined the Interscope "family" in 1992), Tupac Shakur. For this alone, Ted Field should be enshrined in cement on Hollywood's Walk of Fame. Not just his hands. All of him.

Someone who would be glad to do the honors is a smart, passionate anti–gangsta rap activist named C. Delores Tucker, who heads an organization called the Political Council of Black Women. Ms. Tucker is on a crusade, convinced that gangsta rap is one of the forces undermining black kids in America today. She once testified before a congressional committee that "Gangsta music is drugs-driven, race-driven, sex-driven, greed-driven, and violence-driven." And she condemned Ted Field by name as one of "the wealthy mavens of the record industry" who "produce gangsta rap filth . . ."

But Ted Field couldn't care less. His contempt for Delores Tucker and anyone else who cares about the endless stream of violence and depravity he has brought to American kids was perfectly captured in this charming and gracious observation: "You can tell the people who want to stop us from releasing controversial rap music one thing," Field said. "Kiss my ass."

Diane Sawyer

THERE HAVE BEEN MANY dumb celebrity interviews on "news" magazine programs; many interviews that have nothing to do with real news that no self-respecting journalist would ever do. But the "exclusive" interview that Diane Sawyer did with Britney Spears for *Primetime Thursday* on November 13, 2003—for me, anyway—was the day the music died.

Here's a brief exchange between the two divas.

"You can bop me. I have to ask a couple of things about Justin," Diane tells Britney, referring to the singer's old boyfriend Justin Timberlake.

"He's gone on television and pretty much said you broke his heart, you did something that caused him so much pain, so much suffering," Ms. Sawyer says in that same serious tone she uses when interviewing someone like Henry Kissinger. "What did you do?"

Canny and discreet as ever, Britney tries to evade the question, saying only, "He'll always have a special place in my heart."

But this isn't good enough for the tough veteran reporter, who demands facts, not spin. "But you said, 'I've only slept with one person in my whole life, two years into my relationship with Justin.' And yet, he's left the impression that you weren't faithful, that you betrayed the relationship."

"I'm not technically saying he's wrong," Brit tells Di, "but I'm not technically saying he's right, either."

"So, who are the dream guys now? Still Brad?" Diane asks.

"Yes, definitely Brad," Britney responds.

"Ben?" Diane continues.

"Ben Affleck. He's cute," Britney says.

But Diane's relentless search for the truth is only getting started. What about "The Kiss"—the one between Britney and Madonna on a live broadcast of MTV's Video Music Awards show? Diane skeptically observes: "You said there's no tongue action here."

"Oh, of course there was no tongue. Gosh no," Britney insists.

Diane isn't buying any of it.

"Well, it looked like it. It looked like there was," she says before moving on to even more serious subjects, like Britney's ass.

"And you don't like the famous bottom, the world-famous . . . ?" the always-curious Diane Sawyer wants to know.

"The world-famous bottom? *Ewww*, don't say that," Britney tells Diane.

And then comes the payoff, this wonderfully enlightening exchange, about a song on Britney's new CD—specifically, a tune about . . . masturbation.

"I mean, it's not something you openly talk about with a lot of people. It's something sacred," B solemnly tells D.

This leaves Diane—who used to cover the State Department for CBS News and who could have put her foot down and refused to do the Britney interview in the first place, had she wanted to—stunned. "*Sacred*?" she says.

This comeback from Diane flusters young Britney, who still manages to get out, "It is sacred. But in a way, okay, I'm confusing myself right now."

No, it is not exactly Eric Sevareid interviewing Supreme Court Justice William O. Douglas. Still, Britney has no need to apologize for confusing herself. I'm confused, too. I thought Diane Sawyer was a journalist.

David Westin

TED KOPPEL IS WORRIED.

He's worried that television news isn't as serious as it ought to be. He thinks that's the fault of people in the TV news business who believe they can get more viewers if they dumb down the news. And he thinks it's a losing strategy.

Speaking to broadcasters in Los Angeles, on April 20, 2004, the ABC News anchorman said, "When we began taking our journalism more lightly, people began taking us less seriously."

The problem, according to Koppel, is the mixing of news and entertainment, what they call "infotainment," a trend, he said, that was alienating loyal news viewers who expected to get *news* when they turned on a *news* program—not fluff.

"I have no problem whatsoever with entertainers and comedians pretending to be journalists," Koppel said, "my problem is with journalists pretending to be entertainers."

Good for you, Ted. Thanks for saying what needed to be said.

There's just one problem. Ted Koppel, like most of the media elite, is part of the club. And in the club you never push it too far. You never, for example, name names and say exactly who is causing all these problems you care so much about. That would be a violation of club rules, and considered rude.

But I'm sure Ted could have come up with a few names if he really wanted. In fact, he could have started with his own boss, David Westin, the president of ABC News.

At ABC News, the buck stops at David Westin's desk. He can say no to infotainment. He can decree that when an ABC news correspondent questions Britney Spears about masturbation, it gives the viewers reason to "take us [at ABC News] less seriously"—and refuse to put it on the air. But he doesn't do that.

David Westin is what's wrong with television news these days. He's not alone, of course, but he's the one who allows "journalists" like Barbara Walters and Diane Sawyer to incessantly blur the line the way they do. He's the one who goes to the Columbia University School of Journalism to speak about the First Amendment, then goes back to ABC News and green-lights all those silly celebrity interviews you see on *20/20* and *Primetime*.

Once that didn't happen. Once television news presidents were men of great courage and great integrity. Once there was a healthy tension between the presidents of network news divisions, who cared passionately about the integrity of news, and the corporate guys, who cared passionately about the integrity of the bottom line.

After Ted Koppel finished his prepared remarks, a student in the audience asked him what young journalists should do if they find themselves forced to do things that compromise their integrity.

"Quit," Koppel told him, without any frills. "If you start doing those things . . . you're never going to be able to get out from under it."

Once, it actually worked that way. Back in 1965, when his bosses would not run live hearings about the war in Vietnam, you'll recall, CBS News President Fred Friendly, Ed Murrow's former partner, walked away, his integrity intact.

Can anyone even imagine David Westin quitting over principle?

Here's a little experiment: If one of Westin's corporate bosses suggested, "Let's do more interviews with Britney Spears—and this time let's get her to show more skin," which would his response more likely be?

A) "I'm running a news division . . . not a strip show!"

Or

B) "Great idea. I'll get right on it!"

Neal Shapiro

I READILY ACKNOWLEDGE that a lot of you won't care one bit about what Neal Shapiro, the president of NBC News, has done to his news organization. I understand that to a lot of people it's no big deal when the suits on executive row blur the line between news and entertainment. But when they blur the difference between *news* and journalistic *prostitution*, then we all ought to care.

Here's the problem. In the spring of 2004—while another news magazine was covering real news, like the abuses at the Abu Ghraib prison in Baghdad—*Dateline*, which is part of NBC News, had more pressing journalistic priorities. *Dateline* was busy shilling for NBC *Entertainment*—the news magazine devoting hours of programming, *entire editions* of *Dateline,* to pure, unadulterated fluff about the season finale of *The Apprentice* and the final episodes of two long-running NBC hit comedies, *Frasier* and *Friends. Dateline* ran about five hours in all—two full hours of *The Apprentice* "news" *in just one week.*

This caught the eye of TV critics, who saw it for what it was: a news-division president selling out.

"The *Dateline* brand is cheapened every time it's prostituted to shill for other NBC shows, and the last thing anyone at the network should want is to drag down the reputation of NBC News," is how TV critic Phil Rosenthal put it in the *Chicago Sun-Times.*

An "orgy of self promotion," is what Verne Gay called it in *Newsday.* "NBC News disgraced itself."

As I say, I get it; to a lot of people, this may sound harmless enough. Some may even be thinking, "Hey, I like *The Apprentice* and *Frasier* and *Friends*. I'm glad I got to see what goes on behind the scenes of those shows." But there's a reason Tom Brokaw didn't sit down with the contestants from *The Apprentice*; there's a reason he didn't ask the stars of *Friends* "how it feels" to be saying good-bye after so many years. The reason is that Tom Brokaw (and now his replacement, Brian Williams) is a serious journalist and this isn't something serious journalists do. Serious journalists understand that this not only would injure their own credibility, but also the credibility of their entire news division.

Either Neal Shapiro doesn't get it, or, more likely, he doesn't want to get it. It's no small point that his boss, NBC president Jeff Zucker, likes this kind of "cross-promotion." And the way it works in network television news these days is when your boss says "jump," you say "how high," even if—make that *especially* if—you're the president of the news division.

In the world of TV executives, if a show gets big ratings, it was a success—end of discussion. And guess what? "The audience certainly watched [the *Dateline* specials]," Shapiro says. "There's no doubt about that. The ratings speak for themselves."

Yes they do. The ratings were great. And they probably would have been even better if all the contestants from *The Apprentice* or the stars from *Friends* went on *Dateline* naked. But doesn't Neal Shapiro understand that while ratings are important, the credibility of his own news division is a lot more important?

"The practice [of cross-promotion] devalues everything else NBC News does," as Verne Gay of *Newsday* put it."

Call me old-fashioned, but the way I see it, if you're going to sell your journalistic soul, at least sell out for a fancy title, lots of money, and really cool perks. Never mind. That's *exactly* what Neal Shapiro is selling out for.

Anna Nicole Smith

IF YOU GAVE ANNA NICOLE SMITH A CHOICE: Push button number one and you can win a Nobel Prize, or push button number two and you'll be on the cover of *People* magazine—is there any doubt that Anna would trample you, your grandma, and maybe even that silly little dog of hers to get to button number two?

I don't mean to pick on Anna. Really. For one thing, it's way too easy. I'm thinking of the guy who wrote that "her taste for the tacky is only rivaled by her taste for the even tackier." Cheap. True, but cheap.

Still, Anna Nicole Smith represents something important about our culture, something that needs to be talked about. Let's call it the Vulgarization of the Personal—the idea that nothing is private anymore, or should be; that turning one's life into a big fat public spectacle is perfectly okay.

Anna, for sure, isn't alone. There's the "TV personality" who just had to get engaged at the NBA All-Star game so that she could share the moment with the whole world by making sure the proposal was on the big-screen TV hanging over the arena. There's the Hollywood star who has to keep us all up to date about how her pregnancy is going. There are all the other Hollywood celebs who can't wait to go public with news that they were drug addicts or alcoholics but now, just out of rehab this afternoon, have a new mission in life, which is to tell us all about what it was like being a drug addict or an alcoholic.

But when it comes to bizarre self-exploitation, Anna sets the bar as high as anyone. She couldn't just pop up every now and then on Jay Leno's show like all the other less-than-scintillating beautiful people and tell us, say, about her weight *issues*. No, thanks to the cable television E! network, we know (as one of those nasty writers said) that "with the aid of famous Hollywood decorator Bobby Trendy, Anna Nicole has made her mansion into a gaudy wonderland that looks like a Dr. Seuss scene on acid." We know about her leopard-skin wallpaper, about her bed, about her bathroom, about her passing out in limousines, about her yelling at people, about her eating contests, about her toady assistants, about, about . . . about *everything Anna*.

No, Anna Nicole is not public enemy number one. In a lot of ways, she's just like all the other Hollywood narcissists, except with a little less sophistication and style. When you get right down to it, they all have the same egomaniacal compulsion. *"I must tell you about my life because I know that you, an ordinary person, will find me, a celebrity, just fascinating!"*

Actually, no, I don't—and I think I speak for many other Americans when I say that. But let's be perfectly honest: These people can only exist in a culture of voyeurs, a culture where there are enough people who actually care about this stuff. Still, just because people like watching car wrecks, doesn't mean car wrecks are good for us, does it?

But here's the craziest part. When I see Anna Nicole Smith, I think of . . . *Joe DiMaggio*. Seriously! Because he was the opposite of so much of what we see today. Joe was the epitome of style and grace. And if some of that was only a facade, well that just proves the point—that he cared enough to behave with dignity when he was out in public. DiMaggio's personal life was personal. He didn't tell us how he felt about anything, let alone about such painful things as his troubled relationships with family members or the death of the woman he loved.

Where have you gone, Joe DiMaggio? We need you more now than ever.

We all know where Anna is, and that's the problem.

Markos Moulitsas

ON MARCH 31, 2004, four American civilian contractors were on their way to work in Iraq when they were ambushed and savagely killed by a gang of insurgents who shot them and set their cars on fire. A cheering crowd then dragged the bodies into the street and dismembered them before hanging the corpses from a bridge for the world to see.

In the United States, here is how another American, a Chicago-born man in his early thirties named Markos Moulitsas reacted to the news on his Web site, dailykos.com: "I feel nothing over the death of the mercenaries. They aren't in Iraq because of orders, or because they are trying to help the people make Iraq a better place. They are there to wage war for profit. Screw them."

We live in a big country with more than a few nasty, but basically unimportant, screwballs out there; and if Moulitsas simply were one of them, he would not be worth my time or yours. But Markos Moulitsas isn't just another anonymous run-of-the-mill loser. He's a big, important operative—a Demoratic consultant, who has close ties to lots of mainstream Democrats, including Howard Dean, the new head of the Democratic National Commmittee.

And in case you're wondering, dailykos.com is not some obscure little nothing-of-a-site. It's immensely popular, especially with liberals—especially the angry kind. The site gets 400,000 page views a day, which according to people who know about these things, makes it one of, if not *the*, busiest political weblogs on the Internet. When Markos Moulitsas speaks, liberals listen.

And a lot of them apparently like what they hear. As political pundit Michael Barone described it in his *U.S. News & World Report* column on February 12, 2005, Moulitsas's blog "seethes with hatred of Bush, constantly attacks Republicans and excoriates Democrats who don't oppose Bush root and branch."

According to Barone, the "repulsive comment [about the murdered American civilians in Iraq] produced no drop-off in page views." Why? Because the "Democratic Internet constituency was and is motivated by one thing more than anything else: hatred of George W. Bush."

So Markos Moulitsas is in this book not just because he said one vicious and hateful thing, but because whether liberals like it or not, his voice is becoming one of the more important voices of American liberalism, certainly on the Web where's he's already a big star.

Yes, it's true that not many liberals are as crude as Moulitsas. Much as they may detest George W. Bush and his policies, few, hearing that four fellow Americans had been brutally murdered in Iraq, would ever think, let alone actually say out loud: "Screw them."

But here's where it gets tricky. While they may sincerely mourn for those who've died, there's little question that a lot of Moulitsas's readers actually do atively root for bad news—whether it's in Iraq, or Afghanistan, or here at home with the economy. Like Moulitsas, they are pessimistic, defeatist, and way too often, nasty. And in their bitterness, they're for anything that makes George W. Bush look bad.

Consider the elections in Iraq in early 2005. As every dispassionate observer knows, they went remarkably well. Decent people everywhere were stirred by the sight of a people still under siege proudly showing off their purple ink-stained fingers for everyone to see. They had free elections in Afghanistan too, something that never happened under the Taliban. There's even talk of more free elections in the region, in places that have never embraced real democracy. So what's a good liberal to do at such a remarkable historical moment? Give George Bush just a little credit? Some have, of course, but not Markos Moulitsas. Here's what he wrote on dailykos.com: "January was the third bloodiest month for U.S. and allied troops. Will that cease now that Iraqis have voted? Nope. . . . The war will continue unabated."

Maybe it will. But that's not the point. Something good had just happened in Iraq, but Markos Moulitsas and the others like him couldn't be happy even for two seconds. Once upon a time, liberals were the optimistic ones. They were the hopeful ones. They were the upbeat ones. Now, too often, too many of them see darkness wherever they look. Nothing can go right, as far as they're concerned, as long as George Bush is around.

So what do liberals who loathe W have to look forward to, now that their guy lost the presidential election in 2004 and for the first time in a long time some hope is trickling out of the Middle East? Well, with a little luck maybe Iraq will descend into a bloody civil war. Or Iran may blow up in Bush's face. Or maybe North Korea will launch a nuke on Honolulu. Or maybe the stock market will crash. Or there'll be an outbreak of the plague in Kansas.

Hold on. Kansas is a Red State, right? So, as Mr. Moulitsas might—no make that *would*—put it: Screw them.

☞ *51*

Ann Pelo

REMEMBER WHEN you first found out about The Blue Angels, the elite Navy flight demonstration squad that has thrilled generations of American kids since its formation at the end of World War II?

Maybe you ran across a picture of them in a book or in *Life* magazine. Maybe it was seeing them perform their amazing feats of high-speed air acrobatics on TV, or in a classroom film. Maybe, if you were lucky, it was when they came to your hometown for one of their famous shows. However it happened, for most of us, as small kids, watching The Blue Angels was thrilling. These were genuine heroes—men with unbelievable skill, daring, and courage. And even more than that, these were men (and now also women), ready to give their lives to protect our freedoms, if that's what it took.

But that's not how Ann Pelo sees it. She's the co-author of a manual for preschool teachers called *That's Not Fair!: A Teacher's Guide to Activism with Young Children*. In it, Pelo tells us that she has a "commitment to peace and justice"; that she wants "to help shape children's values and to coach them about how to oppose injustice"; and that when she was a kid herself, her family "decried the injustices of the dominant culture," [but] we were still a part of it." Get the picture? Think of "That's Not Fair!" as "Michael Moore for Toddlers."

How do The Blue Angels fit in? Well, Pelo includes a section in her manual where she describes how she handled a situation one day when her tiny charges were out in a park in Seattle, and happened to see the famed flyers practicing their stunts overhead.

"Those are Navy airplanes," Pelo told the little kids. "They're built for war, but right now, there is no war, so the pilots learn how to do fancy tricks in their planes . . ." That was good with the kids, but not good enough for Ann Pelo. The next day when the planes flew over the park again she asked them to "communicate their feelings about the Blue Angels."

"They drew pictures of planes with Xs through them," she reports with satisfaction. ". . . They drew bomb factories labeled: 'No.' (and) 'Respect our words, Blue Angels. Respect kids' words. Don't kill people.' "

They said, "If you blow up our city, we won't be happy about it.

And our whole city will be destroyed. And if you blow up my favorite library, I won't be happy because there are some good books there that I haven't read yet."

Pelo tells us that the children "poured out their strong feelings about the Blue Angels in their messages and seemed relieved and relaxed."

Are you kidding me? Are we supposed to believe that little kids who can't wipe their own runny noses came up with this—on their own? But what's really frightening is that this kind of thing is not an aberration—far from it! As older kids are increasingly fed PC history that relentlessly stresses America's role as an "oppressor," and junior high and high school English classes today are often more concerned with a writer's ethnic background than the quality of his work, more and more of the youngest schoolchildren are being taught by those with an activist leftist agenda. Indeed, "That's Not Fair!" has been described as "exciting and informative" and a resource "to change the world for the better" by the organization that oversees preschool teacher training, the National Association for the Education of Young Children. And here's the best part: it's used by teachers across the whole country.

Once again, it takes an ordinary person with common sense—in this case, a reader of "That's Not Fair!" who felt the need to respond to it on Amazon—to say it best: "The author(s) of this book should never be allowed in front of a group of small children ever again, and neither should any other 'teacher' who would seriously consider using this drivel as a legitimate resource for their classroom. It is frightening and dangerous to even think that teachers would be willing to indoctrinate the smallest children in such a manner, by telling them that the Blue Angels would try to bomb their town. It is ghastly."

John Vasconcellos

CALIFORNIA STATE SENATOR John Vasconcellos is not a bad person. To the contrary, he appears to be a very good person who wishes only the very best things for children and other living things. Unfortunately, John Vasconcellos's ideas about what is good for others have had very, very bad consequences in the real world.

Recently term-limited out of office after more than thirty years representing the Silicon Valley in the California legislature, Vasconcellos likes to describe himself as "a pragmatic idealist," and his Web site adds, "He will probably be best remembered as 'The Johnny Appleseed of Self Esteem.'"

I wouldn't brag about that.

But maybe that's just me. As for Vasconcellos, he remains one of America's biggest cheerleaders for the "self-esteem movement" that he has done so much to promote—and impose on the nation's schools. And even though he's past seventy, he's still fluent in the hip, New Age lingo so common among the many fuzzy thinkers of his part of America. He speaks of "California as the human frontier, seedbed of revolutions in hi-tech, gender, race, self-esteem, global economy, interactive communications, politics"; of "redesigning society to encourage development of healthy, self-realizing, responsible human beings"; and of "developing a new human politics based on belief we human beings are innately inclined toward becoming life-affirming, constructive, responsible, trustworthy . . ." He authors books with titles like *A Liberating Vision: Politics for Growing Humans* and *Welcoming This Next American Revolution: Toward a 21st Century Politics of Trust, Healing and Hope.*

And he'll tell anyone who will listen that his worldview is born of personal experience; that, as a child, "I had been conditioned to know myself basically as a sinner, guilt-ridden and ashamed, constantly beating my breast and professing my unworthiness." But in the glorious 1960s, he attained self-knowledge and understood the power of self-esteem.

I'm happy for him. And besides, this is California, and the dude's just doing his thing.

Except that, far from being some zonked-out idealist, as a powerful California pol, Vasconcellos was in a position to do something about his obsession. In 1986, he founded the California Task Force to Promote Self-Esteem and Personal and Social Responsibility, which, three years later, issued a report declaring self-esteem a "vaccine" that would attack academic failure, drug use, and juvenile crime; and which led to legislation promoting self-esteem-driven curricula in the state's schools.

And as goes California—with its reputation for being on the cutting edge of all things new and exciting—so goes the nation, and the fixation on self-esteem was soon a national phenomenon. By the mid-90s, self-esteem programs were in place in elementary schools in thousands of districts across the nation.

What did this mean in practical terms? As with the self-help books that proliferated at the same-time, such curricula stressed love of self, endlessly repeating affirmations of self-worth. Children's feelings were paramount. "All children are honored," as a bumper sticker in one California community had it; "they're all students of the month," declared the principal of an elementary school in another. "When they don't excel, we say they have potential."

The *Los Angeles Times* described the kids in one L.A. school with especially low test scores spending time in daily "I Love Me" lessons, in which they completed the phrase "'I am ____' with words such as beautiful, lovable, respectable, kind or gifted. Then they memorized the sentences to make them sink in."

The consequences of all this were exactly what anyone with an ounce of common sense would have expected: No fewer than ten thousand research studies have now shown that, in academic terms, self-esteem curricula are worse than useless. By the end of the 90s, test scores, rather than rising, were falling, and the movement had no effect on drug use or crime. Indeed, a University of Michigan study showed that while American students lagged far behind their Asian counterparts in math, they outranked them in only one area—self-confidence.

And why not? With the self-esteem movement having led to rampant grade inflation, kids *thought* they were doing great. After all, as UCLA education professor Sandra Graham put it, in many classrooms, "it's just scripted that if the low achiever does *anything*, you praise them." So if little Mary thinks two and two are five, give that girl a gold star—it'll make her feel good about herself. And if little Johnny says Mickey Mantle discovered America . . . well, if it boosts his self-esteem, then maybe Mickey did discover America.

As the *L.A. Times*'s article summed up this ongoing experiment with American kids, "Encouraging students to love themselves is not paying off in the classroom, educators and researchers say. The time is better spent, they say, on teaching the basics."

No kidding! But, even after all this time, John Vasconcellos still doesn't buy it. "All the research in the world," he flatly declares, "won't change my mind about it."

Maybe that's what prompted one of his last major acts in the State Senate: his introduction in 2004 of a proposed constitutional amendment to lower the voting age, in which sixteen-year-olds would get a half vote and fourteen-year-olds a quarter vote in state elections. Hey, dude, why not? Sure, it would screw up California even more—but, hey, think of what it could do for kids' self-esteem!

Ingrid Newkirk

IF YOU DON'T FOLLOW these things too closely, I guess it's easy to write off Ingrid Newkirk, cofounder, president, and loudmouth-in-chief of People for the Ethical Treatment of Animals, as just another screwball.

After all, isn't PETA the outfit that gets those supermodels to pose nude in antifur ads? Hasn't Newkirk herself written in her last will and testament that when she dies, in order to drive home her pro-animal message, that she wants "the 'meat' of my body, or a portion thereof, [to] be used for a human barbecue?" Hasn't Newkirk also said that when she's gone she wants her skin made into shoes and purses? And isn't she the one who, when she's six feet under, wants her pals to dispatch her no longer living liver to France—as a protest? Against what? What else? *Foie gras*, also known as liver pâté.

Hey I like animals as much as the next guy, but I'm not sending anything to France when I die—certainly not my liver! But all of this is small, not even vaguely controversial stuff, for Ingrid Newkirk. And why should it be, when you consider some of the other things she believes in and has talked about over the years. For example:

"Six million Jews died in concentration camps, but six billion broiler chickens will die this year in slaughterhouses."—Ingrid Newkirk, *Washington Post*, November 13, 1983.

"Even if animal research resulted in a cure for AIDS, we'd be against it."—Ingrid Newkirk, *Vogue*, September 1989.

"There is no rational basis for saying that a human being has

special rights. A rat is a pig is a dog is a boy. They're all mammals."
—Ingrid Newkirk, from same *Vogue,* September 1989.

Okay, maybe the liver-to-France stuff is funny, but I stopped laughing a long time ago. Maybe this woman who equates the slaughter of chickens to the Holocaust, and would ban animal testing that stands to save hundreds of thousands of human lives, and sees a human child as not better than a rat, is an irresponsible zealot and a moral monstrosity—no matter how well-meaning her intentions may be.

Want more? Try this: After learning of a horrific suicide bombing in Israel, Newkirk wrote a letter to Yasser Arafat—*because a donkey was used in the bombing.* "We have received many calls and letters from people shocked at the bombing in Jerusalem . . . in which a donkey, laden with explosives, was intentionally blown up," she wrote to Arafat. "If you have the opportunity, will you please add to your burdens my request that you appeal to all those who listen to you to leave the animals out of this conflict?"

When a *Washington Post* columnist asked Newkirk if she would try to persuade Arafat not to blow up people, too, she replied, "It's not my business to inject myself into human wars."

But what's even worse than Newkirk's ridiculously misplaced sense of priorities is that she and her organization are *not* a joke. To the contrary, in recent years—fueled by clever marketing built around an appeal to people's natural love of animals—PETA has grown into a powerful force, more powerful than you probably think. Its membership now numbers more than three quarters of a million and—because it uses as recruiting tools the shallowest, least informed, most emotionally driven among us, that is, celebrities—PETA's support continues to grow. It proselytizes relentlessly at schools and universities, enrolling the idealistic young in what sounds like the worthiest of causes: the protection of animals. Some years ago, Harvard actually started offering a course in "animal law," and Newkirk readily acknowledges: "We're looking for good lawsuits that will establish the interests of animals as a legitimate concern in law."

PETA's targets are generally corporations that rely on animal products or, even more ominously, scientific research labs that use animals in experimentation; and, with the help of a largely uncritical press, it's had a great deal of success in imposing its radical agenda. It's one thing when, for instance, PETA gets Calvin Klein to stop using fur in its clothes, but quite another when it pressures corporate contributors to stop giving to the March of Dimes because a small percentage of its resources go to organizations that do animal experimentation. That kind of thinking can cost human beings their lives. But Newkirk apologizes for none of it, bragging that "Our opponents know we never let up."

And when legal means fail to get the job done, Newkirk is perfectly ready to endorse far more drastic tactics. While PETA may be best known for such unsavory (but relatively innocuous) "actions" as dousing fur-clad women with red paint or blood, or depositing a dead raccoon on the plate of Newkirk's foe, *Vogue* editor Anna Wintour, the group makes no secret that it applauds those who go much, much further. "I find it small wonder that the laboratories [where they do scientific experiments on animals] aren't all burning to the ground," says Newkirk. "If I had more guts, I'd light a match."

The amazing thing about Newkirk and PETA is that, if you give it even a moment's thought, you'll see that their entire argument makes no sense. After all, violence is part of nature. Animals kill. They eat other animals all the time. It's called "survival of the fittest." What's more natural than that? But when a reporter actually tried to question Newkirk about the obvious contradictions in her "philosophy," she immediately shut him up, demanding: "Stop asking these nutty questions."

And Ingrid Newkirk knows something about nutty.

48 ☞

Robert Byrd

YOU'D THINK THAT Senator Robert Byrd would maybe be just a *little* bit embarrassed.

I mean, there he stands on the Senate floor, week after week and month after month, going on self-righteously about decency and morality, liberally quoting Scripture and Shakespeare and the sages of Ancient Rome.

"Error, wounded, writhes in pain, and dies among his worshippers," he thunders, as once again he attacks American policy in Iraq, and "Today I weep for my country."

While Byrd's fire-and-brimstone act has led liberals to dub the West Virginia senator "the conscience of the Senate," the man does have one mighty colorful and checkered past—and that's putting it generously.

As a younger man, not only was he a member in good standing of the Ku Klux Klan, but he was such a good member that he got promoted to "Kleagle." And in that capacity, Robert Byrd was in charge of recruiting other bigots into the organization, a very important job, indeed. After all, not everybody gets to be a Kleagle; only the ones with those very special leadership skills—the kind that might convince some pathetic yahoo to put on a white sheet and pointy hat.

Years later he explained that he had joined because the Klan "offered excitement" and was an "effective force" in "promoting traditional American values," and described it as a mistake of youth.

Fair enough. We all make mistakes, although (I could be wrong about this) most of us never joined the Ku Klux Klan—either for "excitement," or because it was a good way to pursue "traditional American values," *or for any other reason*! And besides, Byrd left the Klan a long, long time ago, way back in 1943, when he was about twenty-five.

But then in 1971, a letter came to light that Byrd wrote to the Klan's Imperial Wizard three years *after* he left the KKK. Byrd identifies himself as a former Kleagle and says, "The Klan is needed today as never before and I am anxious to see its rebirth here in West Virginia. . . . It is necessary that the order be promoted immediately and in every state in the Union. Will you please inform me as to the possibilities of rebuilding the Klan realm of W. Va?"

And a year after *that*, after his election to the West Virginia State Senate, he wrote that he would "never submit to fight beneath that banner [the American flag] with a Negro by my side. Rather I should die a thousand times, and see Old Glory trampled in the dirt never to rise again, than to see this beloved land of ours become degraded by race mongrels, a throwback to the blackest specimen from the wilds." The boy had a rhetorical touch even then, didn't he?

Nor did Byrd change his tune all that much after his 1958 election to the United States Senate, when he became one of the most adamant members of the Democratic block who fought long and hard against civil rights legislation. He personally filibustered more than fourteen hours trying to defeat the historic 1964 Civil Rights Act. And he holds the dubious distinction of being the only senator to vote against the only two black Supreme Court nominees in U.S. history—Thurgood Marshall *and* Clarence Thomas.

No one in his party, of course, is going to fault him for going against Thomas—or anything else, for that matter. They've certainly never held his sordid past against him. Instead, they've honored him with the posts of majority whip and majority leader. And as recently as 2001, when he twice used the term "white niggers" in a TV interview, he got a free pass from all those, both in the public sphere and the media, who normally eviscerate any public figure who displays even a hint of "racial insensitivity."

Remember Trent Lott?

Little wonder, then, that his liberal friends also don't seem to care that "the conscience of the Senate" has so ruthlessly abused his powerful position on the Senate Appropriations Committee by steering so much taxpayer money to his home state that the non-partisan Citizens Against Government Waste (CAGW) has crowned him "the king of pork." The CAGW points out that, in-credibly, in 2001, "Byrd managed to claw $232 million in pork for West Virginia, or $128 for every single resident." As Byrd himself boasts, in that charmingly folksy way of his, "West Virginia has always had four friends, God Almighty, Sears Roebuck, Carter's Liver Pills, and Robert C. Byrd."

Think that tells you all you need to know about his ego? Think again. The following is a sampling of taxpayer-funded projects Byrd has brought to his home state:

Robert C. Byrd Locks and Dam, Byrd Aerospace Tech Center, Robert C. Byrd Green Bank Telescope, Byrd Industrial Park, Robert C. Byrd Drive, Robert C. Byrd Health Sciences Center of West Virginia, Robert C. Byrd Cancer Research Center, Robert C. Byrd Technology Center (at Alderson-Broaddus College), Robert C. Byrd Hardwood Technologies Center (near Princeton), Robert C. Byrd Bridge, Robert C. Byrd addition to the lodge at Oglebay Park, Robert C. Byrd Community Center, Robert C. Byrd Honors Scholarships, Robert C. Byrd Expressway, Robert C. Byrd Institute (in Charleston), Robert C. Byrd Institute for Advanced Flexible Manufacturing, Robert C. Byrd Visitor Center at Harpers Ferry National Historic Park, Robert C. Byrd Federal Courthouse, Robert C. Byrd Academic and Technology Center, Robert C. Byrd United Technical Center, Robert C. Byrd Federal Building, Robert C. Byrd Hilltop Office Complex, Robert C. Byrd Library, Robert C. Byrd Learning Resource Center, Robert C. Byrd Rural Health

Center, Robert C. Byrd Clinical Addition to the veterans' hospital in Huntington, Robert C. Byrd Industrial Park (Hardy County), Robert C. Byrd Scholastic Recognition Award, Robert C. Byrd Community Center (in the naval station Sugar Grove).

Oh yeah, there's one more thing, something the CAGW calls "a new standard for taxpayer-funded narcissism." It seems that there's a statue of Robert C. Byrd himself in the state capitol—which just happens to violate state law prohibiting statues of government officials until they have been dead for half a century.

"Truth has a way of asserting itself despite all attempts to obscure it," proclaimed Byrd in one of his patented Senate harangues. "Distortion only serves to derail it for a time. No matter to what lengths we humans may go to obfuscate facts or delude our fellows, truth has a way of squeezing out through the cracks, eventually."

Maybe they could inscribe that on the Robert C. Byrd statue at the state capitol . . . or the Robert C. Byrd Federal Building . . . or the Robert C. Byrd Community Center . . . or the Robert C. Byrd Hilltop Office Complex . . . or maybe the yet-to-be-built-but-don't-bet-it-won't Robert C. Byrd King of Pork Museum.

47

Maxine Waters

BACK IN 1992, in the midst of one of the nasty, race-based disputes that have marked her career, one of California representative Maxine Waters's political opponents was reported to have described her—in a private conversation—by using a familiar word that rhymes with "witch." Hearing of this, Ms. Waters professed to be shocked, *shocked,* and, of course, demanded the man's professional head on a platter. "After all," as a *National Review Online* columnist wrote at the time, who wouldn't be "aghast that a woman of such grace, such refinement, such unparalleled gentility should be spoken of in such terms?"

Yes, the columnist was kidding.

In fact, as anyone who's ever seen her in action will tell you, Maxine Waters is about as refined and genteel as a pit bull in a bad mood—and quick to contaminate the public discourse with her big, belligerent mouth. At times, she even embarrasses her fellow race-baiters, which isn't that easy—praising dictators like Fidel Castro while referring to the Republican Party as "the enemy," savaging a moderate Republican like former L.A. mayor Richard Riordan as "a plantation owner," and rushing to bully any fellow Democrats who threaten to think independently on race.

And when her South Central Los Angeles district was laid waste by the devastating riots of 1992, arsonists and looters destroying the livelihoods of thousands of her constituents (a great many of them Korean), her first instinct was to defend the criminals. The riots, she proclaimed, were not even riots at all, but a "rebellion . . . a spontaneous reaction to a lot of injustice and a lot of alienation and frustration." I'm sure that's why so many in the *rebellion* were dealing with all that *injustice* by stealing liquor and TV sets.

As for the drug epidemic in urban America, Waters focuses on the notion—exposed as a hoax by reports in the *Washington Post, L.A. Times,* and *New York Times,* among many others—that the CIA created the problem by promoting drug use in the inner cities. "If I never do anything else in this career as a member of Congress," she angrily tells us, "I'm going to make somebody pay for what they've done to my community and to my people."

She even defends escaped murderer Joanne Chesimard, a former leader of the Black Panthers and the Black Liberation Army, who was sentenced to life in prison for gunning down—at point-blank range—a New Jersey State Highway patrol officer she had already shot and wounded. That was in 1973. Chesimard escaped in 1979 and turned up in Cuba, where Fidel Castro granted her political asylum. And when Congress passed a resolution urging Castro to send her back to America, Waters wrote Castro asking him to let her stay and even compared Chesimard to Martin Luther King. According to Maxine Waters, "She was persecuted as a result of her political beliefs and affiliations."

All of which would be easy to write off as the ravings of a fringe crank, except for one thing: Maxine Waters holds quite a bit of power and influence in her party. And these days, it's almost impossible to find a Democrat in Washington willing to cross her on any issue that involves race. One who dared, Joseph Lieberman, found out just how unpleasant the experience can be. When Lieberman—who had expressed reservations about affirmative action and who gave tentative support to school vouchers—was nominated for vice president by the Democrats in 2000, Waters caused a huge stink, demanding to know why she hadn't been consulted in advance and forcing him to appear before a black audience to explain himself. The *explanation* soon became a *recantation*, as Lieberman disowned the very moderate positions that might have gotten Al Gore and him elected.

"She is one of the most self-serving, hate-filled, race-obsessed politicians in America," as columnist Michelle Malkin puts it, and "the Democratic Party doesn't just embrace her. It kneels at her feet."

Barbara Walters

IF YOU GO TO THE ABC NEWS WEB SITE, you will learn that Barbara Walters is "one of the most highly acclaimed journalists on television."

You will be told that "she has interviewed every American President and First Lady since Richard Nixon."

You will be reminded that "she made journalism history by arranging the first joint interview with Egypt's President Anwar Sadat and Israel's Prime Minister Menachem Begin in November 1977."

You will be informed that "another of her 'firsts' was an hourlong primetime conversation with Cuban President Fidel Castro—an interview which has been printed in half a dozen languages and shown all over the world."

And you will be treated to a list of some of her most important interviews, a list that includes "Russia's Boris Yeltsin, China's Premier Jiang Zemin, Great Britain's former Prime Minister Margaret Thatcher, as well as Indira Gandhi, Vaclav Havel, Moammar Qaddafi, the Shah of Iran and King Hussein of Jordan."

The fact is Barbara Walters has probably interviewed more movers and shakers than anybody else in the world of broadcast journalism.

Still, the ABC News Web site doesn't even begin to capture her real significance in American life—because it doesn't explain how

Barbara Walters, more than anyone else, has helped turn serious television journalism into trivial crap.

Indeed, in her refined, ladylike way, she has done more harm to journalism than did Jayson Blair, the *New York Times* reporter who was exposed as a fraud and a plagiarist. As Eric Boehlert succinctly put it in a piece for *Salon*, Barbara Walters "has long pioneered the transformation of television news into, literally, parlor gossip. Who, after all, better represents the watering down of television news than Barbara Walters?"

If it weren't a rhetorical question, the answer would be: "No one."

It's not just that her questions are so puffball-soft that she makes Larry King look like Bill O'Reilly, although that's part of it. I mean, who will ever forget her riveting, insightful query to Katharine Hepburn: "If you were a tree, what kind of tree would you be?"

Over the years, she has asked equally probing questions of other *newsworthy* celebrities, such as Mariah Carey, Matt LeBlanc, Ben Affleck and Jennifer Lopez, Leonardo DiCaprio, Angelina Jolie, and The Fab 5 from *Queer Eye for the Straight Guy*. Having once interviewed Sadat and Begin, Barbara moved boldly on to Paris Hilton, whom Barbara calls one of "The Ten Most Fascinating People of 2004"—which doesn't say much for 2004 . . . or Barbara Walters.

And when she interviewed rocker Courtney Love, and Ms. Love told her, "You wouldn't be talking to me now if we actually sucked. We don't suck." A brilliant observation, of course, which prompted this equally brilliant followup from Barbara: "What's the opposite of not sucking?"

Gilda Radner, doing Baba Wawa on *Saturday Night Live*, couldn't have made this stuff up.

But Barbara Walters cannot be dismissed simply because she's gone into semiretirement and has, over the years, become so silly. She's done way too much harm to get off that easy.

"Walters had managed to smuggle celebrity past the journalistic guard dogs and into a network news organization without making the distinction that [Ed] Murrow had made between his serious reportage and Person to Person," as Neal Gabler explains in his book *Hollywood Interrupted.* "For Walters, celebrity was serious reportage, and that was why on her *20/20* news magazine program an interview with a movie star shilling his latest picture could be followed by hard news like an exposé on, say, radiation leakage from a power plant or inadequate meat inspection, as if the interview and the exposé were of equal gravity."

Still, Barbara Walters, the pioneer who became a role model for so many others who shamelessly turned celebrity fluff into "serious reportage" never hesitated to play St. Barbara, martyr for journalistic integrity, when *that* suited her purposes.

Back in 2001, when ABC News shuffled its prime-time lineup, Barbara's show, *20/20,* was temporarily moved out of its Friday-night slot, where it had been a fixture for fourteen years. There were lots of news stories about how angry she was, about how hurt she was, about the tears and even about the possibility that she might leave ABC—*over a temporary time-slot change!* She even went on her other show, *The View,* and, sounding like the serious journalist she probably believes she is, Barbara said, "So many of us felt that news is a public trust and should be respected as such, and the perception was that ABC doesn't care about news."

It is truly fascinating how clueless Barbara Walters is. Of course she's right that ABC network executives don't see news as a public trust anymore. That's why from time to time they threaten to cancel *Nightline* and replace it with some kind of entertainment show, which they would have done already had David Letterman taken them up on their very lucrative offer. But what Barbara obviously doesn't grasp is that one of the main reasons the ABC brass doesn't respect news as much as she would like . . . is because of *her;* because she, more than anyone else, has trivialized and cheapened the news. But what is even more fascinating is that so many of Ms. Walters's elite media colleagues actually thought she had a point. The sad fact is that network news has by now been so corrupted by idiocy masquerading as journalism that even the insiders can't tell the difference.

It was all too much for Eric Boehlert, who wrote: "Have any of these commentators, including Dan Rather and Katie Couric, who have rushed to Walters' defense, watched *20/20* lately? Has television news as a profession sunk so low that a show, when not investigating the poor sanitation conditions at discount nail salons, or airing interviews with Macaulay Culkin (Walters: "Tell me about your father"), can suddenly be regarded as a paragon of hard-news reporting? And can it really be possible that a host such as Walters, who's best known for making celebrities cry, is being regarded as a patron saint?"

In the end, of course, it was no big deal. *20/20* went back to its usual time slot and Barbara Walters went back to doing what she does best—asking Leonardo DiCaprio if he has a girlfriend, and grilling actress Anne Heche about her sex life with Ellen DeGeneres.

But a question lingers, one that for all its apparent silliness, really is important: If Barbara Walters were a tree, wouldn't television journalism be a lot better off?

☞ *45*

Ken Lay

KEN LAY WAS Enron's chairman and CEO who claimed he had no idea other top executives of Enron were cooking the books and driving the company into bankruptcy—right under his nose.

Value of Enron stock Lay reportedly sold from 1996 to 2001: $184 million

Amount received in bonuses from 1997 to 2000: $18.1 million

Amount of severance check to each employee laid off since bankruptcy: a maximum of $13,500

Number of Enron employees, mid-2001: 20,600

Number of Enron employees today: 0

44 ☞

Dennis Kozlowski

IN JUNE 2001, Dennis Kozlowski, then the CEO of Tyco, the giant conglomerate that was worth more than Ford and General Motors combined, threw a fortieth birthday party for his wife.

He invited about seventy-five people, hired a band, and had the whole thing videotaped. It was a nice little birthday party and a good time was had by all.

Oh, did I mention that the party was in Sardinia, off the coast of Italy? Or that Kozlowski flew the whole gang in for the party? Or that they stayed at the super-ritzy Cala di Volpe resort, where some rooms go for over a thousand bucks a night? Or that they stayed, not just for the party, but for a whole week of "sailing . . . tennis, golf, eating, drinking. All the things we are best known for," as Kozlowski told his guests? Or that hot models—male and female—

were brought in to run around in togas to give the party an erotic, bacchanalian flavor? Or that the band he hired was Jimmy Buffett's band that played for forty-five minutes and cost $250,000? Or that there was an ice replica of Michelangelo's David that had vodka pouring out of his penis? Or that the birthday cake was shaped like a woman's breasts and had sparklers mounted on the top? Or that the whole shebang cost $2.1 million and that Dennis Kozlowski paid half and charged the other half to Tyco, because about half the guests were Tyco employees, which made the fun-filled getaway . . . *a business function*, which it probably was, since, I'm sure, somebody during that week of sailing, tennis, golf, eating, and drinking said to somebody else, "How's business?"

Gee, I wonder why the very name "Dennis Kozlowski" has become shorthand for wretched excess and shameless greed.

Three years and three months after the birthday bash, Kozlowski was at a different get-together. This one was in a Manhattan courtroom, where, along with his chief financial officer, Kozlowski was on trial for allegedly looting Tyco of about $600 million—by taking unauthorized bonuses and loans from the company and by getting Tyco to pick up the tab for unauthorized personal expenses.

Like what allegedly unauthorized personal expenses? Well, there was the $15,000 nineteenth-century French umbrella stand in the shape of a poodle, the $6,300 sewing basket, the $17,100 eighteenth-century Venetian "traveling toilette box," the $2,200 wastebasket, the $2,900 coat hangers, the $5,900 bed sheets (two sets), the $1,650 appointment book, and the $445 pincushion.

According to prosecutors, there was also the $100 million in loans to dozens of other executives and employees, *which were later forgiven*. And there were the allegations that Kozlowski borrowed about $30 million to buy property and build a house in Boca Raton, Florida, and about $7 million to buy a Park Avenue apartment in New York City, and millions more for other real estate transactions and luxury purchases.

According to Dennis Kozlowski, it was all 100 percent legal. And, who knows, he may even be right; that trial ended in a mistrial. (A second trial was under way in spring 2005.)

But this is not about the trials, past or future; it's not about legalese at all.

No, it's about a man who thought he was Marie-Antoinette, living like there was no tomorrow while his company was gobbling up lots of other smaller companies, then streamlining the new, bigger Tyco conglomerate by shutting down dozens of plants and firing thousands of employees.

In the end, it's about greed and shame—and about a man who was able to rise to the very heights of success, apparently without even knowing what those words mean.

43 ☞

Paul Eibeler

YOU'RE WALKING DOWN THE STREET and you see a great-looking car stopped at a red light. You want it. So you rip open the door, throw the driver out on the street, and take it. Later in the day you see someone you don't like. So you stomp him into the ground. Now the cops have you cornered. No biggie. Just pull out your semiautomatic and blow them all away.

After that, just for fun, you can massacre lots of other people who get in your way—with your sniper rifle or your chainsaw or, hey, if you're in the mood, you can just set them on fire.

Welcome to the vile world of depravity also known as *Grand Theft Auto*, one of the most popular video games on the market—a game that has sold 35 million copies with sales worldwide worth about 2 billion dollars.

It's not for nothing that *Grand Theft Auto* has been called "a cop-killing game" and a "murder simulator." In one scenario, the player walks into a police station, breaks a convict out of jail. and escapes by shooting a bunch of cops.

Should there be a law against this kind of thing? Probably not—censorship tends to lead to more censorship, which makes it a dangerous road to travel. But should we all feel revulsion at this moral garbage that big-time video-game manufacturers are peddling to kids (though nominally they can't sell it to anyone under seventeen)? Damn right we should! And while we're at it, here's another question that begs to be asked: Does everything always have to be about money?

Don't get me wrong. I'm all for capitalism. And yes, I get it: businesses are about the bottom line. Fine. So let's see, would that make it okay if they made a game where players rape make-believe women? Or kill computer-generated gays? Or blacks? Or even dogs? Yet these guys shamelessly go ahead and push a game where it's okay to kill computer-generated cops?

Like everything else rotten that happens, it doesn't happen by accident. There are a whole lot of people at a company called Take-Two Interactive Software—one of the two heavyweights in the video-game business—who are responsible for *Grand Theft Auto*. But Paul Eibeler, because he is both the president and CEO of the company, deserves special recognition. To him, *Grand Theft Auto* means one thing: profits. In 2002 he told an industry magazine that "*Grand Theft Auto* sales have been and continue to be tremendous. This game has been a very compelling experience for the gamer, which has led to the strong success."

No one disputes that for a certain kind of person video-game mayhem and the murder of virtual cops is a "compelling experience." Just as 2 billion dollars in worldwide sales is a "compelling experience" for Paul Eibeler. But a lot of Americans, all that money notwithstanding, still don't get it. One of them, a Methodist minister from Alabama named Steve Strickland, told Ed Bradley of *60 Minutes*, "The question I have to ask the manufacturers is why do you make games that target people who are to protect us—police officers, people that we look up to. . . . Why do you want to market a game that gives people, *even the thoughts* that it's okay to shoot police officers? Why do you want to do that?"

As it happens, the reason *60 Minutes* was doing a story about *Grand Theft Auto* is that Take-Two Interactive now finds *itself* in the crosshairs—the target of a multimillion-dollar lawsuit charging the game provoked an act of horrible violence against police. This is called irony—or in some circles, sticking it to the SOBs!

The civil suit was filed against the makers and marketers of *Grand Theft Auto* on behalf of three men in Alabama—two of them police officers—who were shot and killed by an eighteen-year-old who had been picked up on suspicion of—you got it!—auto theft, and who decided to shoot his way out of trouble. He had no prior police record but says he had been playing *Grand Theft Auto* day and night for a month before the shooting. "Life is like a video game," he reportedly told police after his capture. "Everybody's got to die sometime."

No matter what a jury ultimately decides on whether the people who make *Grand Theft Auto* can be held legally responsible for the killings, the wrenching questions posed by Methodist minister Steve Strickland—about why anyone would want to make a game that targets the people who protect us—ought to cause sleepless nights for Paul Eibeler and everyone else at his company. Because when Strickland poignantly asks, "Why do you want to do that?" it is not just rhetorical. His brother Arnold was one of the murdered policemen.

Gloria Steinem

LET'S SAY YOU'RE A GUY who runs a big, important company, and a woman, who has supported your causes in the past, comes in to see you about a job, which she says she desperately needs because her husband (who eventually kills himself) is out of work and the family needs money to get out of debt. You find her attractive, so, without asking, you fondle her breast. She pushes your hand away and you figure, nothing ventured, nothing gained. You gave it a shot. It didn't pan out. No big deal.

Now let's say that years earlier, when you were the top dog in a much smaller company, you did pretty much the same thing. This time, you're walking through a local hotel, where your company is running a big function, and you spot a woman who works for you. Through an intermediary, you send word that you want her to come up to your room. Since you're the boss, she complies, though she's a bit confused because she's just a low-level employee. In the room, you sit and talk for a while and then you casually pull your pecker out of your pants and make a suggestion regarding what the young woman might want to do with it. She says no thanks, gets up, and rushes out of the room.

Hey, no harm, no foul, right? You didn't force either of the women to do anything. As a powerful male, you made an honest effort to get some nooky in the workplace with a powerless woman. So? It sure isn't sexual harassment; that much we're sure of.

And why exactly are we so sure? Well, because Gloria Steinem herself—one of, if not *the* best-known feminists of our time—has told us it isn't sexual harassment.

Except Ms. Steinem wasn't talking about the president of some hypothetical company who was accused of sexual hanky-panky. She was talking about the president of the United States. She was writing, in a *New York Times* op-ed, no less, about President Clinton, who was accused of playing grab-ass with Kathleen Wiley in the Oval Office and of unzipping his pants in a Little Rock hotel room in front of Paula Jones.

"The truth is," Ms. Steinem wrote on March 22, 1998, "that even if the allegations are true, the President is not guilty of sexual harassment. He is accused of having made a gross, dumb and reckless pass at a supporter [Ms. Wiley] during a low point in her life. She pushed him away, she said, and it never happened again. In other words, President Clinton took 'no' for an answer."

In other words, ARE YOU KIDDING?

But so much for Kathleen Wiley and her alleged non–sexual harassment encounter with President Clinton. What does our feminist icon think about the Paula Jones story?

"In her original story, Paula Jones essentially said the same thing [as Kathleen Wiley], Ms. Steinem writes. "She went to then-Governor Clinton's hotel room, where she said he asked her to perform oral sex and even dropped his trousers. She refused, and even she claims that he said something like, 'Well, I don't want to make you do anything you don't want to do.'"

You see how simple it is, men? Whether you're the CEO of a Fortune 500 company or you're dishing out fries at McDonald's, thanks to Gloria Steinem, you are allowed to grope the woman of your choosing—just as long as you're gentleman enough to take "no" for an answer. And if you do, you're not guilty of sexually harassing anybody. I'm betting many of you didn't know that?

Thanks to Gloria Steinem, every guy in America (and, hey, let's be equality-minded here: every woman, too) now has the right to cop one free feel, no matter how "gross, dumb and reckless" that "pass" might be.

And thanks to Gloria Steinem, and a few others like her, feminism in America is dead.

For years, feminism has been accused of rank hypocrisy, of savaging perceived enemies and giving friends a pass, of twisting facts to suit the feminist agenda. And now, in one fell, idiotic swoop, Gloria Steinem showed the world that it was all true.

There's a name for what Gloria Steinem did. It's called selling out your principles. And she did it—without any pressure, without anyone holding a gun to her head—simply because Bill Clinton was a Democrat who was on her side of issues important to feminists, like abortion. And for that Ms. Steinem became an apologist for the abuse of power. There's a name for that, too, especially when you've ostensibly devoted your life to making sure that women don't get run over by powerful men. It's called hypocrisy.

☞ *41*

Susan Beresford

FOLLOW THE MONEY. It was good advice back in the days of Watergate and it still is today.

Let's say there's some radical group out there throwing its weight around. Follow the money and you'll find a sugar daddy behind the curtain writing big fat checks.

Or some foundation.

Most people by now know, for example, that George Soros is the moneybags behind all sorts of left-wing political groups. But even though he spends millions, he's a bit player compared to the giant foundations with names like Rockefeller, MacArthur, and especially, Ford.

The Ford Foundation, led by its president, Susan Beresford, has become a great big piggy bank for an amazing range of organizations pushing left-wing agendas. It's practically a shadow government— with its own domestic policy, its own foreign policy, and assets put at about $11 billion, which makes the Ford Foundation wealthier than a lot of small countries. And what does Ford do with its money, besides spend it on *Sesame Street*? Well, as *FrontPage Magazine*'s William Hawkins puts it, the Ford Foundation mounts "attacks on American society . . . from every angle."

And most Americans don't have a clue.

Most, for example, probably think the Ford Foundation (if they think about it at all) is part of the car company. It once was, but today, it's totally independent—with roughly a billion dollars to hand out every year. Compare that to the *measly* $25 million Soros gave away to anti-Bush activists in 2004, and you start to understand how big and how powerful Ford and Beresford are.

Beresford is a child of the radical 60s. She graduated from Radcliffe in 1965. And she's got enough money at her disposal to at least try to create a brave new world in her own image. At Ford, she has vigorously pushed a whole bunch of noble-sounding leftist programs—focusing, she proclaims, on "racism, sexism, the environment, peace and justice, among others." Who's not against racism and for peace and justice, right? But follow the money, and it'll lead you right to the heavy hand of liberal PC. As former treasury secretary William Simon says, "under the rubric of the 'public interest,'" Ford is "engaged in a radical assault on traditional culture."

Let us count the ways . . .

Under Beresford, Ford has made the nation's colleges and universities a particular target, pushing radical feminism and multiculturalism and every other strain of fashionable left-wing political activism on campus. You say your school wants money from Ford. Then you have to toe its rigid line on "diversity," which mandates that every grant application include a "diversity table," spelling out for the Ford bean-counters the number of nonwhites and women that will be involved in the project.

The Ford Foundation also doles out big money, either directly or through surrogates, to a broad range of antiwar groups, from liberal to hard Left, including one organization called the Center for Constitutional Rights. This is a group that opposed the invasion of Iraq—on the grounds that it was a "blood for oil" war, and called it "Bush's quest for world domination."

The center also got Ford money "for racial justice litigation, advocacy, and educational outreach activities related to the detention and racial profiling of Arab-Americans and Muslims following the World Trade Center attack"—and used it to file suits against the detention of captured terrorists at Guantánamo.

Ford has also been a longtime banker for anti-Semitic hate groups, like the Jerusalem-based Society of St. Yves and the Palestinian Society for the Protection of Human Rights and the Environment, the latter an organizer of the notorious 2002 UN conference on racism in Durban, South Africa, that became a festival of vicious Israel-bashing.

In 2003, with evidence mounting that Ford money might be ending up in the hands of pro-terrorist organizations, seventeen congressmen issued a public demand that Ford "cease funding of subversive groups." Only then did Beresford agree to stop subsidizing the most notorious of the groups.

In perhaps its most blatantly arrogant display of contempt for the popular will, Ford has for years been at the forefront of the fight to throw open America's borders, donating more than $60 million to the cause. Among other things, it funded the creation of the radical Mexican-American Legal Defense and Education Fund—an organization with unveiled contempt for American traditions and values. No group has had greater success in pushing ever-expanding rights for illegal aliens and the massive expansion of bilingualism in U.S. public schools.

As Dan Stein, executive director of the Federation for Immigration Reform, explained it on Bill O'Reilly's program, Ford's objective is nothing less than "to radically overhaul the ethnic basis of American society . . ."

"Yes," O'Reilly cut in, as if the whole crazy idea wasn't computing, "but they're white—white rich people."

Yes they are, Stein replied. White rich people with "a paternal elitist, leftist liberalism."

And they have the money to make their dreams come true.

40 🫵

Scott Harshbarger

SEXUAL ABUSE OF CHILDREN is a real and terrible problem, one that for too long was swept under the rug. But back in the 80s, when the issue provoked a nationwide wave of hysteria, there were other innocent victims: child-care workers themselves! Decent people from Massachusetts to California, and lots of places in between, were charged, on the basis of outlandish stories and the total absence of any physical evidence, with having committed horrendous crimes against children.

"Believe the Children" became the mantra. "Children don't lie about such things," we heard over and over again. "They don't make this stuff up." And too many prosecutors, for all sorts of reasons, were willing to believe anything the children said—no matter how bizarre the allegation and no matter how much the children were coaxed into saying things even they didn't believe happened.

There were many overzealous, politically ambitious prosecutors behind these cases—"prosecutorial zealots," in the words of the *Wall Street Journal*'s Dorothy Rabinowitz, who won a Pulitzer for her investigative reports on child-abuse cases. They were, she said, "runaway prosecutors who, quite simply, in many cases don't care if you're guilty or you're not guilty." But none was more zealous, or even now remains so unrepentant, as Scott Harshbarger.

Harshbarger was the district attorney of Middlesex County, Massachusetts—not far from Salem, Massachusetts, where during another wave of hysteria they burned "witches" based on other out-landish stories. In 1984, Harshbarger launched his prosecution of the Amirault family, which ran a day-care center called Fells Acres in the town of Malden. The case started with a five-year-old boy claiming that his "pants were pulled down," and, as in the case of the McMartin Preschool in California, which had broken just a few months before, the charges rapidly snowballed, becoming increas-ingly grotesque and bizarre.

After questioning by social workers and police, the children began saying they had been fondled, violated, and photographed at "nude swimming parties," and taken to a "magic room" by a "bad clown," and, finally, that they'd been forced to eat human feces and attacked with knives. There was no physical evidence to support any of it, and though the day-care center was open, with parents and other adults coming in and out all the time, no one had ever seen *anything* to support *any* of the charges.

But none of that gave Harshbarger the slightest pause. As his friend and mentor, former Massachusetts attorney general Francis

X. Bellotti only half-jokingly observed, "I used to say: 'Scott, you never let the law get in your way.'"

With everything he had, Harshbarger went after the Amiraults —sixty-one-year-old Violet, who ran the center, her son, Gerald, and her daughter, Cheryl LeFave, who also worked there. Solely on the basis of the children's stories—including one four-year-old's claim that Violet Amirault inserted a four-and-a-half-inch butcher knife into his anus (without leaving a mark)—they were convicted of sexually abusing some forty children. Gerald got forty years in prison, his mother and sister up to twenty.

Perhaps, given the hysteria of the time, Harshbarger and his underlings should be cut a little slack for their early zeal. Except, even as the climate changed and it became clear how monstrously unjust this case, like others, had been from the start, Harshbarger remained adamant about the Amiraults' guilt.

Never mind that there were tapes of the interviews between the prosecutors and the children, which revealed how the interrogators had been complicit from the outset in shaping the children's incredible testimony. As Dorothy Rabinowitz noted, "The children were making the stories up because the interrogators were saying if you don't help me and tell me, we're going to be so disappointed. You're going to betray your little friends . . . and . . . [yet] none of the jurors ever saw this testimony."

"These were some really egregious interviewing techniques. I was very disturbed," is how an expert hired by 20/20 to review the tapes put it. "The child is repeatedly saying no. I can't even count how many times this child said no. And how many times the question was re-asked and redirected and the child's answers were seemingly not sufficient."

While in other cases, including McMartin, such revelations led to acquittals or had convictions overturned on appeal, Massachusetts prosecutors, led by Harshbarger, continued to fight for nearly two decades to keep the Amiraults behind bars. One judge, throwing out the convictions of the women after a review of the evidence, declared it would be "improper" for them to spend "even one minute more" in prison. Another judge, reviewing the conviction of Gerald Amirault, issued a 140-page ruling in which he labeled the children's testimony "incredible," adding the charges were investigated "in an atmosphere of panic, if not hysteria," and that investigators "just overwhelmed these kids. . . . All of the evidence leads this court to conclude that there is more than a substantial risk that the defendant was unjustly convicted."

You'd think all of this would have been enough for Scott Harshbarger to simply, and finally, let it go. And you'd be wrong. By now, he was the attorney general of Massachusetts, and in that position, as the chief legal officer of the state, he further dug in his heels and appealed the cases. He told the *Boston Globe*, "the Amiraults are right where serious child abusers ought to be." And, in response to Rabin-owitz's stories in the *Wall Street Journal*, he wrote to the paper, comparing the Amiraults to child murderers Joel Steinberg and John Wayne Gacy.

There's a far better comparison to be made—and that is between Harshbarger himself and Inspector Javert, the pathologically obsessed officer of the law in *Les Misérables*, who doggedly pursues a good and decent man for stealing a crust of bread for a hungry child—and after he captures him, locks him up for nineteen years. At least Jean Valjean—the "thief"—was guilty of *something*. The Amiraults didn't do *anything*. As the *Boston Globe*'s Ed Siegel wrote after watching 20/20's story on the Amirault case, "there will be a number of people who might ask of Harshbarger, [and his associates] Reilly and Dolan, 'Have you no decency? At long last, have you no sense of decency?'"

It is likely such a question would be completely lost on Harshbarger, who seems never to have had a doubt about anything he's ever done. After his tenure as attorney general, and failing in a run for governor, he became head of Common Cause, the liberal activist group.

As for the Amiraults, by the time Violet and her daughter were released in 1995, Violet, at age seventy-two, was the oldest female inmate in state prison. Her son Gerald was not paroled until 2003. According to the *Boston Globe*, "Former Attorney General Scott Harshbarger, the Middlesex district attorney when the case was prosecuted, called the decision to release Amirault 'unfortunate.' He was concerned, he said, that the parole decision not be seen as an exoneration of Amirault."

Violet, the mother, died two years after she was released. "Near Amirault's bed at home," the *Globe* reported, "a photograph of a sign harshly critical of her nemesis, Attorney General Scott Harshbarger, provided her comfort, family members said."

39 ☞

Peter Singer

"Peter Singer may be the most controversial philosopher alive;
he is certainly among the most influential."

—*NEW YORKER* MAGAZINE

IT'S THE SECOND PART of that statement that's so scary.

Who is it, exactly, that Peter Singer, Princeton University's Ira W. DeCamp professor of bioethics, influences? Well, other academics, of course, that goes without saying, and the mainstream media, which is constantly airing his views on many of today's thorny, emotionally wrenching issues involving bioethics, medical care, and the meaning of a properly lived life. He's gotten over a hundred mentions in the *New York Times* alone.

I understand that your first instinct may be to say, "Hey, the guy's a *philosopher*, for heaven's sake. What do you mean *scary*? Lighten up! He sits up there in his Ivory Tower and gazes at his navel. Who cares how many stories the *New York Times* has written about him?"

But that would be a big mistake—especially if Peter Singer ever got his way.

You see, Peter Singer calls himself a *utilitarian* philosopher. He makes no secret that his aim is to change the way we look at the world; the very way we live our lives. And he uses "philosophy" and "ethics" to justify behavior that has gotten him labeled not just "the most *controversial* philosopher alive" but "the most *reviled* philosopher in the world" as well.

Fair? You decide.

The Australian-born Singer, who has been called "the godfather of animal rights" first made a splash back in 1975, when he was just twenty-nine years old, with the publication of *Animal Liberation*, the book he himself proudly calls "the seminal work of that movement."

Singer wasn't merely interested in stopping cruelty to animals. He was concerned with something far more ambitious. As he asked in another book, *In Defence of Animals*, why do we experiment with chimps, "yet would never think of doing the same to a retarded human being at a much lower mental level? The only possible answer is that the chimpanzee, no matter how bright, is not human, while the retarded human, no matter how dull, is." In fact, he said, in our behavior we should recognize no distinctions between humans and animals.

In fairness, I think we have to acknowledge that Singer has raised a provocative question: Why is it okay to cut into the head of a very smart chimp, to explore his brain, and yet we consider it immoral to do the same with a human, no matter how slow he may be? Peter Singer is no dummy. But he flatly rejects the basic tenet of Judeo-Christian thought that human life is special, that humans are not comparable to chimps or rats or pigs.

In fact, at the national Animal Rights 2002 conference in McLean, Virginia, he noted that Judeo-Christian ethic teaches not only that humans have souls and animals don't, but also that humans are made in the image of God and that God gave mankind dominion over the animals. "All three taken together do have a very negative influence on the way in which we think about animals," he said.

It's one thing if some run-of-the-mill atheist holds views like this, but when a philosopher of Peter Singer's stature believes that a newborn baby has no greater right to life than any other living being with a similar capacity for reason and emotion—including pigs and cows and dogs—then it's time to fasten your seat belts, because Peter Singer is about to take us on a very bumpy and potentially dangerous ride.

In fact, when Singer made his chimpanzee-versus-retarded-human argument, he was only warming up. His next area of concern—a natural outgrowth of how he sees certain mentally and physically impaired human beings—was euthanasia. But unlike others who support it, Singer sees it as useful not only for the terminally ill, or the infirmed elderly. As he wrote in his book *Practical Ethics*, "Killing a disabled infant is not morally equivalent to killing a person. Very often it is not wrong at all."

Quite simple, as *Reason Magazine* observes, "Fetuses and some very impaired human beings are not persons in his view and have a lesser moral status than, say, adult gorillas and chimpanzees." And as Singer told the animal rights conference—repeating a position he had put forth before, and one that tells you everything you need to know about him—society should allow a "severely disabled" infant to be killed up to twenty-eight days after its birth if the parents decide the baby's life is not worth living. Think of it as a "lemon law"—for certain kinds of "defective" babies.

"Thus he would allow parents and doctors to kill newborns with drastic disabilities (like the absence of higher brain function, an incompletely formed spine called spina bifida or even hemophilia) instead of just letting nature take its course and allowing the infants to die," as the *New York Times* reported.

Peter Singer's critics—especially among the disabled—have charged that if he had his way, he would have approved the killing of a Franklin Roosevelt or a Helen Keller. Not so, says Singer, who insists that it is never justified to kill a disabled person who wants to live—just infants or others who are unable to speak for themselves. In those cases, he says, life and death decisions should be left to parents and doctors—not the government.

Our hearts go out to parents whose babies are born with severe disabilities. Still, it's a good thing that FDR wasn't *born* with polio, or that Helen Keller wasn't *born* deaf, dumb, and blind—because if they were, in Peter Singer's world, they might never have made it out of the hospital. And what might happen if Singer had his way and parents decide they don't want a baby with some other disability? Would it be okay to kill an infant with Down's syndrome? How about one with deformed arms or legs? There's a reason they call it a slippery slope.

Fears about where it all might lead prompted one disabled-rights activist to say that Singer is "the most dangerous man in the world today"—just the kind of review that makes you a superstar in the world of the academy. Still, when Princeton appointed him to his highly prestigious post in 1999—in *ethics*, remember!—it did arouse protests, with some students arguing it was morally repugnant to offer him such an important stage to promote the killing of disabled babies; besides which, such a view was utterly at odds with the university's own strong policy mandating respect for people with disabilities. So Singer was quick to reassure the school that he opposes discrimination against *adults* with disabilities—even though he had no particular problem if someone had done away with them as infants.

There were other protests against him when he lectured in Germany—where they know something about taking human life lightly. It was widely claimed that the policies Singer was pushing were identical to some of those pushed by Hitler before World War II as "mercy killing." What made it truly ironic was that the lesson seems to have been lost on Singer—whose own parents fled Nazi Germany in the 30s and whose grandparents died in concentration camps.

Yet in this country, his stature has continued to grow. He has now written more than two dozen books, giving his "ethical" views on a range of subjects. His most recent, published in 2004, is a Bush-bashing work titled *The President of Good and Evil: The Ethics of George W. Bush*, in which he slams W on everything from tax policy to his position on stem-cell research.

But, really, the book is basically just standard-issue liberal politics, so much less offensive—and important—than much of the other stuff he's done. The real story of the damage Peter Singer continues to impose on civilized culture is found in the petition circulated by those Princeton students who stood up to protest his hiring by a university that was once a bastion of Western thought and culture: "We protest his hiring because Dr. Singer denies the intrinsic moral worth of an entire class of human beings—newborn children—and promotes policies that would deprive many infants with disabilities of their basic human right to legal protection against homicide."

Jim McDermott

IT'S ONE THING to be against the war in Iraq, but it's something else for a United States congressman to stand in Baghdad—right before our troops put their lives on the line—and tell the world that Saddam Hussein can be trusted but the president of the United States can't.

Yet that's just what Congressman Jim McDermott did.

McDermott, who is a far-left-winger and leading member of the "Blame America First" contingent of the Democratic Party, represents a part of Seattle that is not only ground zero for ridiculously overpriced coffee and ridiculously overheated anticapitalist rhetoric, but is also—with the possible exception of Berkeley and a few square miles of Beverly Hills and Malibu—the home of more "progressive" loonies than anyplace else on the Left Coast. So Mc-Dermott fits right in.

A caller to a Seattle radio station once said that George Bush was worse than Hitler—because Hitler, at least, was a self-made man. You can't blame the congressman for that, of course, but it gives you an idea about how some of his "progressive" constituents think.

McDermott makes all the usual noises, for all the usual reasons. He vigorously opposed all attempts to curtail partial-birth abortions. He refused to speak the words "Under God" when reciting the Pledge of Allegiance in the House. He said the Patriot Act "trampled" our "cherished civil liberties."

But then he went to Baghdad and stepped *way* over the line.

On the very eve of the war with Iraq, along with now-former

congressman David Bonior, McDermott consorted with Baathist murderers and allowed himself to be used by Saddam's propagandists.

He said that Saddam Hussein, the ruthless mass murderer and world-class liar, should be taken at his word that he would cooperate with UN inspectors; the same inspectors' work he had consistently thwarted and whom he'd finally expelled from the country. "I think you have to take the Iraqis on their value—at their face value," he told George Stephanopoulos on the ABC News program *This Week*.

And when Stephanopoulos asked, "Before you left for Baghdad, you said the president of the United States will lie to the American people in order to get us into this war, do you really believe that?" McDermott tap-danced for a while and then replied: "I think the president would mislead the American people."

Attacking the president's credibility in Seattle may not be a big deal—something lots of folks do while sipping their grande lattes and Mocha Frappuccinos. But to do it in Baghdad, when he did, was treacherous—and George Will, one of *This Week*'s panelists, wasn't about to let it pass without expressing his disgust.

"Let's note," Will said, "that in what I consider the most disgraceful performance abroad by an American official in my lifetime, something not [seen] since Jane Fonda sat on the antiaircraft gun in Hanoi to be photographed, Mr. McDermott said in effect—not in effect, he said it—we should take Saddam Hussein at his word and not take the president at his word. He said the United States is simply trying to provoke. I mean, why Saddam Hussein doesn't pay commercial time for that advertisement for his policy, I do not know."

McDermott's Baghdad performance was so bad that even Democratic National Committee chairman Terry McAuliffe, who'd earned his stripes defending his pal Bill Clinton, couldn't find a way to put an acceptable face on it. This is very rare for McAuliffe, who usually gets behind anybody or anything that suggests George Bush is a liar. This time, with McDermott, he sheepishly dodged all questions on the subject.

But not to worry, the congressman does have his defenders and devoted admirers. One of them even called McDermott his "highly respected friend" and a man of "honor and integrity." In case you're interested, the devoted admirer was Fidel Castro.

☞ *37*

Al Franken

AL FRANKEN SAYS HE'S A SATIRIST, by which he means he can say nasty things about anyone he wants and then claim it's all in good fun.

Small world. I'm a satirist, too.

Not long ago, I sat down with Al Franken for a one-on-one interview about his life and career. We spoke, appropriately enough, in his radio studio in New York City, where he hosts the *Al Franken Show* on Air America, which is a liberal talk radio network that is carried in several cities.

GOLDBERG: Hi, Al, and thanks for letting me come in and have this chat with you today.

FRANKEN: You're a liar.

GOLDBERG: What do you mean I'm a liar?

FRANKEN: I never said you were a liar, you liar. You're telling lies about me lying about you lying. That's a lie.

GOLDBERG: Okay. But before we actually begin, I need to apologize.

FRANKEN: For what?

GOLDBERG: For listing you all the way down at number thirty-seven. When I started this project, before you went on the air here at Air America, I had you in the top five of all the people who are screwing up America. But I'm afraid that after the presidential election, when it became clear that lefties like you probably hurt Kerry more than they helped him, and that you were becoming more and more irrelevant politically, I had to drop you all the way down to thirty-seven, and if we did this interview next week, you might be number seventy-three.

FRANKEN: You're a big fat idiot.

GOLDBERG: Excuse me?

FRANKEN: Liar.

GOLDBERG: Al. Someone once said that liberals have forgotten how to be liberal, meaning they're no longer open-minded. They think the other side is not just wrong, but morally repugnant. Any thoughts?

FRANKEN: Yes, I think you're a big fat idiot.

GOLDBERG: You just said that!

FRANKEN: No I didn't.

GOLDBERG: Let's move on. You've had quite a career: *Saturday Night Live*, movies, politics, and now your own radio show. What motivates you?

FRANKEN: Well, Bernie, as I'm sure you know, I'm good enough, smart enough, and, doggone it, people like me. That's what motivates me. Knowing how good enough and smart enough I am. And I think, if you send off positive vibes, as I do, people will like you, which is why they like me. I also have lots of self-esteem, which is good. And most of all, I'm not negative.

GOLDBERG: What do you think of conservatives?

FRANKEN: I think they're all a bunch of motherf***ing, Nazi, ass***** who should drink poison and die.

GOLDBERG: How does angry talk like that, which we hear a lot from liberals these days, jibe with your insistence that you're not negative? I don't get it.

FRANKEN: That's because *you* didn't go to Harvard and *I* did. Harvard is where smart people go to college. I went there.

GOLDBERG: That leads me to my next question, Al.

FRANKEN: Liar, liar pants on fire!

GOLDBERG: Right. So here's what I'm wondering: You went to Harvard; Frank Rich, the *New York Times* columnist, went to Harvard; Michael Kinsley, now of the *L.A. Times*, went to Harvard. You're all very smart, but you're all very nasty, also. Why are so many Harvard media guys so mean-spirited?

FRANKEN: Come on, Bernie, you really need to ask that question? Just look at the three of us. We're proof that evolution is only a theory. I mean Frank and I are always goofing on Kinsley—behind his back, of course. The guy makes Richard Simmons look like Sylvester Stallone. He's always nitpicking because somebody used a semicolon instead of a comma. This guy is a *looooo-ser*. So is Frank, but don't tell him I told you.

GOLDBERG: That's quite revealing, Al. Anything else?

FRANKEN: Yes. I'm going to tell you a secret, Bernie, because I like you. WE ALL HATE OURSELVES: Frank Rich, Michael Kinsley, and me. We're self-loathing nerds who can't do much except make fun of other people. Why do you think I call people "liars"? Because it makes me feel better about— ME! Bernie, I'm so SICK.

GOLDBERG: I've never heard you open up like this, Al. Do you really think that you're sick?

FRANKEN: Who said that?

GOLDBERG: You did. You just told me exactly that.

FRANKEN: Have I called you a liar yet today, because if I haven't, I'm about to start.

GOLDBERG: Why are you wearing a tinfoil hat?

FRANKEN: No comment.

GOLDBERG: Okay, Al. Thanks very much for your time. By the way, do you know why you're number thirty-seven on the list of people who are screwing up America?

FRANKEN: No, actually, I don't.

GOLDBERG: Well, you know who Casey Stengel was?

FRANKEN: Sure, that baseball man, right?

GOLDBERG: Right, Al, *that baseball man*. He was the manager of the New York Yankees. Well, Casey walked into spring training camp one year and told all of his players to line up in alphabetical order . . . according to height. He wasn't trying to be funny. Casey spoke gibberish . . . gobbledygook . . . total nonsense. Just like you, Al. And Casey's uniform number was . . . thirty-seven! That's why I gave *you* that number.

FRANKEN: Do you like my hat? It's made out of tinfoil, you know.

GOLDBERG: Thanks again, Al.

FRANKEN: Liar.

Nancy Hopkins

I DON'T KNOW ABOUT YOU, but I'm tired of listening to left-wing feminists complain about how tough they have it and about how the evil sexist patriarchy is conspiring against them. Frankly, I was tired of it twenty-five years ago, but now I'm downright exhausted.

Why now? Because of a particular feminist named Nancy Hopkins. Ms. Hopkins is the MIT biology professor who famously stalked out of a conference in early 2005 because she couldn't endure the *indignity* of Harvard President Lawrence Summers floating an idea she didn't like. What Summers had the gall to speculate on was the possibility—let me repeat, the *possibility*—that there might be innate differences between the sexes in math and science. This *insult* left Hopkins so shaken that she says she almost fainted. No kidding. "When he started talking about innate differences in aptitude between men and women, I just couldn't breath," she said. If she hadn't gotten up and marched right out, she "would have either blacked out or thrown up."

Now there's a strong woman for you!

After she regained what passes for her compusure, Hopkins went to the *Boston Globe* with all the sorded details of what Summers said about men and women. And before you could say "PC Alert" Lawrence Summers—that insensitive brute—was walking around with a target on his back, the object of a campaign to get him booted from his job. Summers, for his part, responded with the guts and character we've come to associate with the leaders of today's great universities: He apologized. Not once. Not twice. But by last count, 12 million times. It's humiliating—a once-courageous

president of a great university practically begging for forgiveness—
for throwing out for consideration a controversial idea!

All this, as you probably know by know, touched off the academic equivalent of World War III. The *New York Times* alone ran
forty thousand stories on the subject, several more stories than the
paper ran on World War II, which just happened to be a real war.
Then in March 2005, Harvard's Faculty of Arts and Sciences passed
a resolution stating very simply and directly that, "The Faculty lacks
confidence in the leadership of Lawrence H. Summers." Harvard
has been around for nearly four hundred years and has seen a lot—
but nothing like that had ever happened before.

This prompted David Bernstein, a blogger and law professor at
George Mason University in Virginia, to beautifully capture the
lunacy of the whole thing. "It's pretty simple, isn't it?" he wrote.
"The far left at Harvard is extremely frustrated with political trends
in the U.S. Their votes and activism against Bush were not only
completely ineffectual, but they don't even have a Democratic governor in one of the most liberal states in the country. So they pick
on the closest thing Harvard has to a powerful right-winger: moderate Democrat and university president Larry Summers, who becomes a stand-in for all evil conservative white men, from Bush on
down. The far-left faculty finally participates in a vote that it can win,
and experiences catharsis; that'll teach the world to ignore them!"

But we shouldn't be too harsh on Harvard's faculty in general or
professor Hopkins in particular. They have an excuse: politically
correct idiocy is a way of life on our most elite college campuses.
Susan Estrich, on the other hand, has no such excuse.

While it's true that Estrich teaches law, part-time, at USC, she
mainly has lived in the real world. In 1998 she managed Michael
Dukakis's presidential campaign—disastrously, but that wasn't entirely her fault. Dukakis helped. More recently she's been a contrib-
utor to Fox News—and more often than not she has something
interesting to say.

But right around the same time Nancy Hopkins was hyperventilating in the East, Estrich was blowing a gasket out West—screaming gender discrimination because, in her view, not enough women were showing up on the op-ed page of her local paper, the *L.A. Times*. In Susan's World, this is practically a crime against humanity. So she launched a vicious personal campaign against the section's editor, Michael Kinsley—the same Michael Kinsley who is about the most liberal, pro-feminist male journalist around. When Kinsley, who is battling Parkinson's, sidestepped Ms. Estrich's demand that he institute a de facto quota to ensure "women's voices are heard in public discourse in our community," she lashed out at him in a private e-mail that didn't stay private for long, writing that "people are beginning to think your illness may have affected your brain, your judgment, and your ability to do this job."

Let me be clear: I have zero affection for Michael Kinsley, a nasty little man who over the years has often shown himself as a mean-spirited intellectual bully. But the behavior of Susan Estrich—so typical of the "victim" feminist's willingness to say just about anything, no matter how contemptible, to achieve her idea of "justice"—is about as low as it gets.

Except that the behavior of professor Hopkins—because it sent so many like-minded elitists into such a tizzy—was just a tad lower, which is why she made The List and Estrich missed out. Barely.

And while these two major-league feminists embarrassed themselves and liberal feminism in general, it took another woman, the gifted essayist Heather MacDonald, to put her finger on the whole sorry situation: "It is curious how feminists, when crossed, turn into shrill hysterical harpies," she wrote, "or, in the case of MIT's Nancy Hopkins, delicate flowers who collapse at the slightest provocation—precisely the images of women that they claim patriarchal sexists have fabricated to keep them down."

35 ☞

Jeff Danziger

LET'S PLAY PRETEND.

Let's pretend that a conservative political cartoonist who detests the liberal politics of, say, Jesse Jackson, portrays him in a cartoon as a semiliterate Uncle Tom, with no shoes and big fat lips. Let's also pretend that in this cartoon ole' Jesse is sitting in a rocking chair in a pair of scruffy blue jeans, muttering, "I DON'T KNOWS NUTHIN' ABOUT affirmative action."

We don't have to pretend how every decent American would react to that, no matter what they think of Jesse Jackson's politics. They'd see this insulting caricature of a black person as shameful and offensive, and would condemn it as the racist slander that it is.

Now let's play real-life.

Jeff Danziger is a liberal political cartoonist who detests the conservative politics of Condoleezza Rice. So he portrayed her as a semiliterate Aunt Jemima with no shoes and big fat lips, who is sitting in a rocking chair. She's holding an aluminum tube as if it were a baby and proclaiming her ignorance of her field of expertise: war and peace.

In Danziger's cartoon, Rice—who is a Russia scholar, former provost at Stanford University, concert pianist, former national security advisor to President Bush, and now secretary of state—is drawn barefoot, wearing a housedress, and saying "I KNOWS ALL ABOUT ALUMUNUM TUBES! (Correction) I DON'T KNOW NUTHIN' ABOUT ALUMUNUM TUBES . . ."

The tubes in question are supposed to be the aluminum tubes that Saddam Hussein had imported—apparently, as it turns out, to make conventional missiles. Ms. Rice had suggested during the lead up to the war that he might have wanted them to make a nuclear device. Get it?

As a *Wall Street Journal* editorial, which pointed this piece of nastiness out, says, "Mr. Danziger, a proud member of the media's 'Bush Lied!' brigade, is making a point about the administration's supposed manipulation of pre-war intelligence on Iraq. The caption is an apparent reference to Prissy, the house slave in 'Gone With the Wind' who uttered something similar about babies."

The real line came when Prissy (played by Butterfly McQueen), who had lied about being a midwife, was so scared at the prospect of actually having to deliver a baby (while Sherman was descending on Atlanta, no less), that she shrieked, "I don't know nothin' 'bout birthin' no babies."

Ah, but the good news is that we're all too sensitive and got the whole thing wrong. I know this, because after it hit the fan, Danziger explained that the cartoon wasn't racist at all, because the idea "was suggested to me by a friend who is African-American."

You can't make this stuff up. Danziger is such a PC liberal that it doesn't even occur to him that black people can be just as bigoted as anyone else—especially when the target is another black person who has a "different" point of view.

"For liberals," the *Journal* notes, "Condi Rice's real crime is bucking Democratic orthodoxy and working for a conservative president. This makes her fair game for race-based attacks even when the issue at hand has absolutely nothing to do with race. She is a black woman who, in Mr. Danziger's view, has wandered off the liberal plantation. And this is his way of putting Ms. Rice and other black conservatives in their place."

Mr. Danziger, I suspect, is many things, but none more than a poster boy—for white liberal racism.

34 ☞

Bill Moyers

I DON'T REALLY WANT to write this one.

Years ago, when I was a CBS News correspondent, Bill Moyers and I were colleagues. I liked him. While too many other network journalists—and their ratings-obsessed bosses—were more than happy doing magazine stories about killer dogs and demented stalkers, Bill Moyers invariably took the high road. In fact, he left CBS News because the network didn't want to do his brand of serious journalism in prime time. It already had one grown-up show, *60 Minutes*, and was looking for "hipper" (more frivolous) paths to pursue. His departure hurt CBS News a lot more than it hurt Bill Moyers.

When I knew him, Bill was not just a smart man; he was also a thoughtful and reasonable man. (Here's where the "but" comes in.) But something happened to him over the years—and to a lot of others on the Left, too.

Charles Krauthammer, the conservative columnist who also is a smart, thoughtful, and reasonable man, calls it "the unhinging of the Democratic Party." Krauthammer believes that "Democrats are seized with a loathing for President Bush—a contempt and disdain giving way to a hatred that is near pathological—unlike any since they had Richard Nixon to kick around."

Krauthammer, who trained to be a psychiatrist, later concluded that this "unhinging" no longer was a "near pathological" condition; it had become a full-blown mental illness. "Bush Derangement Syndrome," he called it, the *"acute onset of paranoia in otherwise normal people in reaction to the policies, the presidency—nay—the very existence of George W. Bush."*

Hello, Bill Moyers!

In fact, Krauthammer's column came in the wake of a speech Moyers gave at a "Take Back America" rally, where, after the usual left-wing stuff—he condemned "the unholy alliance between government and wealth" and mocked the compassionate conservative spin that tries to make "the rape of America sound like a consensual date"—he went over the cliff, into full Bush Derangement Syndrome.

Moyers raved (in that earnest way of his) that "right-wing wrecking crews" were out to bankrupt the government in order to enrich the corporate interests, and that "I think this is a deliberate, intentional destruction of the United States of America."

Charging that conservatives are out to *deliberately* and *intentionally* destroy our country is not, to put it mildly, the language of a judicious man. It is not the way liberals used to talk—or the way they used to be. Yet, like it or not, this is the language of today's Left, and of its high priest, Bill Moyers.

His PBS broadcasts on war and disease and poverty and moral philosophy and (over and over and over) corporate greed, have won him fans among like-minded souls everywhere, from Beverly Hills to New York's Upper West Side; from Malibu to Martha's Vineyard; and, as day follows night, a stretch-limo full of Emmy, Peabody, and Alfred I. DuPont awards.

When the story broke about the abuse at Iraq's Abu Ghraib prison, Moyers was among the first to draw a moral equivalency between the sexual humiliation of Iraqi prisoners and the beheading of American Nick Berg. "All of us," as he put it to a left-wing philosopher who was the guest on his PBS show that week, "have been holding in our heads simultaneously this week those images, the images of the terrorist beheading the young American from Pennsylvania and the images of what happened in that prison. Is one of those atrocities more reprehensible than the other?"

It's enough to make you choke on your Brie and spit up your Chablis. So is this from Mr. Moyers, on those big, bad, racist conservatives: "The Right gets away with blaming liberals for their efforts to help the poor," he tells an interviewer, "but what the Right is really objecting to is the fact that the poor are primarily black."

Bill is entitled to his politics, no matter how odd or how stale they may seem. But this nonsense about conservatives wanting to rape and pillage the land and detesting everybody who is poor, especially when they're also black, is *not* reasonable discourse. It's vitriol. And we already have way too much of that in the national conversation.

The problem is Bill just can't help himself. On Election Night 2004, as the votes were coming in, he was on the *Charlie Rose Show* saying that if Kerry were to win in a tight race, "I think there'd be an effort to mount a coup."

"A coup?" Rose incredulously asked.

"I don't believe the Right wing would accept a Kerry victory," Moyers said in absolute seriousness.

And just a month later, when he announced his retirement from PBS, he went out railing against the usual suspects: the "right-wing media" and how it has become "a partisan propaganda arm of the Republican National Committee."

But let's be generous. Despite some of the nastier things he has said, Bill is not a bad guy at heart. It's just that the "new media" has thrown him for a loop. He liked it better in the old days, before Rush Limbaugh, before Fox News, before interesting and thoughtful conservative bloggers threw their two cents into the national conversation. All these new voices trying to be heard in the marketplace of ideas, I think, has left him a tad disoriented.

Charles Krauthammer has written that Bill Moyers's "deferential demeanor and almost avuncular television style has made him the Mr. Rogers of American politics." Too bad this Mr. Rogers wandered out of his old neighborhood and got lost in some dark alley. Too bad Mr. Rogers became unhinged.

Bob Shrum

IT'S NO SURPRISE that Bob Shrum, the Democratic political consultant, media guru, speechwriter, and all-around liberal superstar,
tends to get such good press. It helps, of course, when you have the
right ideology. But it helps even more when you're part of the club.
And Shrummy (as he is known inside the Beltway) has been in the
club a very long time. In his clips, the same words pop up over and
over: "brilliant," "gifted," "tough-minded."

As one of the key advisors to John Kerry in the last presidential
campaign—and long the alter ego of Kerry's patron and fellow
Massachusetts liberal, Ted Kennedy—Shrum is also often described as "committed," and "principled." The episode usually cited
to back this up is his resignation, "in light of my own convictions,"
from the Jimmy Carter campaign back in 1976, because he felt
Carter was drifting too far to the right.

Virtually every one of the many Democratic candidates he's
handled—including fantastically wealthy ones, like Goldman Sachs
chief Jon Corzine in New Jersey and department-store heir Mark
Dayton in Minnesota—has tried to incite class warfare, pitting the
"middle class" (where by some lucky *coincidence*, most of the votes
are) against the "rich." While this tired, supposedly "populist" attempt to turn one group of Americans against another based on
how much money they have in the bank is silly—especially coming
from guys who have more cash than Belgium—it's pretty much par
for liberal politics.

But what makes Bob Shrum different (though this is one thing
you almost never learn from the media profiles) is that on the do-

mestic issue that matters more than any other—race—his influence has been nothing less than poisonous. Quite simply, just about no one in American politics since the time of George Wallace—no one who graduated from the Harvard Law School and hangs out with so many powerful mainstream "respectable" people, anyway—has been willing to play the race card more viciously or unscrupulously.

I'm not just talking about the usual low-level race-baiting crap that has become commonplace in campaigns, the claims that conservatives are "indifferent to minority concerns" or "would turn back the clock." No, when the "gifted" Shrummy is in the picture, things get a lot uglier than that.

Take the Maryland gubernatorial campaign he ran for Kathleen Kennedy Townsend, Bobby Kennedy's daughter, in 2002. Shrum apparently was concerned that the Republican candidate (who had a black running mate) was making inroads with black voters, so he had his candidate link opposition to racial preferences, the Republican position, to supporting slavery and lynching.

"He opposes affirmative action based on race," Ms. Kennedy said of her opponent in front of a predominantly black audience. "Well, let me tell you, slavery was based on race. Lynching was based on race . . . and affirmative action should be based on race."

So, if you oppose preferences based on race, you're a bigot? That was clearly the message from the "brilliant" Bob Shrum. Incite the crowd, turn the races against each other . . . hey, anything to win an election, right? And just in case you think that this was an aberration, take a look at how Shrum ran the "Campaign to Defeat 209"—the effort put together by liberal activists to block California's 1996 voter initiative aimed at ending racial preferences in university admissions and hiring. As Ward Connerly, the black businessman who was 209's chief supporter, said after voters had passed the measure, its opponents launched "a vituperative barrage of unprecedented ferocity and deception." The most disgusting part of this was a TV ad that Shrum put on the air in the last week of the campaign. Over visuals of burning crosses, Ku Klux Klanners, and shots of David Duke, it intoned: "David Duke wants you to vote Yes on 209."

Get it? Only a bigot of KKK proportions would support an initiative to end racial preferences. The conservative *National Review* called the spot "one of the most demagogic political ads ever to appear on television."

In fact, David Duke actually had been invited to join the debate by students at Cal State Northridge, who opposed 209 and were trying to embarrass its supporters. It was a low-class and stupid thing to do—but they were just college kids, so maybe they would someday learn the difference between decency and indecency.

For Bob Shrum—the "principled" man so admired by "respectable" people and the mainstream media—it's way past too late. A point that didn't seem to faze the liberal elites at New York University, who in January 2005 hired Shrum—"the renowned political strategist," as they put it—as a senior fellow to teach young people about public service. In case you were wondering where the next generation of left-wing class-and-race-warriors will come from—now you know.

Jerry Springer

MY FAVORITE DESCRIPTION of the *Jerry Springer Show* is that it's the television equivalent of a churning mass of maggots devouring rotten meat. Except, of course, that's way too kind to Jerry—and grossly unfair to the maggots.

Sure, we've always had our freak shows, but once upon a time we had to actually leave home and go to some dingy, out-of-the-way corner of the circus to do our gawking. That's why they called it a "side" show. Now, we can sit back, relax, stuff Oreos in our face, and let the freaks right into our living rooms.

And what's really so bad about Jerry? Here's a description of a typical episode from the show's own Web site.

"Debbie is torn between her current husband and her ex-husband, who happen to be buddies when they were in jail together! She admits she has feelings for them both but in the end says her ex is the jailbird for her! Next . . . Loretta has been dating April for 6 months but has also been sleeping with April's sister for 3! She plans to break up the family and leave April for her sister today! Then . . . Lynnette is here to steal her cousin's man, Thaddeus! She has absolutely no remorse for her betrayal but gets a taste of her own medicine when Thaddeus chooses his long time lover, Lynnette's cousin!"

Gee, I don't want to miss that one. But first I need to find an open sewer pipe and wallow in the sludge. Just to get in the mood.

I understand how easy it is to write Jerry Springer off as just some smarmy but harmless guy doing a smarmy but harmless television show. I mean, what could be more harmless than the one he did about the love-struck guy who was happily married for five glorious years—*to his horse?* Given the life-and-death problems we have these days—like terrorism—is this something we really need to worry about?

In a word—*absolutely!*

Let's put it this way: If they had TV in Ancient Rome, the *Jerry Springer Show* would have been the biggest hit in the land—just before the empire came crashing down on itself. I'm not saying that Springer, single-handedly, is going to bring America down. But he's certainly screwing America up!

"Here, every day," as the *City Journal* observes, "in some markets, twice and three times a day—family members blithely detail their shared carnal adventures and morbidly obese, slatternly, foul-mouthed women battle over useless, slack-jawed men; while the audience (whose female members get in on the act by exposing their breasts in exchange for bead necklaces), urge them on with chants of 'whore, whore, whore' or, less creatively, 'Jer-ry, Jer-ry, Jer-ry.' "

I don't want a law against this stuff. I don't want Jerry Springer hauled off by the police. But let's not pretend that this daily menu of toxic waste isn't, at its core, sad and depressing, or that it isn't bad for the collective soul.

But give him this much: Jerry Springer is as good as they get when it comes to making millions off of losers. This is someone who parades these half-wits in front of a national audience, encourages them to humiliate themselves (even if they're too dense to realize what they're doing), and then smiles—no, *smirks* is closer to it—from the corner of the studio as he takes in the whole sorry scene. Even as they hail him with their moronic "Jer-ry, Jer-ry, Jer-ry," he understands what pathetic bastards they all are, the ones in the audience no less than the ones on the stage.

Many years ago—on May 9, 1961, to be exact—a wise man named Newton Minnow, who was the chairman of the Federal Communications Commission, simply but devastatingly described television as "a vast wasteland." "When television is good," he said, "nothing is better. But when television is bad, nothing is worse."

It was true then, and thanks to Jerry Springer (and the other maggots that have descended on the rotten meat), it sadly is even truer today.

31 ☞

Maury Povich

THERE ARE SOME DAYS—I know this will be hard to believe—when Maury Povich actually makes Jerry Springer appear decent. Watch both shows in succession, and you'll discover that there's not enough soap and water in all of North America to make you feel clean—ever again.

I understand that some of you may find this hard to believe, since Povich is supposed to be far more respectable. He's an ex-newsman, after all, turned talk-show host. But the fact is, Maury is just as smarmy as Jerry and also very much in the exploitation-of-losers business, making lots of money off of people whose lives are in some form of chaos or another. And like Jerry, Maury does the usual staples of trash TV shows. He did one, for example, about women who are having sex with their daughters' boyfriends.

Yawn.

And because in the dysfunctional world of morning syndicated television, even something this bizarre feels old—*Didn't I see that one before or am I confusing it with the one about moms who are having sex with the pizza boy?*—and because there's just so much of that crap you can put on without looking like a pervert yourself, Maury used his Ivy League education (he went to Penn) and came up with a surefire gimmick to break through the clutter of daytime TV.

Kids!

Yes, all kinds of kids—white kids, black kids, brown kids, tall kids, short kids, boy kids, girl kids, any kind of kid . . . as long as it's a dysfunctional kid, or a kid who comes from a dysfunctional family. In one way or another, almost every Maury show is about kids these days—kids who dress like whores; kids who are violent; kids who tell their mothers what they can do with themselves; kids who are in gangs; kids who ran away from home.

Maury and the geniuses on his team have figured out that if you can bring children into the picture and toss them into the cesspool in front of a screaming audience, then you've got yourself a ratings grabber. It's a way to separate yourself from all the other television slimeballs—and become a very rich and "successful" slimeball in your own right. Never mind how low you have to sink to get there. When it comes to Maury and kids, almost anything is fair game.

There was one Maury show that wasn't about the usual kind of dysfunctional kid. In fact, it was barely about kids at all, unless you count babies as kids, which is exactly what this show was about. Actually, it was about a certain kind of baby. The kind that is humongous. The kind of baby who is so big and so fat that he looks more like a sumo wrestler than an infant. Of course, the infants couldn't come on the show alone, so they brought their sorry mothers with them, who picked fights with the slugs in the studio audience who were booing the moms for bragging about how they let their kids eat just about anything that isn't nailed down.

This is the kind of show that makes Maury so *special*.

There was three-year-old Jordan—who weighed 117 pounds. There was five-year-old Jessica—who tipped the scales at 205. And just in case someone in the audience was legally blind and couldn't see how big and fat these kids were, Maury made sure there were plenty of close-ups. One tight shot showed a huge baby in diapers, who was devouring a leg of fried chicken, the grease glistening on his fat face.

Of course, at the end of the show, there was that wonderful, warm Maury touch: he brought out the expert who gently advised the moms that letting their kids eat crap all day isn't really healthy.

You see . . . Maury *cares* about kids.

In fact, he cares so much about kids that he came up with a theme show that he runs almost every other day—aimed, *I'm sure*, at helping kids. This one is about . . . paternity tests.

This is how the *City Journal* described Maury's paternity test shows, each featuring five or six depressingly similar segments.

"A woman, usually very young and very often a minority, comes onstage and declares, either angrily or tearfully, that she *knows* a given man is the father of her child. After a couple of minutes of this, the accused male walks out—often, depending on how he's just been characterized, to jeers from the audience—and just as vigorously denies he is the father. The denial routinely involves his using the large photo of the child in question at the back of the set, pointing out how dramatically this or that of the child's features differs from his own. He'll often cast aspersions on the mother's character, too, peppered with variations of the words 'slut' and 'whore.'"

On one show I saw, a married guy swore that he wasn't the baby's father, while the baby's mother swore that he was—that is, when they weren't swearing at each other. "*The baby has to be yours,*" the woman was saying, "*you're the only black guy I ever had sex with.*" To which the black guy responded, in total disbelief: "*You tellin' me I'm the only brother you been with?*" And while these two were yelling at each other, we got the money shot—the live picture of the smiling baby, oblivious to the chaos around him. Then the big moment, when Maury revealed the DNA results. Turned out, the married man really was the baby's father, despite his protestations. Cut, this time to the audience, where we saw Mr. Married Man's wife, looking like she just got hit by an eighteen-wheeler.

And what did Maury think about this? "Don't worry about it," he told the father. "You have a history of taking care of your kids and that's the most important thing."

Yes, taking care of your kids—paying for their material needs and spending time with them is important. But so is *not* running around on your wife and getting some other woman pregnant. But we can't expect Maury to tell the guy that, can we? That would be "judgmental"—and being judgmental in a valueless culture is simply unacceptable, not to mention bad for the ratings.

So instead of judgment we get a commercial. Literally! And as they lead into it, we hear a cheery-voiced, upbeat announcer ask us: "Are you convinced your mother is having sex with your boyfriend or husband? If you are, call the *Maury Show* at . . ."

As Whitney Matheson put it in her *USA Today* column: "Povich's talk show is, without a doubt, the worst thing on television. Period."

But how can that be, as long as Jerry Springer is still alive?

"Don't be fooled by the pressed shirt and pleated khakis," Matheson continued, "*Maury* is miles farther down the commode than *Jerry Springer.*"

I agree. But at least Maury *cares*—about the kids, about their pathetic parents, but mostly, about Maury.

30 ☞

Latrell Sprewell

IN LATE 2004, Latrell Sprewell, who plays basketball for the Minnesota Timberwolves, announced that he had a problem. He was worried about being able to feed his family. At the time he was making $14.6 million a year. But what *really* had Latrell worried is that the Timberwolves wanted to pay him a mere $21 million for the next three seasons, which, if you do the math, you'll realize comes out to a measly $7 million a year.

Latrell said the offer was "insulting."

Why not help the T-Wolves win the NBA title this season, a reporter asked him, and then see what happens? To which Latrell Sprewell responded: "Why would I want to help them win a title? They're not doing anything for me."

Well, that's not exactly true. They are doing something for you, Spree. They're paying you $14.6 mil to play a little boy's game. And they're paying you all that money even though you're the guy who, when you were with Golden State, famously choked your coach because you didn't like his attitude. But I digress. Here's the rest of the Sprewell quotation: "I got my family to feed. Anything could happen."

Spree, my man, if you can't feed your family on $14.6 million a year—or even $7 million—you're not shopping in the right places or your family's eating way too much.

Oh, I forgot taxes and agent commissions. My bad. That would leave Spree with only about $8 or $9 million a year, which means, according to the World Vision relief program, that he could feed his family *and* an entire village—for fifty-seven years! Of course, if he takes the $7-million-a-year deal, he could only feed them for about thirty years.

Sure, people say dumb things all the time, and when given the opportunity to take them back, do just that. Latrell Sprewell, however, is not one of those people. The very next day, he was asked if he regretted playing the "feed my family" card, knowing that thousands of his fans in Minnesota were out of work, with winter on the way. "That's where I can be if something happens to me," Sprewell replied.

This is precisely why we desperately need some organization that does nothing but throw charity dinners for down-on-their-luck needy athletes like Latrell Sprewell.

Some of us remember a time in this country when athletes could actually relate to their fans, when even famous athletes lived in the same communities as the people who went to see them play, when some ball players took public transportation to the game. They got paid more than some guy hauling ice, but not that much more. A lot of players had to take jobs in the off-season to make ends meet. As recently as the 1970s, Pittsburgh Pirates third baseman Richie Hebner was a part-time gravedigger. Boy, have times ever changed! Take just one half of one percent of Sprewell's $14.6 million and you've got $73,000—which is more than most fans earn in a whole year at real jobs. And most fans don't have a yacht or a fleet of cars, including a Rolls-Royce and a custom-designed Lamborghini. Spree does.

Still, we shouldn't fault Sprewell or any other athlete for being rich. That's capitalism. And we shouldn't condemn them, either, for spending their gazillions any way they want. It's *their* money. But we can fault them for a few other things that have turned sports ugly—like cheating, then justifying it on grounds that everybody else is doing it. Steroids, anyone? And we can fault them, too, for the "look at how great I am" routines we have to endure whenever some egomaniac catches a two-yard pass then parades around the field like he just found a cure for cancer. And while we're at it, we can fault Latrell Sprewell for being so self-absorbed that he doesn't know how good he has it, and for the contempt he, and others, show their fans, without whom there would be no big-time professional-sports industry in this country.

For the record, most athletes are good guys. A lot of them do charity work. They go to hospitals or do public service ads for the United Way. They high-five their fans after a game, sometimes throw them a jersey. I've seen Sprewell in post-game TV interviews and thought, *Is this the same guy who choked his coach?* He always came across as a thoughtful and decent guy. But it's tough to ignore an athlete who can be as dense as Sprewell seems to be. When he asked, "Why would I want to help [my team] win a title?" the answer was simple: If not for yourself and your teammates, then do it for the fans—because they're the ones who scrimp and save to take their kids to just one game a season; because they're the ones who have to pay the exorbitant ticket and parking and soda and hot dog prices so that guys like Latrell Sprewell can get their millions. That's why!

I'm not saying Spree is the biggest villain in big-time sports. There are plenty of other athletes vying for that honor. There's Todd Bertuzzi, the hockey player who snuck up on a guy from the other team, grabbed his shirt, then delivered a roundhouse sucker punch that left his victim with a concussion and a broken neck, not to mention unconscious—an especially cheap and violent shot even for someone in his line of work. There was Pete Rose—who gambled on baseball games! And there are God knows how many home-run sluggers who have pumped themselves up with banned substances and pose a far greater threat to the integrity of their sport than Latrell does to his. Still, when it comes to greed without shame, a cancer that is eating away at our love of sport, Latrell Sprewell is one of the guys leading the league.

After all, as Rick Reilly, the *Sports Illustrated* columnist, put it: "On the official Ten Most Selfish, Greedy, Spoiled to the Spleen, Multimillionaire Athletes You'd Most Like to See Thrown to a Dieting Lion list, you'd have to rank Latrell Sprewell one through at least eight."

John Green

THE HEADLINE WRITERS called it the "Fracas at the Palace." David Stern, the commissioner of the National Basketball Association, said it was "an unprecedented fiasco." The guys who keep track of these things concluded it was "the nastiest incident in the NBA's 58-year history."

Tens of millions of us saw the video of the brawl in Detroit, the one that was ignited by a disgruntled fan, John Green, who threw his cup of beer at a player named Ron Artest of the visiting Indiana Pacers. After that, as they say, all hell broke loose. Not only was it the worst fight in NBA history, it is believed to be the most violent episode between fans and professional athletes in U.S. sports history.

But the really bad news is that the episode in Detroit was only the most visible example of something gone very wrong throughout the world of American sports, a part of our culture that is supposed to entertain us and at times even inspire us. The sad fact is that incivility—obnoxious and provocative behavior on the part of fans—is pervasive in stadiums and arenas around the country. Most of it never makes the papers or the evening sports shows. But it's there, at almost every game.

Take your kid to a pro football game sometime, and there's a good chance you'll hear the guys in the next row screaming that some player who just fumbled is a "f***ing moron." Or go to your local Little League ballpark. The ump makes a "bad" call, and the next thing you know, a bunch of loudmouth parents are at his, and each other's, throat—literally. It almost makes fifty thousand fans chanting in unison that "Boston sucks" at Yankee Stadium seem as carefree as "Take Me Out to the Ballgame" during the seventh-inning stretch.

Players complain that in recent years the heckling has turned especially vile. Richard Jefferson of the New Jersey Nets says that he has heard fans ridicule a player for having a mentally handicapped child. A month before the basketbrawl incident in Detroit, during a preseason game, a fan threw a bottle toward the visiting team's bench. An NBA referee says, "Some official in a major sport is going to get killed. You can see the craziness in the stands. You can feel it." ". . . some spectators, nurtured at the teat of Jerry Springer, begin to believe that they are, in fact, part of the game. They hurl invective, then beer and feel frustrated that they can't get even more involved," is how Jack McCallum put it in a piece for *Sports Illustrated*.

Today, we live in an age of entitlement. Not all fans, of course, but way too many believe that if they feel like saying it, they should go right ahead. They're entitled. But until recently, sports was different. It was a refuge, the place where we got away from all the other crap polluting our culture. Now it's become a great big arena where we can say anything we want, as loud and nasty and ugly as it may be, simply because we want to.

Which brings us back to John Green, the Detroit fan who threw the beer that started the whole thing. When the Detroit Pistons management informed Green that his season tickets would be revoked, this is what he said: "If they ban me, they should ban Artest [and the other players involved in the fight]. Otherwise it's unequal, it's discrimination . . ."

Get it? John Green is the victim here! All he did was instigate a brawl that could have turned into a full-scale riot. After all, he did pay for his ticket. He is entitled to express himself. He is a fan, isn't he?

Julian Bond

I FIRST MET JULIAN BOND in the mid-70s, when I was a young reporter with CBS News in Atlanta and he was a young politician flirting with the idea of running for president of the United States.

One day, on the road, we were chatting about something or other when he casually said, "When I was a kid, Albert Einstein came over to my house one day, and he told me . . ."

Before he could go on, I jumped in with, "*Who* came over to your house one day?" He couldn't have said "Einstein." No ten-year-old kid knows *Albert Einstein*. But after repeating that it was indeed Albert Einstein who came over—to visit his friends Mr. and Mrs. Bond, and young Julian, too—he went on to make his point. "Einstein told me: 'Never memorize anything you can write down.'"

I'm not sure, so many years later, why he told me that story, but what I'll never forget is the way Julian Bond so effortlessly dropped Albert Einstein's name into the conversation, with no more emphasis than if he were saying, "Billy Johnson, my friend from next door, came over to my house one day to watch TV." He wasn't bragging, just telling a story. Maybe because he was just a kid at the time, maybe because his parents were well educated he was used to meeting important people, the visit apparently was no big deal to him.

But it was a big deal to me, who came from a tenement in the Bronx. Growing up, I didn't know anybody famous, and I admit it, I was impressed—with Julian Bond. He was smooth. He was cool. And he was very smart. He carried himself in a classy way. Maybe that's why whenever we would bump into each other, I would embarrassingly address him as "Mr. Bond," stretching out his last name—*Hello, Mr. Bonnndddd,* I would say in a cheap English accent, trying to mimic the way villains would address *James* Bond, who was very big in the movies at the time.

Julian Bond, as they say, was a man of great promise. Today he is the chairman of the NAACP—and, I am truly sad to say, the individual more responsible than anyone else for undermining the civil rights organization's moral foundation.

Once, the NAACP, which is the oldest and largest civil rights group in America, was also the most respected. Once, great men ran the organization and no matter how bad things were for black people, they took the high road. Like the old Julian Bond, they not only were smart, they were also dignified. They were the kind of men who changed America; the kind of men who good, decent people, black and white, admired and respected.

Today, the NAACP no longer has any special moral standing. Today, it's just one more highly politicized special interest group, like the abortion lobby or the teachers union. More than anyone else, Julian Bond hijacked the supposedly nonpartisan NAACP and set it down firmly inside the left wing of the Democratic Party.

And like so many other supposed progressives, Julian Bond seems to be mired in the past. For Bond, when it comes to race, it's as if not much has changed in the past forty years, except now the bigots wear suits and ties. But let Julian Bond speak for himself.

In 2001, he had this to say about the president and his new administration: "They selected nominees from the Taliban wing of American politics, appeased the wretched appetites of the extreme right wing and chose Cabinet officials whose devotion to the Confederacy is nearly canine in its uncritical affection."

And during the presidential campaign of 2004, Bond continued down the same old road, saying the Republican Party's "idea of equal rights is the American flag and the Confederate swastika flying side by side." Republicans, he said, "want to write bigotry back into the Constitution."

He also said that Republicans "appealed to that dark underside of American culture, to that minority of Americans who reject democracy and equality. They preach racial neutrality and they practice racial division."

Never mind that his overheated rhetoric can only breed ill will and suspicion between the races—for Julian Bond it is always 1965 and America is Selma, Alabama.

"How ironic," Rod Paige, president Bush's (then) education secretary and lifelong member of the NAACP, wrote in the *Wall Street Journal*, "that [Bond and then NAACP president Kweisi Mfume] would direct this vitriol at a president who has appointed more African Americans to high-profile posts, has committed more funds to fight AIDS in Africa, has championed minority home-ownership, and has supported more trade and aid for African and Caribbean nations than any other administration. . . . Sadly, the current NAACP leadership has managed to take a proud, effective organization in a totally new direction: naked partisan politics, pure and simple."

When I contacted Julian Bond in the summer of 2004, he was gracious and gentlemanly. About that "Confederate swastika" quote, Bond had this to say: "I've read that I've accused Republicans of being Nazis because I've spoken of their fondness for the Confederate swastika. While you or others may find that rhetorically over the top—it seems a stretch from that to calling them Nazis."

Really? Can such a smart man *not* see how a reasonable person would connect the dots between "Confederate swastika" and come up with "Nazi"—even though, as he says, he never actually used the word? Can such a smart man *not* understand how "over the top" rhetoric often produces "over the top" reactions?

Sorry. But it doesn't take an Einstein—or the old Julian Bond—to figure that out.

27 ☞

Paul Begala

BY NOW IT'S OLD NEWS that Paul Begala, the CNN commentator and a primary architect (along with business partner James Carville) of Bill Clinton's rise to the presidency in 1992, is a left-wing hate-monger. So it could be that what he wrote back in November 2000—a column equating Bush voters with bigots and murderers—may also seem a bit old.

Still, it's more than worth revisiting, not for the sake of nostalgia, but for some insight about a man so many liberals still hold in high regard—and mostly, for some insight on *today's* liberal mind in general.

The story begins in the days right after the chaotic election of 2000, when we still didn't know who the next president would be. On MSNBC, Mike Barnicle, the commentator, held up a map of the United States, and noting the Red States (for Bush) in the middle of the country and the Blue States (for Gore) on the coasts, said that this was evidence of a cultural divide in America—"Wal-Mart versus Martha Stewart," as Barnicle put it, "family values versus a sense of entitlement."

This is when the fun begins. Maybe the Martha Stewart–Wal-Mart thing wasn't such a big deal, but the crack about "family values versus a sense of entitlement" deeply offended Begala's liberal sensibilities. So he responded. Not in some free-for-all TV slugfest, where people tend to say things off the cuff and in the heat of the moment—but in a written column, a week later.

"Yes, Barnicle is right when he notes that tens of millions of good people in Middle America voted Republican. But if you look closely at that map you see a more complex picture. You see the state where James Byrd was lynch-dragged behind a pickup truck until his body came apart—it's red. You see the state where Matthew Shepard was crucified on a split-rail fence for the crime of being gay—it's red. You see the state where right-wing extremists blew up a federal office building and murdered scores of federal employees—it's red. The state where an Army private who was thought to be gay was bludgeoned to death with a baseball bat, and the state where neo-Nazi skinheads murdered two African-Americans because of their skin color, and the state where Bob Jones University spews its anti-Catholic bigotry: they're all red too."

Peggy Noonan, the *Wall Street Journal* columnist and former Reagan and George H. W. Bush speechwriter, showing considerable restraint, called Begala's piece "a remarkably hate-filled column." Michael Kelley, writing in the *Washington Post*, noted the obvious: that Paul Begala can be counted on to explore "the lowest level of the sewer. But even for him, the passage above must stand as the ultimate smear."

Linking Republicans who did absolutely nothing wrong (except, of course, vote for George W. Bush) with bombers and racists and homophobes was indeed a smear in a hate-filled column. Except, as you might have guessed, Paul Begala didn't quite see it that way.

"I'd like to report a mugging," he began a followup column. And guess who got mugged? Right, Paul Begala himself. What Mike Barnicle said about family values versus entitlement, Begala wrote, was both superficial and wrong. "To show an equally superficial—and equally wrong—view of Middle America, I listed a series of atrocities that occurred in states that voted Republican for president: a black man who was lynched, men who were murdered because others thought they were gay, right-wing terrorist bombings. Both before and after that parade of atrocities, I made it clear that I did not think those places could be judged solely by those monstrous crimes."

What do you suppose Paul Begala would say if someone like Rush Limbaugh or Sean Hannity had written the following: "New York—the state where a Jewish rabbinical student was stabbed to death by a black man who was part of a frenzied anti-Semitic black mob—was a blue state (that voted for Al Gore). California—the state where rioters hauled an innocent, helpless man out of his truck and beat him senseless with a brick—was a blue state. The states with the most people on welfare—they're blue states, too."

And what would Paul Begala say if Rush or Sean tried to worm his way out of the firestorm that he alone created by saying, "I was mugged by those mean liberals who distorted what I said."

I'll tell you *exactly* what Paul Begala would say: "Be a man. Admit what you did. Admit that you *intentionally* tried to smear innocent people in the most shameful way. For cheap political gain!"

As one of the premier smear-artists of our day, Paul Begala has been called "the Joe McCarthy of the Democratic Party." While the comparison may be a tad unfair—to the late senator—let me put a question to Begala that was once put to McCarthy, a question that very much applies today:

"Have you no sense of decency, sir? At long last, have you left no sense of decency?"

Dr. Martin Haskell

DOCTORS HAVE BEEN some of humanity's most noble servants.

Doctor Albert Schweitzer won a Nobel Prize for his work with the needy in French Equatorial Africa, then used his prize money to build a colony, so lepers could live in peace.

Doctor Jonas Salk freed humanity from the scourge of polio.

Doctor Robert Gallo has been a tireless fighter in the long campaign against AIDS.

Then there's Doctor Martin Haskell.

Dr. Haskell's claim to fame is that in 1992 he pioneered the procedure known as partial-birth abortion. He is also responsible for creating the technical term—"dilation and extraction" (D&E)—that the defenders of this procedure use to obscure what it actually means: the killing of a fully formed, preborn human being, accomplished by the insertion of scissors into the base of the head, followed by the suction machine sucking out the brain.

Frankly, I don't care how anyone feels about abortion. Reasonable people, as they say, may disagree. But this is something else entirely. This is something that is as barbaric as it seems. And unlike many of the procedure's defenders—like NARAL Pro-Choice America president Kate Michelman—Dr. Haskell never has pretended the procedure is rare or that it is performed primarily to safeguard the health of the mother. Dr. Haskell has personally performed the procedure over a thousand times, usually on healthy women.

This is how Dr. Haskell explained, in a 1993 interview with *Cincinnati Medicine,* how he began using the procedure: "I noticed that some of the later D&Es were very, very easy. So I asked myself why can't they all happen this way. You see [with] the easy ones . . . you'd reach up and grab the foot of the fetus, pull the fetus down and the head would hang up and then you would collapse the head and take it out. It was easy. At first, I would reach around trying to identify a lower extremity [a foot] blindly with the tip of my instrument. I'd get it right about 30–50 percent of the time. Then I said, 'Well gee, if I just put the ultrasound up there I could see it all and I wouldn't have to feel around for it.' I did that and sure enough, I found it 99 percent of the time. Kind of serendipity."

Well, doc, if you could just wait a little while until the baby was born, and put a bullet in its head, that would be even easier!

Ten years later, in 2003, at a national conference of abortion providers, Haskell narrated a video of the procedure, walking the audience through it step by grisly step. When he was done, the unborn child destroyed, his audience applauded enthusiastically.

Every person in that crowd deserves to be on The List. But Dr. Haskell is an eminently worthy stand-in for the whole sorry bunch.

25 ☞

James Kopp

ON OCTOBER 23, 1998, antiabortion extremist James Kopp murdered Dr. Bernard Slepian, a Buffalo-area gynecologist who performed abortions.

Kopp was hiding in the woods near Dr. Slepian's house—armed with his Russian-made assault rifle—waiting for the doctor to come into view. Inside the kitchen, Slepian was microwaving a bowl of soup while talking to his wife and one of his four children. When he walked across the room and appeared in the crosshairs, Kopp fired a shot, hitting Dr. Slepian in the back and killing him.

"I consider this a crime of the worst magnitude," district attorney Frank J. Clark told the *Buffalo News*. "A man was gunned down in his own home, while his family was there. It was an assassination."

Prosecutor Joseph Marusak told the judge, "I equate this to an act of religious terrorism. We've got someone shooting and killing in the name of God and the name of Jesus Christ."

As for Kopp, he said it was his reverence for life that made him do what he did. He also said he didn't really mean to kill the doctor; he wanted to wound him.

The jury didn't buy it. Kopp was convicted of murder and sentenced to twenty-five years to life—a small price to pay, as far as he was concerned. "Why should the safety of Dr. Slepian be put over the safety of unborn children?" he asked. "I wish I could do ten life sentences or ten death penalties to save them."

This made a lot of sense to Kopp's supporters, who affectionately referred to him as "Atomic Dog." Words fail in the face of such chilling hypocrisy and self-delusion. Save us, please, from James Kopp and all the other murderous zealots out there who have convinced themselves that they have the right to play God!

24 ☞

Lee Bollinger

THE BEST WAY to talk about Columbia University President Lee Bollinger, the most dogged defender of racial preferences on American campuses, is to start by talking about Jennifer Gratz.

Unlike Bollinger, Jennifer Gratz isn't the sort of person the press usually pays attention to. She doesn't get referred to as "a distinguished academic," and no one gives her awards and honorary degrees. Nor has she ever been asked to serve on corporate boards or the board of Britain's Royal Shakespeare Company. In fact, when she was growing up in a working-class Detroit suburb, the daughter of a retired police sergeant and a secretary, Jennifer Gratz's dream was pretty basic: she was hoping to be the first member of her family to get a college degree.

She knew her family couldn't afford a swank school like Harvard—where Lee Bollinger's daughter went—but Jennifer Gratz was still aiming high. A hard worker who played by the rules, she graduated in the top four percent of her high school class, and served as vice president of her student council. "I wouldn't ask any more of my own daughter," her former assistant principal told the *Washington Post*.

Why was Jennifer Gratz in the *Washington Post*? Because at seventeen, she applied to the school she'd always dreamed of attending, the prestigious Ann Arbor campus of her state's taxpayer-funded university—the University of Michigan. And like too many other kids, she was rejected for the worst of all possible reasons: because of the color of her skin.

At first she was hurt and disappointed when her application was rejected. But later she became shocked and angry when she learned that other kids who were clearly less qualified *had* been admitted, and for the same reason—the color of *their* skin.

At the time, 1997, the president of the University of Michigan was Lee Bollinger, a longtime proponent of racial preferences—a term the Left routinely rejects (even though that's exactly what it is) in favor of either *affirmative action* or the more current and (in their view) less threatening *diversity*. "Diversity is not merely a desirable addition to a well-run education," Bollinger has said, "it is as essential as the study of the Middle Ages, of international politics, and of Shakespeare."

So when Jennifer Gratz filed suit against the school, Lee Bollinger became not simply just another backer of racial preferences; he became America's foremost and most tireless public defender of the practice. Over the six years that *Gratz v. Bollinger* made its way through the courts, Bollinger gave countless interviews, passionately arguing for a system that rewards some students for an accident of birth and punishing others. While the antipreferences side based its case on simple fairness, citing the "equal protection" guaranteed by the Fourteenth Amendment to the Constitution as well as the Civil Rights Act of 1964, Bollinger insisted that diversity—having different-colored faces on campus—took precedence.

As for the other kind of diversity—the diversity of ideas, which sounds like a pretty important concept on a college campus—well, that's not the kind the Lee Bollingers of the world seem to care very much about. If the faculty is overwhelmingly left-of-center, and if that represents an obvious and glaring lack of ideological diversity, that's just fine with them. But for the cause of racial diversity, Bollinger pulled out all the stops, rallying as many of America's elite as he could round up. As the *St. Louis Post-Dispatch* observed, "Bollinger, as much as any other individual, drove a defense that eventually enlisted hundreds of businesses, military leaders, state attorneys general, universities, labor organizations and members of

Congress that filed pro-university 'friend' briefs with the Supreme Court."

By the time the case was decided, in June 2003, the university had spent more than $10 million of public funds on the case—five times more than their opponents. And while the Supreme Court ruled in a 6–3 decision that the specific bean-counting formula the university had used to reject Gratz and others was illegal, it said that schools could still "consider race and/or ethnicity as one of many factors in making admissions decisions through a 'properly devised' admissions program. . . ."

In other words, they could keep doing exactly what they had been doing, but they should find a less obvious way of doing it. "As a consequence of Bollinger's firm decision to defend affirmative action," as the Michigan student paper says admiringly, "universities around the country have been able to enact policies to ensure racial diversity within the student bodies."

Though technically she won her case, the ruling came far too late for Jennifer Gratz. She had already graduated—from a less prestigious school.

Of course, you can make the case that since blacks have been historically discriminated against in our society, there should be some kind of remedy, like affirmative action. But what Lee Bollinger never seemed to understand—or certainly never seemed to care very much about—is that in the days when the old boys network threw its weight around and helped kids get into college, it wasn't just black kids who got the short end of the stick—it was also white blue-collar kids, just like Jennifer Gratz. The old boys network never looked out for *them*. They got screwed under the old system and now they were supposed to just smile and walk away when they got screwed under the new system? They were supposed to *understand* that Lee Bollinger was doling out racial goodies *for the sake of the nation*, while never paying a price himself? In fact, after the *Gratz* decision, Bollinger was even more celebrated by the

cultural elites than before—which got him an even more prestigious job, as president of Columbia University!

Still, Jennifer Gratz has said that she supports the concept of affirmative action, that she's all in favor of creating greater opportunities for minorities, but that it should be based on income and not on
race. Why should a better-qualified blue-collar white kid have to
step aside for a less-qualified upper-middle-class black kid?

Or, as Jonah Goldberg put it in a piece for *National Review
Online*: "If the choice is between an abstract black and an abstract
white and they are for all intents and purposes otherwise indistin-
guishable, I'm not going to freak out if the black kid catches a
break, even if it violates the principle of colorblindness. But I'd be
even more in favor of a poor white kid from Oklahoma [or Michi-
gan] catching a break at the expense of a black dentist's kid."

Oh, yeah, one more thing: Did I mention that Bollinger's own
son attended the University of Michigan at Ann Arbor? I wonder
how much chance there ever was that *he'd* get turned down because
of the color of *his* skin?

☞ *23*

The Unknown
American Terrorist

IN THE MIDDLE OF THE NIGHT, on August 1, 2003, a big luxury
condominium complex under construction in a picturesque canyon
in San Diego went up in flames, sending fire two hundred feet into

the sky. You could see the glow from miles away. It was such an inferno, firefighters couldn't get anywhere near it.

When the sun came up, and they surveyed the damage, nothing was left. Every one of the two hundred and six units had been reduced to smoldering rubble. And then, nearby, the firefighters saw something else—a banner, twelve feet long, with a message.

IF YOU BUILD IT, it read, WE WILL BURN IT. And a taunting postscript: THE ELFS ARE MAD.

The ELFS are members of an underground band of radical environmentalists—ELF is short for Earth Liberation Front—which first surfaced in the mid-90s and whose stated mission is "to inflict economic damage on those profiting from the destruction and exploitation of the environment." ELF members in one cell may not even know their fellow "green anarchists" in another. They're "unknown" ecological terrorists. And the FBI hasn't been able to stop them.

Damage in the San Diego fire was put at $50 million, "far and away the most destructive act of eco-terrorism in U.S. history," according to Bryan Denson, a reporter for the *Oregonian* in Portland, one of the most knowledgeable journalists in the country on the subject of the Earth Liberation Front and other domestic terrorist organizations.

In a story for *Maxim* magazine in March 2004, Denson writes, "If, as FBI officials claim, stopping ELF is indeed one more front in the larger war on terror, then we are losing miserably. With a loose command structure even more impenetrable than al Qaeda's, ELF has managed to elude authorities at every turn. Although no ELF attack has yet claimed a human life, law enforcement officials say it's only a matter of time before someone is killed."

This is the same group that first made headlines back in 1998 when it set fire to a ski resort that was under construction in Vail, Colorado, causing $12 million damage. They did it, the ELFS said, to save the Canada lynx, which roamed the area.

But it was during the summer of 2003—the Summer of Fire, as it's been called—that the Earth Liberation Front earned its reputation as the most destructive, and most elusive, band of homegrown terrorists in the entire United States.

Just three weeks after the San Diego fire, the ELFS struck again. This time they hit one of the largest SUV dealerships in the country, in West Covina, a suburb of Los Angeles.

This time, Denson reports, firefighters arrived to a scene that looked more like a war zone in Iraq than a place that sells cars. "Hummers were burning all over the lot like an ambushed convoy. When the firefighters hit a cluster of brand-new $50,000 Hummer H2s with high-pressure water, the exotic metals in the steering column exploded. Flaming plastic dripped from bumpers and splashed to the ground like lava; tires blew apart yards from their feet."

And once again, when the smoke cleared, there was another message for everyone to see. This time it was spray-painted in red and blue right onto the surviving vehicles. SUVS SUCK. FAT LAZY AMERICANS. EARTH RAPER.

And again it was signed, ELF.

It had been a busy night for the ELFS. They hit three other car dealerships in the area within hours of each other, spray-painting and setting on fire about 125 SUVs. Damage was put at nearly $5 million.

But now something else was becoming clear to the authorities, beyond the actual damage: It wasn't just *what* was going up in flames; it was *where* it was going up in flames. Now they weren't just hitting remote targets in the isolated great outdoors. Now they were hitting major population centers in the suburbs.

ELF was taking their war to where Americans lived. And no end was in sight.

Almost before the charred ruins from the August fires had cooled down, the Earth Liberation Front struck again, in September and

October: more luxury homes were set on fire in San Diego; a Wal-Mart was vandalized in Indiana; there was an attempt to burn down a factory that pumps bottled water in Michigan.

But in 2004, federal agents made a tiny dent in their war against ecoterrorism. They arrested William Cottrell, a twenty-three-year-old graduate student who was enrolled at the California Institute of Technology, on charges that he helped firebomb and vandalize those 125 SUVs in Southern California one year earlier during the Summer of Fire. At his trial, Cottrell testified that SUV dealers were "evil." That little observation, along with his own testimony that he took part in the vandalism (though he insisted he had nothing to do with the firebombing), was enough to convict him, and on April 18, 2005, Cottrell was sentenced to just over eight years in prison.

But, the authorities say, several accomplices got away and are in hiding, maybe overseas. And because the ecoterrorists operate without a structure, without a president or a recording secretary, authorities have been fighting a losing battle, the Cottrell conviction notwithstanding. Trying to catch these guys, the former FBI chief of domestic terrorism has said, is "sort of like grasping at smoke."

22 ☞

Michael Newdow

BACK IN 2002, after a three-judge panel of the Ninth Circuit U.S. Court of Appeals, by far the nation's most liberal, declared the words "under God" in the Pledge of Allegiance unconstitutional, we were all forced to make the acquaintance of one Michael Newdow, the California atheist who brought the case.

Over the time since, as the case made its way to the U.S. Supreme Court and Newdow made his way through countless TV studios, we have learned a fair amount about him. We've learned that Newdow, who is both a doctor and a lawyer, is a well-spoken and passionate advocate for his cause, a true antireligion zealot. We've learned that he is doing this because "I don't believe in God. And every school morning my child is asked to stand up, face that flag, put her hand over her heart and say that her father is wrong." And, oh, yeah, we've also learned that, in fact, neither the nine-year-old daughter in question, nor the child's mother, who has actual custody, has any problem at all with reciting the Pledge.

I'm not a lawyer or a constitutional scholar, so I'm not about to argue the fine legal points of whether those two words—"under God"—amount to an unconstitutional "establishment" of religion, although I don't see how they do. Unfortunately, we got no help from the Supreme Court, which never decided the fundamental issue, ruling instead that Newdow had no legal grounds to challenge the Pledge of Allegiance in the first place since he's not the girl's custodial parent—thus tossing out the Ninth Circuit's decision. But after the Supreme Court dismissed his case, Newdow promised he'd be back. And, God bless him, on January 4, 2005, he was.

This time, he didn't go to court alone. This time, he rounded up eight atheist coplaintiffs—all of them custodial parents or the children themselves—and went to federal court in Sacramento, California, where he filed another suit challenging the Pledge of Allegiance. Heaven knows where it all will lead, but if Newdow gets another crack at the highest court in the land, anything is possible. Yes, as the justices walk into the chambers, a marshal intones, "God save the United States and this Honorable Court," which would indicate Newdow might not have a prayer of winning. But sooner or later, with new justices coming and going, he just might. And if he does, rest assured that we all would have to endure the spectacle of him and his fellow atheists celebrating yet another triumph of what they see as open-mindedness and tolerance over the forces of ignorance.

But you know what? People like Newdow have it exactly backward. As members of proudly aggrieved minorities, they regard themselves as brave and noble, true defenders of freedom, for pushing an agenda that runs roughshod over the values and beliefs of their fellow citizens; because Newdow was offended by "under God," he'd see to it that no one got to recite the words.

Yet genuine tolerance is grounded in respect for the opinions and beliefs of others, even when—gasp, call the ACLU!—the others in question happen to be the majority!

Look, I understand the obvious: that atheists don't want some invisible man who lives in the sky, as they put it, so much as mentioned in public school, or in any other public arena, for that matter. But are these two little words really such a big deal? Is this a battle that has to be fought? Is it worth the friction that it has caused? Like the insistence by the intolerantly tolerant that we say "Happy Holidays" instead of "Merry Christmas"—something even non-Christians have happily repeated for generations—it needlessly sets us at one another's throats. As Judge Ferdinand Fernandez warned in his dissent to the Ninth Circuit's original ruling on Newdow's case, such a decision would have far-reaching consequences, starting with the banning of patriotic songs in public places. "'God Bless America' and 'America the Beautiful' would be gone for sure," he observed.

Can anyone really make the case we would be better for that? Is that anyone's idea of freedom?

Judge Roy Moore

LET'S SAY a liberal judge went way beyond the usual activist stuff. Let's say he not only "interpreted" the law to fit his own politics—which happens all the time—but went a giant step further. Let's say he flat-out disregarded the law by refusing to obey a ruling handed down by a higher court. And let's say he did it simply because he was convinced that he knew what was right and what was wrong and that's all that mattered.

If that happened, conservatives would be up in arms. And they'd be right! They'd say this is a huge part of what's wrong with America today—activist judges taking the law into their own hands and thumbing their smug noses at anyone who disagrees with them. And they'd be right about that, too!

So what should we make of Judge Roy Moore, the chief justice of the Alabama Supreme Court, until he was removed from office for defying a federal judge's order to remove a Ten Commandments monument from the rotunda of the State Supreme Court building?

Let me be absolutely clear: This is not about whether the federal judge made the right decision in ordering the 2.6-ton monument removed. Nor is it about whether there's a place, in general, for symbols like the Ten Commandments inside our courthouses. On that, reasonable people may disagree.

No, this is about something much simpler. It's about respecting the law. Disagree or not with the order that the monument had to go, it was a higher court's ruling—and Judge Moore refused to obey it. Period.

On November 14, 2003, Alabama's nine-member Court of the

Judiciary listened to arguments from both sides—on whether or not he had the right to disobey a higher court's ruling—then, in a unanimous decision, decided he didn't, and removed Roy Moore from office. Afterward Moore was defiant, claiming, "It's about whether or not we can acknowledge God as the source of our law and our liberty. That's all I've done. I've been found guilty." No, judge, that's not all you've done. If it were, you'd still be on the bench. What you did was break the law by disobeying a federal judge's ruling.

Ordinary citizens may practice civil disobedience and risk punishment for what they see as a greater good. But judges can't. Imagine if not just one, but hundreds of judges all over the country did what Judge Moore did—and not just in matters involving religion, but in a whole variety of cases. We would have anarchy.

Judge Moore, of course, has many conservative defenders—people of faith who see their traditional values under attack in many areas of our culture. I don't disagree with that. But what Judge Moore did should enrage true conservatives—in fact, it ought to make them even angrier with the judge than liberals were. Liberals, after all, usually like judicial activism—so long as they've got activist liberal judges handing down rulings they agree with. But conservatives have long rightly objected to it on *principle*, and sorry, but you can't tailor your principles to fit the circumstances. That's called hypocrisy. Worse, in this case it's a formula for chaos.

As John Gibbs, the assistant attorney general of Alabama, eloquently summed up the case against Judge Moore before the panel that would determine his fate, "What message does that send to the public, to other litigants? The message it sends is: If you don't like a court order, you don't have to follow it." What Judge Moore did, he added, "undercuts the entire workings of the judicial system."

Amen.

Howard Dean

WHILE HE WAS CAMPAIGNING for president and still the Democratic front-runner, Howard Dean was riding high and could afford to be generous, but that wasn't in his nature.

After he finished a speech at the community center in the little town of Oelwein, Iowa, he asked the crowd, which was overwhelmingly in his corner, if there were any "questions, comments, or rude remarks" anyone had in response to what they had just heard.

With that, Dale Ungerer, a sixty-six-year-old retiree and Bush supporter from Hawkeye, Iowa, got up and said what a lot of Americans had been thinking.

"Please tone down the garbage, the mean-mouthing, the tearing down of your neighbor and being so pompous," Mr. Ungerer said. "You should help your neighbor and not tear him down."

To which Howard Dean bluntly replied: "George Bush is not my neighbor."

"Yes, he is," Ungerer went on, prompting Howard Dean to angrily tell him, "You sit down. You've had your say, and now I'm going to have my say."

The Dean crowd loved it. They cheered—none of them, I suspect, realizing that what had just occurred was very revealing about their guy—and very bad for the candidate who was supposed to be unbeatable.

Forget the fact that he had just told a senior citizen to sit down and put a sock in it, already not the smartest thing to do in the world of politics. Maybe even worse, he had brashly, and without the slightest hint of embarrassment, rejected the idea that the president of the United States was his neighbor, with shared values and shared concerns for the well-being of the country. Why? Because, well, because they simply disagreed about things.

It would have been one thing, if, say, George Bush believed in slavery. Or if he thought gays should be taken out and shot. Then I wouldn't want to call him my neighbor, either. But this was something else entirely. This was the language of anger and arrogance, a language in which Dr. Dean was fluent.

A week later, Iowans went to their caucuses, and front-runner Howard Dean was history. This time it was the voters who told *him* to "sit down" and be quiet. He only got 18 percent of the vote in a state where three-quarters of the Democrats said they were against the war in Iraq and *he* was the only major candidate who opposed it from the outset. The much overplayed "scream" after the defeat was only the icing on the cake, because by then, it was already over.

But here's the depressing part: Millions of liberals loved his angry-man persona. Hey, he was angry with George W. Bush and conservatives, and that was A-OK with them. All that anger was fine—right up until it became painfully obvious that in the real world of politics, too much anger is a big, fat liability. In the end, the problem for them wasn't that Howard Dean was smug and mean, without even the pretense of respect for anyone who disagreed with him; it was only that he was unelectable.

Of course, Howard Dean didn't invent anger in politics. But more than anyone else in recent years, he aggressively tapped into it—and in his own dark way, "legitimized" it, at least for his rabid supporters. Like their leader, they didn't see their political opponents as neighbors, either, but as "the enemy"—the very term Dr. Dean used to describe George Bush—not *opponent* but *enemy*. Even Nixon would have been stunned. He only talked that way in private.

"In the past I have thought of him as an angry little teapot, but that is perhaps too merry an image," Peggy Noonan wrote of Dr. Dean. "His eyes are cold marbles . . . and he holds himself with a kind of no-neck pugnacity that is fine in a wrestling coach or a tax lawyer but not in a president."

And while Dean may never have personally called George Bush a moron or a Nazi—at least not that we know of—he certainly made it easier for all the haters to say exactly that. And while he may not have come up with the idea for the bumper sticker so popular in certain liberal suburban neighborhoods during the campaign—"Friends Don't Let Friends Vote Republican"—it perfectly mirrored his smug intolerance.

Politics was never a pretty, polite game, but it became a lot uglier and a lot nastier than it had to be, thanks in large part to the "angry little teapot" who might have quietly gone home to Vermont after the election and done everybody a great big favor. But no. In February 2005, Howard Dean was back, emerging from the ashes to announce, "I hate Republicans and everything they stand for" and then becoming head of the Democratic National Committee—a grand victory for all the other "angry little teapots" on the Upper West Side of Manhattan, in San Francisco, in Beverly Hills, and one or two other places, if not for the Democratic Party itself.

☞ *19*

George Soros

IN AN AGE OF RECKLESS SLANDER, no charge is so vicious as the one that has become so common on the American Left: that their political and ideological opponents are Nazis.

As columnist John Leo says, "Almost every prominent member of the Bush administration had been identified with some Nazi or other . . . As a test of the state of 'Bush the Nazi' rhetoric, I went to Google, and typed in 'Bush is a Nazi' and got 420,000 hits, well behind 'Hitler was a Nazi' (654,000 hits), but then Hitler WAS a Nazi and had a 75-year head start."

Then again, there are slanderers and there are *slanderers*. Which brings us to George Soros, who may be the most influential Bush-hater of them all. When Soros talks about George Bush and the Nazis in the same sentence, you have to wonder: a) is he losing his marbles, or b) does he, like a lot of other hard-core Lefties, figure that linking Bush and Hitler is just telling it like it is?

Unfortunately, Soros is not some glassy-eyed radical spouting off in some dingy corner of the World Wide Web. George Soros is loaded. He's worth about $7 billion (give or take a billion). He is a very big player in the world of finance and Democratic politics. He is polished and moves in respectable circles. He sits down with important journalists who hold him in high regard. So when he talks, people listen.

And in an interview with the *Washington Post* during the 2004 presidential campaign, George Soros said, "When I hear Bush say, 'You're either with us or against us,' it reminds me of the Germans."

Gee, what Germans could George possibly be talking about? Well, here's a hint: According to the *Post*, Soros believes that the Bush White House is guided by a "*supremacist* ideology" (my emphasis).

Germans. Supremacists. Why is the word *Nazi* popping into my head?

Well, because, as the *Post*'s Laura Blumenfeld writes, Soros "hears echoes in [the Bush White House's] rhetoric of his childhood in occupied Hungary . . . It conjures up memories, he said, of Nazi slogans on the walls, *Der Feind Hort mit* ('The enemy is listening')."

"My experiences under Nazi and Soviet rule have sensitized

me," Soros tells the reporter, effortlessly linking Bush to *both* the Commies *and* the Nazis in just one little sentence. And he said it, the reporter tells us, "in a soft Hungarian accent."

Boy, am I glad that Soros is sensitive. I'd hate to think of what he might say about George Bush if he were *in*sensitive.

Soros spent about $25 million trying to defeat Bush, an effort he called "the central focus of my life" (and he was the big money behind the relentlessly anti-Bush, left-wing political outfit MoveOn.org). Not only has he helped make Bush = Nazi talk commonplace and mainstream, he has helped make it *respectably* mainstream.

For the record, Soros insists that he never compared George Bush to the Nazis, only that Bush reminded him of "the Germans."

Really? Which ones? Heidi Klum and Steffi Graf?

A piece of advice, Mr. Soros: Knock it off—before somebody calls *you* a German.

☞ *18*

Al Gore

OKAY, IT'S NOT EXACTLY A NEWSFLASH that politicians will say and do just about anything to get elected.

But there may never have been a pol who actually lived that truism more fully than Al Gore. Of course I'm referring to the *old* Al Gore—the wooden and ever-calculating Al Gore; the "lock box" Al Gore; the Buddhist fund-raising, Internet-creating, *Love*

Story–poster boy Al Gore. The one we came to know and loathe during the eighties and nineties. *That* Al Gore!

That was the Al Gore who, at the 1996 Democratic National Convention, recounted the story about how his sister started smoking as a teenager and died from lung cancer at age forty-five in 1984. "Three thousand young people in America will start smoking tomorrow," Gore passionately told the delegates in the hall and the millions of Americans watching at home on television. "One thousand of them will die a death not unlike my sister's. And that is why until I draw my last breath, I will pour my heart and soul into the cause of protecting our children from the dangers of smoking."

This was Al Gore, morally outraged and wanting everyone to know it.

So how do you figure this? In 1988, when he ran for the Democratic presidential nomination, the same Al Gore boasted to a crowd in North Carolina, right there in the heart of tobacco country, "Throughout most of my life, I raised tobacco. I want you to know that with my own hands, all of my life, I've sprayed it, I've chopped it, I've shredded it, spiked it, put it in the barn and stripped it, and sold it."

And this, remember, was four years *after* his sister's death.

You don't have to be a cynic to conclude that Al Gore was *for* tobacco when he thought that would help him get votes, and *against* it when he thought *that* would help him get votes—and to hell with principle. In fact, you'd have to be pretty naive to think anything else. But Al Gore had a different explanation, something about how it took a while for the death of his sister to sink in and for him to do the right thing. It was the "numbness" after his sister's death, he said, that made him slow to get out of the tobacco business and stop taking money from tobacco companies. "Sometimes you never fully face up to things that you ought to face up to," he said.

Then there was Al Gore on *Meet the Press*, dodging a simple question about abortion.

On July 16, 2000, during the presidential campaign, Tim Russert asked Gore about a federal law that prohibits the execution of a pregnant woman.

RUSSERT: Right now there's legislation which says that a woman on death row, if she's pregnant, she should not be executed. Do you support that?

GORE: I don't know what you're talking about.

RUSSERT: It's a federal statute on the books that if a woman is pregnant and she's on death row, she should not be executed.

GORE: Well, I don't know what the circumstances would be in that situation. I would—you know, it's an interesting situation. I'd want to think about it."

Most reasonable people, regardless of whether they're Democrats or Republicans, liberals or conservatives, would have had a quick, easy answer, without the pregnant pause: Don't execute the woman—at least until after she gives birth; to kill her before would be to kill the innocent unborn child.

Or he could have had some fun with Tim. He could have said, "Tim, who are we kidding? By the time her appeals run out, the kid will be twenty-one. Next question."

But Al Gore had other things on his mind. As you watched the interview, you could almost see the wheels turning inside his head: *"Gee, if I say the decent and common-sense thing, that you can't execute the woman because that would also kill the completely innocent baby . . . my supporters at the abortion lobby might get real mad at me . . . because I'd be acknowledging that the fetus has rights . . . and if a fetus has rights, what does that mean for abortion? What should I do?"*

So again, Al Gore sacrificed principle for a kind of popularity, and said, "I want to think about it"—a process that didn't take very long, because the very next day he issued a *clarification,* saying, "The principle of a woman's right to choose governs in that case."

Al Gore gave the abortions-rights lobby the answer it wanted: that fetuses have no rights, that they aren't people in any sense of the word, that if the woman tells the warden, "Kill me now," then the unborn kid—even though he or she is guilty of nothing—takes the lethal injection along with Mommy.

Back then I wondered what Al Gore would be like if someone let him out of his cage; if he were unencumbered by personal ambition; if he were unleashed and could say whatever he felt like saying. What would the *real* Al Gore sound like? Well, after he lost by a whisker in 2000, we all found out. He came out of seclusion after the Florida recount, a free man. Out was the wooden man of caution. In was a new man with no controlling legal authority to keep him in check and no feminist consultant to tell him how to dress.

So who *was* this new Al Gore? Someone who made even most Democrats long for the old one, that's who. The new Al was a fire-breathing dragon that didn't even *fake* moderation anymore.

During the 2004 presidential campaign, the new Al Gore didn't really *speak* at rallies—he *bellowed*, like a beast unchained. In Nashville, he ranted at a crowd that President Bush "betrayed this country!" by going to war in Iraq. Iraq might indeed be a big mistake, but . . . *betrayed*? That would make the president guilty of . . . *treason*, right?

At New York University, "reaching decibel levels usually reserved for ball games and boxing matches," as one news item put it, he called for the resignation of top Bush officials, including Donald Rumsfeld and Condoleezza Rice. "How dare they subject us to such dishonor and disgrace!" he shouted. "How dare they drag the good name of the United States of America through the mud of Saddam Hussein's torture prison!"

In another stem-winder, Gore said that George W. Bush "created more anger and righteous indignation against us as Americans than any leader of our country in the 228 years of our existence as a nation because of his attitude of contempt for any person, institution or nation who disagrees with him."

You really have to wonder about a guy who condemns the president of the United States more often and with much more enthusiasm than he condemns, oh let's just pick a name . . . Osama bin Laden!

It's enough to make you miss the old Al Gore, the one always ready to pander to any group at any time for a few votes; the one who would exploit his dead sister to win an election; the one who couldn't figure out if an innocent fetus should be put to death because his mother killed somebody. I don't know about you, but I liked *that* Al Gore, the toady par excellence, a lot better than the one we've got today.

And consider this: Let's say the *old* Al Gore had won in 2000 instead of barely losing, then, unchained and free to be himself, turned into the *new,* bellowing Al Gore right there in the Oval Office. Talk about your scary scenarios.

☞ *17*

Al Sharpton

AL SHARPTON COULD HAVE BEEN SOMEBODY. Not just a contender for the presidency, a run nobody in his right mind ever took seriously; or the host of a cable-TV reality show; but somebody who made a real lasting difference in this country. He's got charisma, a way with words, and he can belt out a message. Americans might have listened to him and might have taken him seriously.

He could have used all that charm to speak some of the hard truths about personal responsibility—as, in recent years, he sometimes has. In July 2004, for example, Sharpton told the *New York Times* that he agreed with Bill Cosby, that "We didn't go through the civil rights movement only to end up as thugs and hoodlums." Give credit where credit is due.

But mainly, over the years, what we've gotten from Al Sharpton is the tiresome blame game, the same old song and dance about white racism and indifference to "people of color." Who, besides Al Sharpton, cares how many "black or brown" people were in Howard Dean's cabinet when he was governor of Vermont? I don't think even "black or brown" people give a damn.

What a waste!

And Sharpton doesn't even pretend to be consistent. Even though he has become America's most visible gladiator against bigotry, real or imagined, somehow he manages to make accommodations for *certain* major-league bigots—the kind he surely would publicly condemn, in front of TV cameras, of course, if only they were white.

Take the late and not-so-great Khalid Muhammad, best known for his gay-bashing, Jew-hating, anti-Catholic tirades. Not only did the Reverend Sharpton share a stage with this vicious screwball, he actually praised Muhammad as "an articulate and courageous brother."

Then there's that other tower of virtue, Tawana Brawley, the black girl who famously claimed that a gang of white men raped her. Al Sharpton, the gladiator, went running to her defense, and— even as it became increasingly clear that, in fact, Tawana Brawley had not been raped by white guys or by anyone else—Sharpton (as a court subsequently ruled) went ahead and slandered and defamed one of the innocent men supposedly involved.

On January 12, 2003, sixteen long years after she perpetrated the hoax, Tim Russert, on *Meet the Press*, gave Sharpton an opportunity to do the right thing and apologize for his role in fanning the racial flames, something that, for years, he had steadfastly refused to do.

Dream on, Tim. "To apologize for believing and standing with a woman, I think all of us need to take women's claims more seriously," he told Russert without so much as a wink.

And when Russert pressed Sharpton a few more times, finally asking, "No apology for Tawana Brawley?" Sharpton replied: "No apology for standing up for civil rights."

Let's see if I understand this: A black girl makes up a story, says six white guys gang-banged her, a grand jury determines it never happened, Al Sharpton loses a defamation case in court, and to him this is "*standing up for civil rights*"? Martin Luther King Jr. must be spinning in his tomb. As Peter Beinart put it in the *New Republic,* "According to Al Sharpton, the behavior of Al Sharpton is synonymous with the cause of civil rights, and therefore any criticism of Al Sharpton is, by definition, an attack on racial justice."

Then there was Sharpton's role in the Freddy's episode—and the eight dead people in its wake.

In 1995, Freddy's Fashion Mart, a Jewish-owned discount clothing store in Harlem, reportedly gave its subtenant—a popular black-owned record store—an ultimatum: pay more rent or move out. When the owner of the record store refused to pay, Freddy's— or, others say, the landlord of both properties, a black Pentecostal church—planned to evict him.

Presto, a picket line appeared outside the store set up by an organization run by Al Sharpton. Soon after that, rallying his forces outside the store, the reverend declared, "We will not stand by and allow them to move this brother so that some white interloper can expand his business."

The pickets marched outside Freddy's for months. Customers going into the store were spat upon and called names like "traitor" and "Uncle Tom." One man reportedly shouted, "Burn down the Jew store."

On December 8, 1995, at 10:12 in the morning, one of the protesters did just that. He burst into Freddy's and announced, "It's on now. All blacks out." He then shot four employees, poured paint thinner on several bins of clothing, and set the store on fire. Seven innocent people, and the gunman, died in the blaze.

Despite his "white interloper" remark, Al Sharpton denied he egged anybody on, telling reporters, "I am a preacher, not a prophet. I could not know in advance what this was going to come to."

Being Al Sharpton means never having to say you're sorry.

Which is just fine with the political and media establishment. Al Gore, Bill Bradley, and Hillary Clinton, to name just a few—when they need black votes—make the pilgrimage to Harlem to kiss the reverend's ring. John Kerry pays homage and lets him speak at the party's National Convention. Journalists don't press Sharpton on his anti-Semitic remarks. Jeff Jacoby, the conservative writer, nailed it in the *Boston Globe:* "If Sharpton were a white skinhead, he would be a political leper, spurned everywhere but the fringe. But far from being spurned, he is shown much deference. Democrats embrace him. Politicians court him. And journalists report on his comings and goings while politely sidestepping his career as a hate-mongering racial hustler."

Indeed, as Al Sharpton's most fawning apologists, the elites routinely make the case that he's a voice for the voiceless, and all that—and that all the other stuff is "ancient history." They talk rhapsodically about the new Al Sharpton.

But can there really be a *new* Al Sharpton as long as the old one is so blissfully unrepentant, so adamantly unwilling to take any responsibility for the Tawana Brawley mess, for the escalation of racial tensions that led to the deaths at Freddy's, and for, as Peter Beinart put it in the *New Republic*, all the other "moral train wrecks that dot his career"?

It calls to mind a line that Christopher Hitchens, the journalist and author, came up with for the *Wall Street Journal*: "It's always interesting when people don't seem to feel shame or embarrassment—and it's often not a very good sign."

16

John Edwards

I GUESS YOU COULD SAY we owe John Edwards some thanks. Though it's an open question whether he's the most shameless millionaire trial lawyer in America over the last couple of decades—there is a lot of competition, after all—he's definitely the one who's brought some long-overdue attention to the way people like him do what they do: which is win enormous financial rewards by ignoring the facts to play on juries' emotions, and, in the process, do great damage to countless blameless medical practitioners and the patients they serve.

Don't get me wrong, there are many legitimate, often heartbreaking, cases of medical malpractice, and those who are victimized by it deserve fair compensation. But thanks to people like Edwards—for years, the top personal-injury lawyer in North Carolina—malpractice law has moved far beyond a search for justice into something more like a treasure hunt. And, ultimately, all of us pay the price, both literally, and in the sense of living in a society where emotion increasingly trumps reason.

Take Edwards's very first case, the one that made his reputation. His clients were the parents of a child born with cerebral palsy. Edwards claimed the baby got that way because the doctor waited too long to perform a cesarean. In his closing argument, Edwards told the jury that the child "speaks to you through me. And I have to tell you right now—I didn't plan to talk about this—right now I feel her. I feel her presence. She's inside me, and she's talking to you."

As the lawyer for the other side later said, it was "just such a blatant appeal to emotions, like putting up a sign: 'I'm appealing to your emotions.' But John could get away with it." Or, in the words of a former state court judge in North Carolina, "He has an ingratiating way, particularly with jurors and particularly with women on juries."

In fact he was so ingratiating that the jury came back with a $6.5 million verdict in the case, the first of many huge awards Edwards would go on to win.

There's just one problem: According to the overwhelming weight of evidence, the medical care in such cases has nothing to do with the fact that the child is born with cerebral palsy. In fact, studies have found that the vast majority of children born with cerebral palsy suffered fetal brain injury long before labor began. One statistic is especially revealing: In 1970, cesareans accounted for only 4 percent of deliveries in the United States, while they account for about 25 percent today—yet the incidence of cerebral palsy hasn't dropped at all!

You think that may have had something to do with why, according to the *New York Times*, in that first case, Edwards had to have his investigators interview *forty-one* obstetricians before they could find *one* to put on the witness stand supporting his position?

Then, again, a few inconvenient facts didn't even slow Edwards down, let alone stop him, any more than it's stopped him from claiming, over and over and over again, that in the courtroom he defended *ordinary* people against the interests of the powerful.

Well, let's look at the actual consequences of trial lawyers like John Edwards on the lives of *ordinary* people. For one thing, ordinary women in labor today are far more likely to be subjected to the major surgery of cesareans, not so much for *medical* as for *legal* reasons. (Doctors call it "defensive medicine"—decisions made primarily to avoid litigation and not based strictly on medical considerations.) Doctors are afraid they'll get sued if they *don't* do a cesarean. What if something goes wrong during the delivery? What if *anything* goes wrong? Do a cesarean, and you cut the chances of spending your life in a courtroom. After all, it's a fact that while doctors are often sued for *not* doing a cesarean, they're almost never sued for doing an *un-necessary* cesarean. Even worse, with as many as 76 percent of American obstetricians reporting having been sued, fewer and fewer young doctors are going into this vitally important area, leaving entire regions of the country without adequate obstetric care.

But such lawsuits are hurting the nation in another, less obvious but no less important way—by reinforcing the false idea that there's always someone to blame when things go wrong. The fact is, sometimes there's not.

"What is truly shameful is the way plaintiff's bar has used cerebral palsy to grow rich," as William Tucker put it in a *New York Post* column on February 10, 2003. "Cerebral palsy is a condition for which no one is to blame. Yet the plaintiff's bar continues to ravage doctors and hospitals because that's where the money is. . . . Malpractice suits over cerebral palsy are a cynical, unprincipled exploitation of nature's tragedies."

Strong, resourceful people understand that life can be hard, and it's not always fair, and when things go wrong, they don't point fingers. They deal with it. John Edwards, meanwhile, sues the Red Cross for unknowingly transmitting the AIDS virus through tainted blood products.

And what have been the consequences of all this on John Edwards personally? "The revenue that he was producing was an out-of-body experience," recalls one of his former law partners. "John would pick up an $800,000 fee for making a few phone calls." "He paints himself as a person who was serving the interests of the downtrodden, the widows and the little children," as North Carolina defense lawyer Dewey W. Wells told the *New York Times*, while, in fact, ". . . he was after the cases with the highest verdict potential." Though Edwards refuses to disclose his net worth, it has been estimated at anywhere from $12 million to $60 million.

More important, Edwards's law career—both his reputation as a fighter for the "little guy" and the fortune (and contacts) he made during those years—have been the foundation of his political career. His campaigns overwhelmingly have been financed by trial lawyers who, in John Edwards, have a champion in the fight against meaningful reform of the legal system. And lawyers, just for the record, are now the largest contributors to the Democratic Party in general.

And just as bad, Edwards hasn't hesitated to introduce his brand of smarmy emotionalism into the national political arena, either. Who can forget his reaction to the sad news in the closing weeks of the 2004 presidential campaign that Christopher Reeve had died? "If we do the work that we can do in this country," Edwards told a rally of supporters, "the work that we will do when John Kerry is president, people like Christopher Reeve are going to walk, get up out of that wheelchair and walk again."

This is just the kind of thing John Edwards would say to one of his gullible juries! The man is as cynically unscrupulous as they come, a latter-day two-bit snake-oil salesman. And for all his supposed respect for "the little guy," John Edwards clearly believes the little guy is an idiot. I'm not surprised by what he did—just that he didn't also promise to cure dandruff and raise the dead if he and Kerry were elected.

"In my 25 years in Washington, I have never seen a more loathsome display of demagoguery," is how Charles Krauthammer (who also is paralyzed) characterized it in his syndicated column. "Hope is good. False hope is bad. Deliberately raising for personal gain false hope in the catastrophically afflicted is despicable. . . .There is no apologizing for Edwards' remark. It is too revealing. There is absolutely nothing the man will not say to get elected."

All in all, it's easy to understand those doctors who, at the AMA's 2004 annual meeting, proposed a resolution saying that, except in emergencies, it should be okay to refuse to treat certain trial lawyers and their families. But, no, after heated debate, the proposal failed. The doctors were too ethical.

At least someone is.

15

Ted Rall

EVEN ON THE FURTHEST FRINGES of the America-bashing Left, distinctions have to be made: there is loathsome and there is *beneath* loathsome. And then there's *Ted Rall*.

Rall is the editorial cartoonist, columnist, radio commentator, and all-around creep, whose work often borders on the psychopathic. He is to reasonable debate what hyenas are to opera.

On May 3, 2004, while the nation was mourning the death in Afghanistan of Pat Tillman, who gave up a big-salary pro football career to fight for his country, Ted Rall produced a cartoon that summed up his special brand of "social commentary." "You may remember Pat Tillman, the NFL pro who enlisted in the Army rather than accept a $3.6 million football contract," read the words above the first crudely drawn panel, which showed Tillman at the Army recruiting station. "Never mind the fine print," Rall has him telling the recruiting officer. "Will I get to kill Arabs?"

Over the next three panels, Tillman is depicted as a dupe, "a cog in a low-rent occupation army that shot more innocent civilians than terrorists to prop up puppet rulers and exploit gas and oil resources" and as an "idiot" who "got killed by the Afghan resistance."

"Today's disgusting diatribe against Pat Tillman," as Andrew Sullivan wrote on his Web site that morning, "is so vile, so utterly devoid of any argument but personal malice and hatred, some form of protest is surely merited." He urged readers to contact the Universal Press Syndicate "that peddles the poison that Rall lives off," to express their revulsion.

But the problem with Ted Rall is not simply that he's a vicious, conspiracy-minded hate-filled jerk. It's also that his "commentary" is seen in some circles as respectable and legitimate. His stuff, after all, appears not in crank anarchist flyers no one sees, but in 140 newspapers across the country, including the *Los Angeles Times*, the *San Jose Mercury News*, and, yes, occasionally, even in the *Sunday New York Times*. He is a two-time winner of the Robert F. Kennedy Journalism Award and has been a finalist for the Pulitzer Prize.

And though his diatribe against Tillman was so offensive that most outlets refused to run it, it was by no means an aberration. Just the next month, in fact, when Ronald Reagan passed away, Ted Rall was at it again, this time in the guise of a columnist. As the rest of the nation, including onetime political opponents, celebrated the life and career of the former president, Rall ranted that Reagan was in Hell, "turning crispy brown right about now." In response to the outrage that followed, which Rall seemed to enjoy, he kept piling it on: "Reagan was a public figure and he was an idiot." "We hated him during the dark days he made so hideous, and, with all due respect, we hate him still." "The man was the scum of the earth."

There's more. In Rall's twisted view, George Bush is *worse* than Saddam Hussein. As he wrote when Hussein finally began facing justice in an Iraqi courtroom: "Saddam Hussein, influenced by fascism, ordered the deaths of tens of thousands of people, fought two disastrous wars, turned his nation into an international pariah and ruined his country's economy.

"In other words, his record is identical to George W. Bush's.

"As we saw at his 'arraignment' before a U.S.-picked Iraqi puppet tribunal last week, however, there is a difference between the two men. Hussein is much smarter, funnier and more erudite than Bush. When Saddam pointed out that Bush was the real criminal, who could argue?"

And when George W. Bush won reelection, Ted Rall was right there with another piece of brilliant analysis. "So our guy lost the election," he wrote. "Why shouldn't those of us on the coasts feel superior? We eat better, travel more, dress better, watch cooler movies, earn better salaries, meet more interesting people, listen to better music and know more about what's going on in the world. If you voted for Bush, we accept that we have to share the country with you. We're adjusting to the possibility that there may be more of you than there are of us. But don't demand our respect. You lost it on November 2."

Rall obviously doesn't see himself as the aforementioned all-around creep that he so obviously is. Instead, he calls himself "America's B.S. Detector" and makes no secret of the fact that he thinks he's smarter than the rest of us, whom he views as hopelessly naive. "My theory is that essentially, people don't like to think they're living in a country that's led by an evil, dictatorial madman," as he puts it. "But they are, they are living in Nazi Germany, in Stalinist Russia."

When Rall produced his sickening cartoon about Pat Tillman, many *hopelessly ordinary* Americans did indeed decide they weren't going to take it, and bombarded Rall's syndicate with angry messages of protest. And on the Internet, someone posted a parody of the offensive cartoon that was smarter *by far* than anything Ted Rall has ever done. "You may remember Ted Rall," it says, over Rall's original drawing, very slightly altered so it now depicts Rall in his editor's office, "the no-talent cartoonist who makes his living mocking the sacrifices of the dead." "Actually," it goes on, "he's a cog in a low-rent anti-American movement that practices moral equivalency and emboldens those who would terrorize America."

14 ☞

Mary Mapes

MARY MAPES, DAN RATHER'S PRODUCER at CBS News, is mainstream journalism's worst nightmare: someone so zealous that her actions lend weight to every question about fairness that has been raised about the entire news industry.

Gives Mapes credit. She set her sights high. She was out to bag the president of the United States of America. "Do NOT underestimate how much I want this story," she wrote to a colleague. And if she had to use "dubious" documents to do it, well, so be it.

Her story, which aired on *60 Minutes Wednesday* just fifty-five days before the 2004 presidential election and claimed George W. Bush dodged his National Guard Service in the early 70s, set off a firestorm. Unfortunately for Mary Mapes and CBS News, the documents that were supposed to back up those allegations were apparently as phony as a six-legged hound dog in a rented tuxedo at a Fourth of July picnic in Amarillo, as Mary Mapes's correspondent on the story, Dan Rather, might put it. Except he not only didn't put it that way, what he did, along with Mapes, was stubbornly stick by his guns that the documents were genuine, even though everybody and his dumb cousin had serious suspicions right after the piece aired that they weren't.

Mapes and Rather said they had complete confidence in the story because they had complete confidence in their "unimpeachable source"—who turned out to be about as reliable as a cheap watch at the bottom of a swimming pool. Oh yeah, he also had a long history of detesting George Bush, which was no secret, either; and he actually asked Mapes to put him in touch with a top operative in the Kerry campaign, which, incredibly, she did.

Now, of course, Mary Mapes is Dan Rather's *former* producer, fired outright for her leading role in the most public, humiliating, reputation-trashing screw-up in CBS News history.

So, how could something this bad happen? Turns out, there's something about Mary that helps answer that question.

"She went into journalism with an ax to grind, that is, to promote feminism—and radical feminism, I might say—and liberalism," is how someone who knew her quite well put it. That the "someone" is her own father, Don Mapes, is sad. It seems that they had a falling-out years ago. But whatever his reason for speaking up, apparently he knew what he was talking about.

"She went into journalism to change society," is how anchorwoman Susan Hutchison, a former colleague at KIRO-TV in Seattle described Mapes.

Another former colleague, Lou Guzzo, said that Mapes "always was very, very cause-oriented." Advocates in the world of journalism, he said, are fine, "but if you're as liberal and activist as Mary and work on the news rather than the opinion side, it creates problems."

It sure does. As John Fund of the *Wall Street Journal*, who talked to Mapes's former colleagues, noted, "Some told me that the seeds of CBS's current troubles may have been planted more than 15 years ago when Ms. Mapes was a hard-charging producer at KIRO. Before she left Seattle to become a producer at Mr. Rather's 'CBS Evening News,' Ms. Mapes produced a sensational report on a killing of a drug suspect by police that rested on the shoulders of an unreliable source whose story collapsed under cross-examination. Sound familiar?"

And exactly what happened to Mary Mapes after she went on the air at KIRO with a lame story based on an unreliable source? Nothing. Except, eventually, CBS News hired her, where it was déjà vu all over again, this time with the National Guard story.

According to CBS News, Mapes had been working on the story on and off for more than five years. A lot of marriages don't last that long. More than five years is not journalism. It's an obsession. Captain Ahab wasn't as fixated on Moby-Dick as Mary Mapes was on George Bush.

The independent panel CBS brought in to investigate the mess concluded that it was a "myopic zeal" to be first with the story that led CBS News down the perilous road that has done so much damage to its credibility—and that it could not say that political bias played a role in the debacle.

Really!

It's true there was no smoking gun—no memo from Mapes to Rather saying, "Hey Dan, let's screw Bush." But that's not how bias works at places like CBS News. There are no conspiracies. No secret meetings in dark offices where collaborators give secret handshakes and map out plans to bring down their enemies. Instead, it's groupthink. It's the mindset of the elite newsroom, the bubble in which Mary Mapes had been operating at CBS News since they hired her from KIRO in 1989—a place where no one saw her obsession as an obsession, because like Mapes, many of them also wanted the anti-Bush story to be true.

Most of the time the bias is not so obvious as it was this time. Most of the time it doesn't blow up in everybody's face. That's the good news. The bad news is . . . it's always there. Always. Which is why the question that lingers after the scandal is only indirectly about Mary Mapes. The question that is still with us today is how many *other* Mary Mapeses are still out there in the news business, passing off ideologically driven stuff as honest news?

Andrew Heyward

FIFTY YEARS AGO, Harry Truman memorably described leadership with character with just four simple words: "The buck stops here." And he meant it.

As I write this in April 2005, Andrew Heyward is still the president of CBS News, a job, you would think, that also requires a certain amount of leadership with character. Heyward is a smart man. Harvard, Phi Beta Kappa. But he must have been absent from school the day they taught about Truman and leadership and the kind of dignity that comes with having the moral courage to do the right thing.

Of all the entries in this book, this is by far the hardest for me to write. Not only did I work closely with Andrew for twenty of my twenty-eight years at CBS, but I also considered him one of my closest friends. I think I know him better than anyone at CBS News. I know beyond question that he knows right from wrong in the world of news. But I also know that, like so many other businessmen, when his own personal interests are involved, he'll do what he has to do, and leadership with character be damned.

I guess this is not an uncommon trait in human beings. To some extent, we all look out for Number One. That's how we survive in this world. But it seems to me that more and more in our culture—especially in our corporate culture—looking out for Number One has become an art form at which too many executives have become way too adept. Which is why we have fewer and fewer leaders with character today, the kind who are willing to say, "The buck stops here," and mean it.

Over and over in recent years, we've seen executives of large companies callously treat longtime employees like dirt when it serves their larger needs: relocating their factories to other countries, engineering massive layoffs, or simply shifting responsibility for disastrous decisions to less-powerful underlings. Nothing personal, of course—just business. Yet when *they* screw up, when the companies they run lose billions, when their incompetence drives the price of their stock down and hurts millions of shareholders, and finally when somebody more powerful says it's time for *them* to go, they stroll into the sunshine with multimillion-dollar golden parachutes—and the best I can figure, feel no shame about it at all.

This is a large part of the reason why so many of us think back so fondly on characters of days gone by—men like Will Kane, the Marshall in *High Noon*, who, at great danger to himself, stood up for what he knew was right. Or Atticus Finch who took on an ugly culture in *To Kill a Mockingbird*, because it was the right thing to do. Men like that were never abundant, but they are in desperately short supply these days.

My old friend Andrew Heyward is not a bad person. Actually, he's a nice guy capable of great kindness. But in his professional role, I'm sorry to say that he is a fitting representative for all those cover-your-ass, me-first corporate types.

According to none other than Dan Rather, Andrew Heyward—who fired CBS producer Mary Mapes and demanded the resignations of three other friends and colleagues involved in the Memogate scandal—was himself neck deep in the mess from the start. Rather told the *New York Times* about a conversation he had had with Heyward—*before* the phony story ever got on the air: "I said: 'Andrew, if true, it's breakthrough stuff. But I need to do something unusual. It may even be unique. I have to ask you to oversee, in a hands-on way, the handling of this story, because this is potentially the kind of thing that will cause great controversy.' He got it. He immediately agreed." And let's be clear about another thing: In the world of television news, stories don't get on the air by magic. Someone has to give the final okay. In the case of the *60 Minutes* story that might have brought down the president of the United States, Andrew Heyward, as president of CBS news, was that someone.

So, if four of Heyward's friends and colleagues had to go, why didn't Andrew Heyward have to go, too? Because, his boss, Leslie Moonves, said, "Andrew's failures were trusting lieutenants with orders that were not being carried out." The same could be said of everyone who trusted Mary Mapes, the discredited producer of the piece, but that wasn't enough to save any of *them*. As a leader, Andrew could have said, "The buck stops here"—but there would have been a price to pay for that.

The right thing, of course, would have been for Andrew Heyward to resign. It would have been the noble thing to do. Captains, after all, are expected to go down with the ship—especially when they helped run it into the iceberg. Heyward, instead, found a seat in one of the lifeboats, along with the women and children.

☞ *12*

Dan Rather

IN AUGUST 2004, when the Swift Boat Vets for Truth were taking aim at John Kerry and causing a lot of damage, a prominent journalist told a national magazine: "In the end, what difference does it make what one candidate or the other did or didn't do during the

Vietnam War? In some ways, that war is as distant as the Napoleonic campaigns."

What the prominent journalist didn't bother revealing is that at the very time he was saying John Kerry's Vietnam record was irrelevant, he himself was working on a story that would air on a major national television news program *just one month later*, about—take a deep breath!—George W. Bush and what he did or didn't do during the Vietnam War.

If you haven't guessed, the prominent journalist was Dan Rather.

So how is it that when John Kerry was taking fire from critics, Dan thought Vietnam was irrelevant—but just one month later, when George Bush was in the crosshairs, Vietnam was as relevant as could be?

Could it be that Dan Rather was taking sides, that he was recklessly using his substantial power to further a liberal Democrat's cause at the expense of a conservative Republican?

Naah!

Just ask Dan Rather, who, whenever he's been questioned over the years about liberal bias, has always given the same answer: "I'm in favor of a strong defense, tight money, and clean water. I don't know what that makes me. But whatever that makes me, that's what I am."

With all due respect, what that makes you, Dan, is disingenuous at best and delusional at worst. Does anyone really believe that Rather would have run with the dubious documents if he got them from an "unimpeachable" *conservative* source who was out to get *John Kerry*?

There's not much point in rehashing the whole sordid affair. But even if we choose to be generous and conclude that Dan Rather was nothing more than the innocent dupe of an overzealous producer who may have had her own political agenda, he is still accountable—for his key role in the shameful cover-up.

"I don't cave when the pressure gets too great from these partisan political forces," Rather told the *Washington Post*, even when it was becoming more and more obvious that the memos were forgeries. And to the *New York Observer:* "This is your basic fogging machine, which is set up to cloud the issues, to obscure the truth."

That would be 100 percent true—if he were talking about himself!

Dan, *you* were the one who put the phony memos on the air; it was *your* partisan "unimpeachable source" who was clouding the issue and obscuring the truth; it was *you* who aggressively circled the wagons and defended the story for nearly two weeks, it was *you* who cheapened the network's flagship broadcast—the CBS Evening News—by continuing to run ludicrous one-sided stories defending your original screw-up on *60 Minutes Wednesday*, actually claiming with a straight face that if the memos did indeed turn out to be fake—*after everybody this side of Pluto already figured out that they were!*—that you wanted to be the one to break the story.

Sure, even the best reporters can get fooled from time to time, and yes, a case can be made that some Bush-hater took Dan Rather for a ride. But let's not pretend that Dan got into the car at gunpoint. He was a willing passenger—*because he desperately wanted the story to be true.*

And let's be fair: this isn't Dan's problem alone. When Rather first came under fire, the two other network anchors came galloping to his defense. One of them, Tom Brokaw, decried the "kind of political jihad" against Rather as "highly outrageous."

We have come to expect members of the club to stick together in times of crisis—clan rules require such loyalty. But no, Tom, it's not a "political jihad" against Dan Rather to raise legitimate questions—about why he got taken by such obviously phony documents just fifty-five days before the election, or about why he thought Vietnam was so unimportant when the charges were aimed at a Democrat and why he thought they were so important when they were aimed at a Republican.

This is both their bias and their arrogance. And in the end, with all the new media out there, it may also be their downfall. If Dan Rather and the others think they can continue to dismiss legitimate criticism of their motives . . . *they're dead wrong*!

Yes, as many have pointed out, Dan had had a distinguished career, covering every major story since the assassination of JFK. He has shown tremendous courage in going to some very dangerous places to get the news, and he's interviewed some of the most important people in the world. And all of this will be part of his legacy. But so will Rather's dark side, his stubborn unwillingness to take serious criticism seriously. In Dan's world it's always those vicious, nasty partisan political forces that are out to get him.

After his four colleagues were shown the door in the wake of the debacle over the memos, Rather issued a statement to the entire staff of CBS News. In part, it said, "My strongest reaction is one of sadness and concern for those individuals whom I know and with whom I have worked. It would be a shame if we let this matter, troubling as it is, obscure their dedication and good work over the years." Translation: Sorry you got canned, but I still have a job, now let's move on.

So what are the chances, now that the reputation of CBS News is in shreds, that he will take a long, hard look inward—not just at "myopic zeal" and where it can lead, but at his own biases, and those of his colleagues, and where they so often have led? As Dan himself might put it: "Take a hard look at ourselves? Respect our critics? Boy, you got a better chance of slow dancin' with a porcupine at Buckingham Palace during a lunar eclipse—and likin' it!"

Noam Chomsky

THERE'S A CHANCE that you've never heard of Noam Chomsky—unless, of course, you hang out on college campuses in places like Berkeley or Palo Alto or Cambridge, Massachusetts, where Chomsky is as big as Elvis was in Las Vegas. Maybe bigger.

In fact, the *New York Times* has called him "arguably the most important intellectual alive." The *Chicago Tribune* says Chomsky is cited more than any other living author and shows up eighth on the all-time most-cited list, right after Sigmund Freud. He's also a hit in France and Germany, where his ideas—which are spread through his many books and countless speeches and interviews—are especially highly regarded.

Okay, Noam Chomsky is a very big deal in certain places. So why is he on The List?

Because, in many ways, he is the epitome of what, in a sane world, would be a complete contradiction in terms: the anti-American American intellectual. Here's a man who has prospered in America beyond all reason, yet looking at his country, Chomsky sees ugliness, greed, and moral corruption. This is a guy who apologizes for the world's most bloodthirsty dictators and then, without blinking, calls the United States "a leading terrorist state."

There are, sad to say, far too many "intellectuals" who think just this way, and you can find them teaching kids at universities all over the country. But Chomsky is a special case. He is, remember, the most revered and influential leftist intellectual going.

Noam Chomsky made his name long ago in academic circles for his work on linguistics at MIT. But he achieved true superstar status not for that, but for his relentless, vicious attacks on all things American: American society, American values, American behavior in the world.

So what exactly is Chomsky's message? It is that America (way) more often than not is wrong, small-minded, petty, and venal. "When you come back from the Third World to the West—the U.S. in particular," as he once put it, "you are struck by the narrowing of thought and understanding, the limited nature of legitimate discussion, the separation of people from each other."

This is a man who has never met an American policy he liked, a point driven home by Stefan Kanfer—who contrasted Chomsky's stated views with reality—in a piece for the conservative magazine *City Journal*. "The cold war? All America's fault: 'The United States was picking up where the Nazis had left off.' Castro's executions and prisons filled with dissenters? Irrelevant, for 'Cuba has probably been the target of more international terrorism (from the U.S., of course) than any other country.' The Khmer Rouge? Back in 1977, Chomsky dismissed accounts of the Cambodian genocide as 'tales of Communist atrocities' based on 'unreliable' accounts. At most, the executions 'numbered in the thousands' and were 'aggravated by the threat of starvation resulting from American distraction and killing.' In fact, some 2 million perished on the killing fields of Cambodia because of genocidal war against the urban bourgeoisie and the educated, in which wearing a pair of glasses could mean a death sentence."

Chomsky is always happy to come out against tyranny and brutality—and for him that will always mean, first and foremost . . . the United States of America.

In fact, nothing in his long career was quite so nauseating as his analysis of 9/11. No one was so quick to rationalize the terrorist attack that killed thousands in New York, Washington, and Pennsylvania, by calling attention to the "far more extreme terrorism" that is the United States foreign policy.

Sound familiar? It's not for nothing Michael Moore has been referred to as "Chomsky for children."

But, as with Moore, it's a lot harder to laugh when you consider the consequences of Chomsky's behavior. In the words of the conservative social critic David Horowitz, "The most devious, the most dishonest and—in this hour of his nation's grave crisis—the most treacherous intellect in America belongs to MIT professor Noam Chomsky."

☞ *10*

Ralph Neas

IF YOU JUST WENT by its name, you'd think the People for the American Way was one of those organizations involved only in selfless good deeds, like the March of Dimes or the Boy Scouts.

Oops—hold on! You can't say "selfless good deeds" and "Boy Scouts" in the same breath anymore—not since those *despicable* Scouts became a target of liberal groups for their supposed antigay bigotry and their unapologetic belief in God.

Which brings us right back to the People for the American Way—and its aggressive, self-righteous guiding spirit, Ralph Neas. It will come as no surprise to anyone familiar with Neas's career that the Boy Scouts have been on his hit list—part of a long hit list of organizations and individuals with a conservative orientation he has sought to demonize and, in some cases, destroy. Ralph Neas, you see, is one powerful guy, who wields tremendous influence in the halls of Congress. He's got the clout to mobilize all sorts of liberal interest groups, which then go out and hammer just about anyone who fails their liberal litmus tests.

Of course, there is a place for lobbyists in the legislative process. They represent points of view that need to be heard. But Neas's tactics—his calculated disregard for basic fairness—have served only to stink up the process.

"Politically speaking, he's Edgar Bergen and Senate liberals are his Charlie McCarthys," as the *Wall Street Journal* nicely sums up Ralph Neas's approach to the politics of personal destruction. "He gives them their attack themes, and they then repeat them to skewer some hapless nominee who thinks a judgeship is going to be the capstone of his career."

Over the years, Neas and his Charlie McCarthys famously went after two nominees to the U.S. Supreme Court—Robert Bork (whom they defeated) and Clarence Thomas (whom they did not), viciously attacking both of them. But Neas reached a new low in his 2002–03 campaign to derail the appointment of a U.S. district judge named Charles Pickering, who had been nominated to serve on the U.S. Court of Appeals. Pickering is not merely a decent man, but an exceptionally principled and brave one: a white Mississippian who, after the state's public schools were ordered desegregated, broke with his neighbors to send his children to the local school with black kids and subsequently, at great risk to his own life, testified in court against one of the most violent racists in the state.

But none of that mattered, because he's a conservative.

Pickering had been a judge for about forty years, and by most accounts he had a distinguished career. Not distinguished enough, though, for Ralph Neas and his cronies, who went through Pickering's record, case by case, and came up with a real juicy one—one involving three white bigots who burned a cross on the lawn of a mixed-race couple. Pickering had sentenced one of the young men, a twenty-year-old, to two years and three months in prison—

instead of the seven and a half years that had been recommended by the Clinton Justice Department. Pickering said it was a fair sentence, because it was the man's first offense and also because the other two defendants, including the seventeen-year-old ringleader, had already plea-bargained their way to complete and total freedom (no prison time at all). The man standing before Judge Pickering in his courtroom wasn't so lucky. "You're going to the penitentiary for what you did," Pickering lectured the man at his sentencing. "We've got to learn to live, races among each other. And the type of conduct you exhibited cannot and will not be tolerated."

This wasn't good enough for Ralph Neas. His *coddling* of a cross-burner made Pickering unfit to serve on the Court of Appeals, which, after all, is just one level below the Supreme Court of the United States.

Apparently, Ralph Neas felt he knew more about the judge than some of the people from his hometown of Laurel, Mississippi—black people, at that. "I can't believe the man they're describing in Washington is the same one I've known for years," said Thaddeus Edmonson, a former president of the local NAACP and member of the Laurel City Council.

Deborah Gambrell, a black attorney and a Democrat, told Mike Wallace on *60 Minutes* that she thinks Pickering got a raw deal from those Democrats in Washington. "This man makes for a level playing field," she said of Pickering, "and that's the thing that I admire about him."

And longtime civil rights activist Charles Evers praised the judge as "the man who helped us break the Ku Klux Klan."

Yet even that didn't stop two Charlie McCarthys—Democratic senators Pat Leahy and Charles Schumer—from doing Neas's talking for him, endlessly repeating the fiction that Pickering was soft on cross-burning racists. And a couple of other Charlie McCarthys—*New York Times* columnists Maureen Dowd and Frank Rich—simply echoed the smears without bothering to find out for themselves who Judge Pickering really was. And why should they? He was a conservative who "went easy" on a cross-burner, wasn't he? That was enough for them.

When a frustrated President Bush bypassed the confirmation process and granted Pickering a temporary "recess appointment," Neas's reaction was as ugly as everything that had come before: "Announcing this appointment as Americans prepare to celebrate the birthday of Martin Luther King is an insult to his memory, and to all Americans who are committed to equal justice under the law."

This was around the same time, incidentally, that Neas, the supposed champion of equal rights, was bitterly opposing a voucher program that would give inner-city children in Washington access to educational choice, claiming, "it would set a terrible precedent for public school systems around the nation."

If, as the saying goes, you can know someone from his enemies, there are also times when you know them even better from their friends. Senator Edward Kennedy, one of his closest allies, calls Neas "the 101st senator for civil rights."

In December 2004, Judge Pickering decided he had had enough. He gave up his temporary appointment to the U.S. Court of Appeals and announced his retirement from the bench.

Jonathan Kozol

NOT LONG AGO, a young man named Dan Gelernter wrote a piece for the *Weekly Standard* about what it felt like to be a conservative in his upscale, overwhelmingly liberal public high school in Connecticut. "The teachers are predicable liberals," he wrote, but "the students are more worrying."

He told about lunchtime at school with his friends, where politics is often on the menu. "Most lunch table liberals say that they do not love America, and would not defend it. One boy says he'd just as soon live in Canada. They can't understand why I should be so enthusiastic about our country."

While he was writing the piece, a close friend asked what it was about. "To put it briefly," Gelernter writes, "I said, 'It's about kids who don't love their country.'" To which his friend replied: "Do they have to love their country? Is that a requirement?"

Not that Gelernter was surprised. This is fairly typical stuff coming from hip, smart kids in well-to-do liberal suburbs these days. Try telling one of them that you get goose bumps when you hear "God Bless America," and he'll think you're hopelessly uncool (at best), maybe even a borderline fascist.

Why? Because in Dan Gelernter's school, as in many others around the country, teachers trash America and its values as a matter of course. "As computer geeks used to say," Gelernter writes, "garbage in, garbage out.

"We are taught U.S. history out of politically correct textbooks. . . . They take care not to offend America's past enemies, but don't seem to worry about offending Americans. . . . Perhaps needless to add, there are no lessons on the virtue of patriotism. Like the textbooks, my teachers are extremely charitable when discussing American enemies; from the Soviet Union to the Vietnamese Communists, they all get the benefit of the doubt."

To be sure, there are a number of ways that the American education system has broken down over the years. Far too many of today's schools are violent, and far too many are filled with kids who don't care much about learning. Yet, what may be even worse, and in the end even more dangerous, is that so many of today's schools are turning out "smart" kids with little understanding of how precious their heritage is.

How did it happen?

It's a complicated question. But an excellent place to start is with one man who, despite his considerable popularity in some circles, you may not know. His name is Jonathan Kozol.

Kozol is the patron saint of today's powerful liberal educational establishment. For decades, on the lecture circuit, in the press, and in books with heart-wrenching titles like *Death at an Early Age* and *Savage Inequalities*, which focused mainly on poor and minority kids, he has preached his version of how kids should be educated, and his influence today is immense. Kozol is a fierce opponent of traditional learning, which he says deadens children's souls. He believes that education cannot and should not be politically neutral. Indeed, the once-outrageous idea that teachers should use their classrooms to espouse liberal/radical political views—i.e., to *propagandize*—can be traced directly to Jonathan Kozol. His views on the subject are laid out in his influential book *On Being a Teacher*, which was written following a visit to Cuba in the mid-70s.

"There is a sense, within the Cuban schools," he wrote admiringly, "that one is working for a purpose and that that purpose is a great deal more profound and more important than the selfish pleasure of an individual reward."

"Kozol brooded over the ideas he'd taken away from Cuba and molded them into a new theory for reforming American education," as conservative education writer Sol Stern put it in the *City Journal*. "Taking as his starting point the crude Marxist view that education in all societies is 'a system of indoctrination,' 'an instrument of the state,' he worked out a method by which teachers could subvert capitalist America's bad indoctrination and—cleverly and subtly—substitute some good left-wing indoctrination in its place."

A typical chapter in *On Being a Teacher* is called "Disobedience Instruction"—about how important it is for students to have skepticism of authority. Kozol writes about "those ordinary but pathetic figures who went into Watergate to steal," and the ones who went "into My Lai to kill—among other reasons, because they lacked the power to say no." He says teachers should talk to their students about the architect of the Holocaust, Adolf Eichmann, whose "own preparation for obedient behavior," Kozol says, "was received in German public schools"—which produced "good Germans, or good citizens, as we in the United States would say."

"All the book's model lessons aim to teach little children to withstand America's state-sponsored brainwashing and to open them up to the self-evident truths of feminism, environmentalism, and the Left's account of history," according to Sol Stern. "At the end of the book, Kozol thoughtfully provides a long list of left-wing publications and organizations—including the information agencies of the Chinese and Cuban governments—where teachers can get worthwhile classroom materials."

What's so alarming is that, because Jonathan Kozol is so admired in the education establishment, his ideas are put into practice every day in classrooms all across America, from high school all the way down to preschool.

As young Dan Gelernter asks, "What will become of a country whose youngest citizens have been taught to have so little affection for it?"

☞ *8*

Paul Krugman

PAUL KRUGMAN of the *New York Times* is often described as the most influential liberal columnist in America. I'm not sure if that speaks worse of the *New York Times* or of today's version of liberalism.

For the record, it's not Krugman's left-wing political opinions that are so offensive—although they *are* pretty offensive—but the nasty way he expresses them, and his stubborn refusal to credit his foes with anything resembling decency or principle. From his lofty perch at the *Times*—on the page that within recent memory was home to thoughtful, reasonable liberal voices like Tom Wicker and James Reston—Krugman cheapens the national debate by hyperventilating twice a week about the "lies" and manifold other deceits of the Bush Administration. "If he were a cartoon character," as Bruce Bartlett writes in TownHall.com, "he would probably look like Donald Duck during one of his famous tirades, with steam pouring out of his ears every time he hears someone say 'tax cuts' or 'George W. Bush' or 'supply-side economics.'"

In fact, anyone looking for evidence of how completely a once great newspaper and a once admirable political philosophy have lost their bearings, need look no further than Krugman's collected columns. They are so full of mean-spiritedness and paranoia, so lacking in elementary civility, they "should be of interest only to sadists and shrinks," as the *Weekly Standard*'s Andrew Ferguson put it.

Another critic, David Luskin, went so far as to compare Krugman, who is also a professor at Princeton, to another Princeton economist of days gone by—John Nash, the central character in the book and movie *A Beautiful Mind*, who, you may recall, descended into madness. "There are a couple of very real differences between the minds of Paul Krugman and John Nash," Luskin wrote. "First, Nash made a fundamental contribution to the science of economics. Second, Nash lived out his paranoid delusions in private—not every Tuesday and Friday on the pages of the *New York Times*."

When he started in 2000, even the *Times* couldn't know what it was getting. Since Krugman, after all, is an economist, he was expected to write mainly about, well, economics. And while he's done plenty of that—ripping the Bush tax cuts, slamming Bush's desire to "privatize" a small part of social security, and making lots of hopeful predictions, most of them wrong, about how under the Republicans the economy was about to tank—economics is only part of his larger obsession, which is the "radical right," and how it is leading us into a Dark Age of Repression. This delusion, which has made him a superstar on the Left, seems to occupy his every conscious moment, and he can't understand why everyone else doesn't share it.

"We need above all sunlight!" he told the Web site MediaChannel in the summer of 2004. "We need to see what is actually going on. When are people going to wake up?" He even goes after the mainstream media, regularly lashing out at journalists for—I'm not making this up—*being lapdogs of the Right*, and for failing to sound the alarm about how dreadful things are in this country under George W. Bush. During the campaign for the Democratic presidential nomination in 2004, his litmus test for potential candidates was not how they would conduct the war on terror, or even the economy, but whether they "are willing to question not just the policies but also the honesty and motives of the people running our country."

Reading his stuff, there are more than a few sensible people who fear he's already gone off the deep end. A former classmate of Krugman's at MIT, an economist named Arnold Kling, wrote a rather touching open letter to his old friend, begging him to get a grip and start using his power a bit more judiciously. "We can have a constructive discussion" on such matters as tax policy or Iraq or school vouchers, Kling wrote. "I can cite theory and evidence . . . and eventually one of us could change his mind, based on the facts." Or alternatively, they could do it Krugman's way, having an argument that "shuts off any constructive debate. It dehumanizes me to the point where I am not even given credit for knowing what my own motives are . . ."

And Kling finally asks: "Paul, my question for you is this: Do you see any differences between those two types of arguments? I see differences, and to me they are important."

You have to feel sorry for Kling, because trying to reason with Paul Krugman is like trying to reason with a taco. And besides, why should Krugman listen to anybody, given that he already knows that he's right about everything? Meaning what? Well, as he told the German magazine *Der Spiegel*, "I now find myself once again the lonely voice for truth in a sea of corruption. Sometimes I think that one of these days I'll end up in one of those cages on Guantánamo Bay. But I can still seek asylum in Germany. I hope you'd accept me in an emergency."

Just between us, Mr. Lonely Voice for Truth in a Sea of Corruption: things being as bad as they are here in the United States, why wait for an emergency?

Margaret Marshall

IF YOU WERE LOOKING to find a single person who sums up the most annoying attitudes of the liberal elites—their insularity, their sense of moral superiority, and mostly their smug certainty that they're a lot smarter than the rest of us—you couldn't do much better than Margaret Marshall.

Educated at Harvard (where she later served as general counsel and vice president) and Yale (where she's now a trustee), Marshall, who's married to the ultraliberal former *New York Times* columnist Anthony Lewis, is almost a parody of the liberal intellectual. As the Associated Press observes, she has "been an activist her whole life, defines herself by it." "She is just passionately committed to the idea that second-class citizens and a permanent underclass is not only cruel to the people who find themselves at the bottom," adds her friend, Laurence Tribe, of the Harvard Law School, "but degrading and dehumanizing to those who happen to be at the top."

Of course, she not only has every right to believe that, but she has every right to work to change the system by making the case for her beliefs. That's the American way. But Margaret Marshall goes a lot further than that. Instead of working to persuade her fellow citizens, she feels free to dictate to everyone else what kind of America they should live in.

Oh, I almost forgot: Margaret Marshall is chief justice of the Massachusetts Supreme Court—in which capacity, she authored the bombshell 4–3 decision legalizing gay marriage.

This makes her a very important person, indeed, because while this was a close ruling in only one state, it was a decision with far-flung implications. What happens, for instance, if a gay couple, married in Massachusetts, moves to Georgia? Is the marriage also legal there? Does a gay marriage in Massachusetts have to be honored in *any* other state, under the U.S. Constitution's "full faith and credit clause"? Is it reasonable for just four judges in one state to cause so much uncertainty in the rest of the country?

Apparently, it didn't bother Chief Justice Marshall that, according to every survey, an overwhelming majority of Americans oppose this dramatic a change in the culture—or even that, just a few years ago, such a "right" had never occurred even to most gay people. For Marshall it "affirms the dignity and equality of all individuals" and shows "we are a nation of equal justice under the law"—and that was that. In fact, her opinion went so far as to compare opposition to gay marriage with the evil of racism—and just to make sure no one missed the point, her court decided to have gay marriages begin on the anniversary of the Supreme Court's historic *Brown v. Board of Education* decision, which banned segregation in the nation's public schools.

As the *Washington Times* notes, in its amazing arrogance and complete indifference to the popular will, "the ruling called to mind Clinton crony Paul Begala's infamous 1998 line about presidential executive orders: 'Stroke of the pen, law of the land. Kinda cool.'"

Opponents pointed out that Marshall should not have even ruled on the case in the first place, since her biases on the subject were not exactly a secret. She had even gone so far as to give a speech in May 1999 to the Massachusetts Gay and Lesbian Bar Association, suggesting legal strategies to challenge existing law.

But to Marshall—poster child for judicial activism run amok— mere appearances mattered a lot less than changing the world according to her own views about right and wrong.

As for my own take on the subject: When it comes to marriage, frankly, I don't care if Adam marries Eve—or Steve. But unlike the over-the-top activist judges, I also respect the views of those tens of millions of Americans whose value system and religious convictions lead them to hold exactly the opposite view. The fact is, it takes someone totally blind to the realities of America—someone like a left-wing ideologue—to simply dismiss those who oppose gay marriage as narrow-minded bigots.

As David Reinhard of the *Oregonian* in Portland has put it: "[The decision] ignores the deep religious and moral objections to homosexuality and the difference between race and homosexuality, it brushes off concerns about the traditional family, it suggests our laws and institutions cannot reflect the public's moral sentiments on sexual issues. But rewriting laws and minting new rights is a job for lawmakers or constitutional conventions, not judges . . .

"As one of the Massachusetts Four's colleagues wrote in dissent: '. . . Today, the court has transformed its role as protector of individual rights into the role of creator of rights.'"

Besides which, if anyone is going to get into the rights-creation business and otherwise make crucial, society-altering decisions, a bunch of Massachusetts liberals are the last ones I'd want doing it. William F. Buckley said it as well as anyone: "I'd rather entrust the government of the United States to the first 400 people listed in the Boston telephone directory than to the faculty of Harvard University."

Ironically, one unintended consequence of what Margaret Marshall and her colleagues wrought is how badly, so far, their decision on gay marriage has backfired. In November 2004, anti–gay marriage propositions won in all eleven states where they were on the ballot—with broad public support! And, speaking of unintended consequences, they may actually have helped President Bush win reelection.

After the votes were in, David Keene, chairman of the American Conservative Union, wrote a letter to Chief Justice Marshall, "thanking" her for the court's decision to legalize gay marriage. "Had it not been for your courageous decision to ignore the will of the people of the Bay State," he wrote, "turn your back on 4,000 years of Judeo-Christian moral teaching, and unilaterally impose your own progressive personal opinions on the law, marriage might never have become the defining issue of the 2004 presidential election."

Naturally, gay-rights activists were not amused. They were screaming bloody murder over the outcome of the votes on the anti–gay marriage initiatives, calling their foes the usual nasty names.

But the real lesson they should draw has to do not with bigotry, but with civics: This is what happens when you use judges and courts to undermine the democratic process. The way to change the system is to persuade your fellow citizens, not bully them.

6

Jimmy Carter

JIMMY CARTER has been involved for a long time with Habitat for Humanity, building homes for underprivileged people and urging others to do the same. For this he deserves enormous praise.

Now let's get to everything else Jimmy Carter has done.

No need to waste much time on his presidency. Suffice it to say there were the long lines at the unemployment office, the long lines at the gas pump, the exorbitant interest rates that made the wise guys in the Gambino crime family blush, the hostages in Iran, and, of course, The Speech, in which he called on the American people to snap out of their *malaise*, which they did, just as soon as they tossed Jimmy Carter out of office. Other than that, it was a pretty good presidency.

So what liberals do, instead of giving him credit for his job in the White House (which even they can't bring themselves to do) is point to his *post*-presidency. Jimmy Carter, they say, is the most successful *ex*-president in memory.

Nice try. But as they might say down home in Plains, Georgia, "that dog won't hunt."

Never mind the good notices he gets in the mainstream press, never mind even the Nobel Peace Prize he won in 2002 after years of campaigning for it, a good case can be made that Jimmy Carter has done even more damage since he left the White House than he did in it. And that's mainly because, in his role as world citizen, he has regularly lent critical support to regimes that have no use for democratic values, and even less for the United States.

He's even made a habit of ignoring the crimes of many of these regimes against their own citizens. "The ex-president is known as Joe Human Rights," as *National Review Online*'s Jay Nordlinger puts it, "but he's mighty selective about whose human rights to champion. If you live in Marcos's Philippines, Pinochet's Chile, or apartheid South Africa, he's liable to care about you. If you live in Communist China, Communist Cuba, Communist Ethiopia, Communist Nicaragua, Communist North Korea, Communist . . . : screw you."

So whom has Carter given a free pass? Well, there was Romania's brutal Communist dictator Nicolae Ceausescu, who was executed by his own people, who Carter once proclaimed, believed "in enhancing human rights"; there was Syria's dictator Hafez-al-Assad; and Haiti's dictator Raoul Cedras; there was even North Korea's "Great Leader" Kim Il Sung, of whom Carter said, "I find him to be vigorous, intelligent, surprisingly well informed about the technical issues, and in charge of the decisions about this country. . . . I don't see that they are an outlaw nation." Then, of course, there are those of our neighbors to the south, for whom Carter has long had special affection: former head Sandinista Daniel Ortega and the ever-popular Fidel Castro.

And whom has Carter gone after with special zeal? Number one on his list is Israel. Long lavish in his praise of Yasser Arafat, Carter told his biographer, Douglas Brinkley, that the Palestinian uprising known as the intifada "exposed the injustice Palestinians suffered, just like Bull Connor's mad dogs in Birmingham."

You see, to Jimmy Carter, who still lives off his role in the Camp David peace accords, the Israelis—who have done everything in their power to secure peace, short of committing national suicide—are like those jack-booted racist thugs, stomping on decent people seeking nothing more than simple justice.

And what other country gets the short end of Jimmy Carter's stick? You got it! His own! As the essayist Lance Morrow observed in *Time* magazine, Jimmy Carter has long acted as an "anti-president," peddling his own foreign policy that is regularly inimical to that of the United States. Before the First Gulf War, he actually wrote to members of the UN Security Council, trying to undermine the first Bush administration's (ultimately successful) policy. And, as the world knows, he's been consistently bitter in his denunciations of the second Bush administration's war in Iraq; not only saying it was based on "lies and misrepresentations"—most Democrats do that—but repeating the outrageous claim that George W. Bush only wanted to finish what his daddy started.

Little wonder that at the 2004 Democratic Convention, Carter was to be found sitting alongside his good friend Michael Moore.

The United States, of course, will survive Jimmy Carter. Some of the countries where he's pitched in to help straighten things out may not be so lucky. Take Venezuela. In August 2004, Carter helped monitor the vote to recall anti-American, pro-Castro President Hugo Chavez. When Chavez's government declared he had received 58 percent of the vote—contradicting exit polls showing him *losing* by 17 points—it seemed clear the fix was in. The next day, when demonstrators peacefully assembled to protest the results, and demand a recount, they were attacked by rifle-bearing Chavez supporters. "Later that morning," the son of a woman shot down in the demonstration wrote in the *Wall Street Journal*, "the most important [election] observer, former President Jimmy Carter, declared that he was shown the computer tally by government supporters and everything seemed in order. Mr. Carter then left Venezuela and the opposition groups that had put their faith in him to facilitate a peaceful resolution to the crisis. Mr. Carter, who was vociferous and insistent about patience, transparency and hand-tallies during the Florida recount, left Venezuela to attend Mrs. Carter's birthday party."

Just a month later, in September 2004, during the run-up to the U.S. presidential election, Jimmy Carter—ever on the lookout for election fraud—said that Florida lacks "some basic international requirements for a fair election" and that "the disturbing fact is that a repetition of the problems of 2000 now seems likely, even as many other nations are conducting elections that are internationally certified to be transparent, honest and fair."

Let's see if I have this right: The presidential election in Venezuela was on the up and up, according to Jimmy Carter, but the one then upcoming in the United States of America, in 2004, was in danger of being rigged!

Sounds like he may be ready to put in for another Peace Prize.

5 ☞

Anthony Romero

I'VE NEVER BEEN a card-carrying member of the American Civil Liberties Union, but for many years I liked what the organization was doing.

As a strong free-speech advocate myself, I supported the ACLU when it defended the right of Nazis to march through Skokie, Illinois, a town heavily populated by Jews, including many who survived the Holocaust. True, I wouldn't have shed any tears if, say, a tornado had kicked up and killed every last one of the brown-shirted bastards as they goose-stepped through town. Still, if the government can stop Nazis from marching, I figured, whom else can it stop?

I'm also with the ACLU when it musters the courage—as it occasionally does—to speak up for college kids who get in trouble with the "speech police" for saying something that offends the hypersensitive on campus, something about race or sex or gay rights.

And even though I'm personally for the death penalty, I even liked the fact that the ACLU fought against it, arguing that it amounted to cruel and unusual punishment. That kind of lively debate is good for our democracy.

So let's be fair, over the years the ACLU has done a lot of good.

But let's also face facts: it's also done a great deal of bad, particularly in recent years; things that are deeply offensive not only to ordinary Americans but also to common sense and common decency.

Like what?

The ACLU sued the Boy Scouts of America and got them

kicked out of a city park in San Diego, where they had camped out for decades, on the grounds that it was a religious organization.

The ACLU has argued that even a *moment* of silence in public schools can amount to the "establishment of religion" and is therefore unconstitutional.

The ACLU forced the county of Los Angeles to take a tiny cross off its seal, on the grounds that it violated the separation-of-church-and-state doctrine, even though it represented the *historical* founding of Los Angeles by Catholic missionaries and wasn't advocating *religion* in any way.

The ACLU has argued that a doctor should not be allowed to tell a wife that her husband has the AIDS virus, because "the benefits of confidentiality outweigh the possibility that someone may be injured," as an ACLU spokesman explained it.

And the ACLU has even defended the loathsome North American Man Boy Love Association—an organization that "celebrates the joys of men and boys in love"—arguing that just because one of its members read material on the NAMBLA Web site and then, with a friend, went out and kidnapped, sexually assaulted, and killed a ten-year-old boy, NAMBLA cannot be held responsible for helping incite the murder. Even pedophiles have First Amendment rights, the Massachusetts ACLU argued.

And now we have the ACLU, in all its high-mindedness, aggressively taking on the most urgent issue of our time: the war on terrorism.

Thanks in large part to its national director, Anthony Romero, a soft-spoken, obviously intelligent man who took over just before September 11, 2001, "In the nearly three years since the mass murder of 3,000 innocent people on American soil by fanatical Muslim terrorists, there is not a single law or policy that the ACLU has supported that would help prevent a bloody repeat of September 11," as Michelle Malkin pointed out in her syndicated column on July 28, 2004. Indeed, thanks to Romero, the ACLU has become an organization "that maintains dangerously absolutist positions," as Malkin put it, on all sorts of measures aimed at fighting terrorism.

Under Romero, who certainly means well, nothing is quite perfect enough for the ACLU. In fact, in late 2004, the ACLU flat out rejected over one million dollars from the Ford and Rockefeller foundations—because the money came with anti-terrorism strings attached. It seems that, like every other organization the foundations support, the ACLU would have to sign a piece of paper that says, "By signing this grant letter you agree that your organization will not promote or engage in violence, terrorism, bigotry or the destruction of any state, nor will it make sub-grants to any entity that engages in these activities." Pretty basic stuff, right? Well, no. Not to the ACLU. "What do they mean by terrorism?" Romero wanted to know. "What constitutes support for terrorism?" To Anthony Romero, and the other absolutists at the ACLU, the foundations' attempt to make sure their money stayed out of the hands of terrorists amounted to nothing less than a threat to civil liberties and free speech!

So, what does the ACLU see as its job, during this extraordinarily dangerous period in our history? As Anthony Romero himself says, it is "to defend ourselves against John Ashcroft (who has since resigned as attorney general) and a government that tramples on the Constitution in the name of national security."

Well, here's a bulletin, Mr. Romero: The ACLU doesn't have a monopoly on virtue. Most Americans are decent people who care about civil liberties, too. It's just that most of us understand that in times like these, when Muslim fundamentalists want to kill us and our children, honest mistakes might be made from time to time. It was a lot worse under Abraham Lincoln during the Civil War, when even he suspended all sorts of civil rights—for the sake of the nation—and the *United* States and its people came out of that war even stronger in our support for civil liberties.

Sure, at some point, the FBI may ask a librarian for information on what some suspected terrorist was reading. Maybe the suspect will be an Arab and maybe some Arab organizations will cry "discrimination." Sorry. It's a small price to pay for living in a free country that happens to be at war. And it would also be nice if we got a little less whining from the ACLU about profiling at the airport and a little more visceral outrage at the Islamic fascists who would like nothing better than to kill every last one of us *infidels*.

I'm not a lawyer, but I get it. We all get it: If the government is allowed to "trample" on the rights of any one of us, then none of us is safe from government tyranny. To which I say, bullshit. We live in a different world than we did on September 10, 2001. It would help if everyone, starting with Anthony Romero and the ACLU, would be a little more understanding, a little more flexible, a little *less* absolutist. Right now the number one civil right most Americans care about is the one about our ass not getting blown up by some lunatic who thinks he's doing it for Allah. We'll worry about who's looking over our shoulder at the library when things calm down.

Jesse Jackson

WHEN I WAS IN HIGH SCHOOL and college in the '60s, the issue that galvanized the nation more than any other—even more than Vietnam—was civil rights. In the '70s, as a correspondent with CBS News, I covered the tail end of the civil rights movement. Along the way, I met wonderful, courageous people like John Lewis, who was one of the leaders of the historic 1965 march from Selma to Montgomery, a man who was brutally beaten by Alabama state troopers as he and thousands of others came across the Edmund Pettis Bridge. Today, he's a United States congressman. I met Daddy King, Martin Luther King's father, and covered stories at the Ebenezer Baptist Church in Atlanta, where his son had preached. I listened as the parishioners sang "We Shall Overcome"—and was moved, literally, beyond words.

The extraordinary dignity of the people in that church and in the civil rights movement in general had everything to do with my belief that, despite the fact that I was a news reporter, there were not two sides to this story. Equal rights for everyone, was, after all, the most compelling moral issue of our time. It was a battle of good versus evil, as corny as that may sound today. Either black Americans were full citizens or they weren't. You were either with Dr. King and his followers or you were with Bull Connors and the other bigots. It really was as simple as that.

And then Martin Luther King was gunned down and somehow

Jesse Jackson became the most prominent voice of black America. And that's when a movement infused with nobility began to lose not only its luster, but its moral authority as well. That's when the great civil rights movement that made America a better place devolved into something else entirely—eventually something partisan, nasty, and divisive.

Looking back, there are a number of reasons for this, but a lot of it has to do with the leadership—or lack thereof—of Jesse Jackson. Like Marlon Brando's character in *On the Waterfront*, Jesse could have been a contender. He could have been a champion, a worthy successor to Martin Luther King.

Instead, he became the "black leader" who, choosing to downplay the significant progress in racial relations in this country, endlessly plays the blame game, pointing to conservatives, Republicans, rich people, business types, and the like for all sorts of perceived wrongs; and who, in the eyes of many—and not all of them conservatives— has used his status and power to shake down corporate America with not-so-veiled threats of boycotts, for the benefit of minorities who also happen to be close to Jackson personally. In Jesse's world, yesterday's "racist corporation" is today's big donor to the Reverend Jackson's coffers.

While Jesse Jackson has always denied this charge, there is no question that he was a key figure in changing the entire tone of the movement. Where Martin Luther King reached out and appealed to the decency in all of us, Jesse Jackson, instead, gives us provocative sound bites designed to draw the cameras his way. Where Martin Luther King told us about his dream and beseeched a nation to make it a reality, Jesse Jackson is content simply to stir things up. "In South Africa, we call it apartheid. In Nazi Germany, we'd call it fascism. Here in the United States, we call it conservatism," he once said. During the Florida election mess of 2000, Jackson was at it again, saying George W. Bush "would preside but not govern because he took this [election] by Nazi tactics."

This kind of talk may win Jackson the applause of some blacks, who, hungry for a leader, apparently will take anything they can get—not to mention from the dwindling number of white liberals who also think conservatism equals fascism. But most of us wised up to Jackson's act a long time ago. We know full well that calling a conservative a Nazi is on the same moral plane as some bigot in the bad old days calling Jesse Jackson a nigger. Both are expressions of mean-spirited ignorance.

But unlike the white racist, Jesse Jackson is no fool—quite the opposite. He doesn't really believe that conservatives are like Nazis; that they want to round up millions of black people and throw them in gas chambers. No, in his case, the words are mere hyperbole, simply part of a strategy. His style is designed to play on white guilt and, that failing, to intimidate, to get his way by dividing us, and to hell with racial harmony.

Booker T. Washington, the great black educator who devoted his life to bringing free black people into the mainstream of American life, once said: "There is a class of colored people who make a business of keeping the troubles, the wrongs and the hardships of the Negro race before the public. Having learned that they are able to make a living out of their troubles, they have grown into the settled habit of advertising their wrongs—partly because they want sympathy and partly because it pays. Some of these people do not want the Negro to lose his grievances, because they do not want to lose their jobs."

He could have been talking about Jesse Jackson.

☞ 3

Ted Kennedy

A MAN OF "CONSCIENCE" has to do what a man of "conscience" has to do.

And, as everyone knows, the unofficial "conscience of the Democratic Party" is . . .

Ted Kennedy.

Of course, given his past, there is something amusing and even perverse about calling Ted Kennedy the "conscience" of anything. Can you say *Chappaquiddick*? Or, before that, *Harvard cheating scandal*, when the young Teddy got another, presumably smarter, student to take his Spanish exam for him? And then there's the well-deserved reputation as a big-time drinker and world-class skirt chaser.

Okay, you say, but all that happened a long time ago and, anyway, it's what he's done *inside* the United States Senate that makes him the "conscience" of the Democratic Party.

Fair enough. So let's take a look at *that* Edward Kennedy, the one who doesn't simply *speak* but *intones*, and, when the stakes are high, *intones* with great moral authority. Let's look at *that* "conscience of the Democratic Party."

Here's a Kennedy sampler, a highlight reel of some of his greatest hits, beginning in 1988, with his hit on Judge Robert Bork.

Judge Bork, you'll recall, was up for a seat on the U.S. Supreme Court when a morally indignant Senator Kennedy said that if Judge Bork were on the high court, America would be a place where "women would be forced into back alley abortions, blacks would sit at segregated lunch counters," and "rogue police would break down citizens' doors."

Of course, it's hard to fathom that Kennedy really believed such things. But if he had to portray the judge as a bigot, and otherwise malign him, in order to keep him off the court, well then, a man of "conscience" has to do what a man of "conscience" has to do. Never mind that Bork was a distinguished Court of Appeals judge and a respected professor at Yale. It didn't matter. Thanks to Ted Kennedy, the very name *Bork* became a *verb*, glibly used to describe what happens to a nominee who finds himself in Ted Kennedy's crosshairs: he gets "borked"!

A few years later, in 1991, Senator Kennedy tried to "bork" another nominee to the Supreme Court, Clarence Thomas. This time it didn't work, even though Kennedy gave it his best shot, mustering his usual moral authority as he again tried to destroy a man whose real crime was not simply that he was a conservative—which would have been more than enough for Kennedy to tear him down—but that he was a *black* conservative, an unforgivable sin in liberal circles.

"I wonder, in this day and age, whether women are prepared to sit still while the United States puts Clarence Thomas on the Supreme Court of the United States," he said, portraying the nominee as the kind of monster who makes women afraid to show up at the office, the kind of man "who fills every workday with anxiety about when the next offensive action and the next embarrassing incident will occur . . .

"Few of us would buy a home in a community near a nuclear waste dump," Kennedy said, "even though the risk of radiation may be extremely small. We don't allow cancer-causing pesticides in our food supply, even though the risk of illness is . . . small. . . . None of us would board an airplane if we had reasonable doubt about the competence of the pilot. We do not take these actions because the action is not worth the risk if we are wrong. The Senate should apply the same test to the nomination of Judge Clarence Thomas."

Can you imagine if a conservative had said the same about a black liberal up for a seat on the Supreme Court? *"You wouldn't want to take a chance living next to a nuclear waste dump . . . and you wouldn't want to take a chance putting a (black liberal) sexual harasser on the high court."*

But a man of "conscience" has to do what a man of "conscience" has to do.

And it was reassuring to see how concerned Ted Kennedy was about the well-being of women—almost as reassuring as learning that the night his nephew, William Kennedy Smith, picked up a woman in a Palm Beach bar, whom he was later to be accused (and acquitted) of date-raping, the companion with whom he had gone out drinking was the ever-responsible man of conscience, his uncle the senator.

The latest highlight on the Ted Kennedy reel, of course, involves George W. Bush and Iraq. In September 2003, the senator was claiming that the Iraq War was "a fraud made up in Texas to give Republicans a political boost." This is pretty serious stuff—charging that the president of the United States went to war in order to win reelection. And exactly how would that work? Let's see, President Bush takes the nation to war, an enormously risky political proposition, says the reason we're going to war is that Saddam has weapons of mass destruction, even though the president *knows* the weapons don't really exist, and that sooner or later, certainly before the election, *everyone* will know they don't exist . . . and he does this "to give Republicans a political boost"?

Am I missing something?

Then, three months later, in December 2003, Senator Kennedy, again claiming the high moral ground, says that President Bush's Iraq policy is enough "to make the Statue of Liberty weep."

I doubt that the women and girls who were raped during Saddam's reign of terror would agree with the man of conscience about that. I'm not sure the Kurds who got gassed by Saddam would agree, either. Or the families of the 300,000 or so dead people found in unmarked mass graves in Saddam's Iraq. But what do any of them know? They're not the "conscience" of anything.

On May 10, 2004, Kennedy struck again, using the same modus operandi—vicious partisanship masquerading as moral indignation. Even before the facts were in on Abu Ghraib, Kennedy took to the floor of the Senate and said, "On March 19, 2004, President Bush asked: 'Who would prefer that Saddam's torture chambers still be open?' Shamefully, we now learn that Saddam's torture chambers reopened under new management—U.S. management."

Taken together, this long history of partisan vituperation tells a story—a story of who this "liberal lion" Ted Kennedy really is. When on the attack, as he so often is, Ted Kennedy is "a distillery of meanness," in William F. Buckley's perfect description.

Then again, as Senator Kennedy and his supporters will tell you: These are dangerous times, and a man of "conscience" has to do what a man of "conscience" has to do.

2 ☞

Arthur Sulzberger

THERE'S A FAMOUS STORY about Arthur "Pinch" Sulzberger Jr., publisher of the *New York Times*, but for anyone concerned about the state of journalism in this country, it bears repeating.

Often.

It seems that back in the 60s, when young Pinch was such a committed student activist against the war in Vietnam that he was twice arrested in antiwar protests, his exasperated father, then-*Times* publisher, Arthur Sr., asked him a simple question: "If a young American soldier comes upon a young North Vietnamese soldier, which one do you want to see get shot?"

Pinch didn't even hesitate. It was, he said, "the dumbest question I ever heard in my life," adding: "I would want to see the American get shot. It's the other guy's country."

What's important about this is not that, as a very young man, in a very turbulent time, he held such views; so did a lot of others who now look upon much of what they believed in their younger years with at least a twinge of embarrassment. No, what's important—and shocking—is that Sulzberger himself told the story only recently, to a pair of sympathetic journalists, without even a hint of embarrassment!

To the contrary, on the basis of everything he says and does, Sulzberger seems to believe more than ever that he has all the answers; and that those on the Left are, by definition, the good guys, and those on the Right the bad ones.

And as the man in charge of the nation's most powerful and influential newspaper—the one from which almost all the other major news outlets, including the networks, slavishly take their cues—he has probably done more than anyone to destroy the confidence of millions of ordinary Americans in the fairness and basic integrity of the so-called mainstream media.

The *Times* has always been a liberal newspaper—that's not the issue. In fact, until recently, it enjoyed the respect of all sorts of people, even those who strongly disagreed with its editorial views, because it admirably fulfilled its basic mission: in the words of the founder of the *Times* dynasty, Pinch's great-grandfather Adolph S. Ochs, "To give the news impartially, without fear or favor, regardless of any party, sect or interest involved."

Pinch himself quoted those words on January 17, 1992, when he took over as publisher from his father. He then proceeded to make a mockery of them.

"We can no longer offer our readers a predominantly white, straight male vision of events," Sulzberger himself proudly acknowledged at the time he became publisher; adding soon after that: "If white men were not complaining, it would be an indication we weren't succeeding and making the inroads that we are."

Indeed, Sulzberger is a fervent believer in every kind of diversity—except the most important kind of all: the intellectual and ideological kind. Since he's taken over, despite the paper's claims to journalistic statesmanship, a chief principle at the *Times* has been its dedication to cheap partisanship—even when it comes at the expense of its own credibility. Here's an example, provided by the *Weekly Standard*—an editorial about Senate filibusters that ran in the *Times* on January 1, 1995, three years into Sulzberger's reign as publisher:

> In the last session of Congress, the Republican minority invoked an endless string of filibusters to frustrate the will of the majority. This relentless abuse of a time-honored Senate tradition so disgusted Senator Tom Harkin, a Democrat from Iowa, that he is now willing to forgo easy retribution and drastically limit the filibuster. Hooray for him. . . . Once a rarely used tactic reserved for issues on which senators held passionate views, the filibuster has become the tool of the sore loser, . . . an archaic rule that frustrates democracy and serves no useful purpose.

Yes, it's an editorial. The *Times* has every right to its opinion. Okay, so now consider this second editorial, which was in the paper on March 6, 2005—on the very same subject:

> The Republicans are claiming that 51 votes should be enough to win confirmation of the White House's judicial nominees. This flies in the face of Senate history. . . . To block nomi-

nees, the Democrats' weapon of choice has been the fili-
buster, a time-honored Senate procedure that prevents a bare
majority of senators from running roughshod. . . . The Bush
administration likes to call itself "conservative," but there is
nothing conservative about endangering one of the great institutions of American democracy, the United States Senate,
for the sake of an ideological crusade.

This is so much par for the course at today's *New York Times* that
the *Weekly Standard* ran those two editorials under the headline
"Obligatory *New York Times* Hypocrisy Item."

Over Sulzberger's reign at the pinnacle of the *Times* masthead,
he has had four top editors. The paper truly hit rock bottom with
the third of these, Pinch's ideological soulmate Howell Raines, a
mean-spirited bully. Raines's enthusiasm for using the *Times* news
pages to aggressively push his own ideological crusades—from
racial preferences to gay marriage to even something so petty as
getting women into the Augusta National golf club—was matched
by a management style that turned much of the newsroom against
him. When the paper was rocked by the Jayson Blair scandal, it was
this last jolt that ensured Raines's departure—probably even more
than the fact that the scandal was itself a result of the Sulzberger/
Raines mentality, with excuses having been repeatedly made for
Blair, a young black reporter with a long record of shoddy journalism, that would have been inconceivable had he been white.

Since Raines's departure, under the more moderate Bill Keller,
there have been some improvements; notably, the hiring of a public
editor, who has often been sympathetic to reader complaints, including those from conservatives about the paper's more outrageous
examples of bias.

However cosmetic, the changes are welcome. Still, the paper is a
far cry from what it once was—and will surely remain so as long as
Pinch Sulzberger is in place. Because while editors come and go, he

is the constant—the *Times* version of a permanent government— and he remains unapologetically dedicated to using the paper's influence to impose his notion of the way America ought to be—on all the rest of us.

☞ *I* ☜

"*They are possibly the dumbest people on the planet. . . .*"

MICHAEL MOORE,
SPEAKING OF HIS FELLOW AMERICANS

A FINAL WORD

FOR TOO MANY YEARS NOW, the cultural elites have been working overtime trying to portray all those *hicks* in flyover country as grotesquely distorted fun-house mirror images of who they really are, without the fun part.

If Middle Americans oppose gay marriage, they must be homophobes. If they don't like the sex jokes at eight o'clock at night on network TV, they're squares. If ordinary Americans think gangsta rap is foul and degrading, they're racists who don't understand black culture. If Red State America thinks our "best" universities are dominated by left-wing ideologues, they're anti-intellectual dolts. If they think feminists have gone too far, they're sexists.

But none of this tells us very much about *real* ordinary Americans. What it tells us a lot about, though, are the cultural elites themselves, those cloistered liberals who, as Tom Wolfe once put it, "do not have a clue about the rest of the United States" and "who are forever trying to force their twisted sense of morality onto us, which is a non-morality. That is constantly done, and there is real resentment."

Yes, there is real resentment, indeed. Middle Americans resent the smug condescension the elites routinely dish out from their cocoons in Manhattan and Hollywood. They resent the authors and journalists who call them "ignorant" because they don't see things the way the elites do. They resent the elites snickering at them because they like to bowl and eat at Red Lobster. They resent the notion that because they go to church every week and take the Bible seriously that there's something creepy about them, and that because they fly the American flag on the Fourth of July they're simple-minded hayseeds.

And it's precisely because of this snobby, elitist attitude that even when I agree with liberals on this issue or that, I don't like being associated with them. I'm with Tom Wolfe, who said, "There is something in me that particularly wants it registered that I am not one of them."

So, what is it that so many ordinary Americans want? It's actually pretty simple. We want a little more appreciation for the values that most of us—liberals as well as conservatives, Democrats as well as Republicans—used to take for granted: civility, mutual respect, a semblance of decency and yes . . . a little old-fashioned love of country, too.

Is that asking too much?

A NOTE TO YOU, THE READER

AS I SAID IN THE INTRODUCTION to this book, there won't be two people in the whole country who agree with every name on my list of 100. So please tell me who you would put on *your* list; that is, the one or two or twenty people *you* think are screwing up America, and—in a few words—why.

There's no reason I should have all the fun.

Thanks.
Bernard Goldberg